ANALYSIS OF THE BRITISH CONSTRUCTION INDUSTRY

The book deals with the British construction industry as a whole rather than individual firms or projects. It is descriptive, analytical and sometimes critical of aspects of the industry, although often with some constructive proposals. It makes use of and interprets statistics and other data to help to understand what the industry is, what it does and how it works.

In the earlier chapters the characteristics of the industry and its place in the economy are defined and the factors determining the demands on the British industry, the process by which they are met and the resultant output in Great Britain and abroad are examined. Then the structure of the contracting industry and the professions is described. There are chapters on forecasting and on costs and prices. The links between demand, output and resource use are analysed. In the last part of the book the resources of manpower, including an attempt to analyse data on productivity, materials, plant and machinery and finance, are considered as inputs to the construction industry. Finally, the research and development effort of the industry is investigated and suggestions made of some areas requiring further research.

Dr Patricia M. Hillebrandt has since 1967 been an economic and management consultant specialising on the construction industry. Educated at University College London (1948-52) and the London School of Economics and Political Science (part-time 1954-8) she has previously been employed as economist to the contracting firm Richard Costain Ltd (1957-62), by the National Economic Development Office (1962-7) and as Senior Lecturer at the Bartlett School of Architecture and Planning, University College London, developing the economic component of an MSc in construction economics and management (1967-80). Since 1980 she has devoted herself to her consultancy work in Great Britain and abroad and to writing.

She was consultant to NEDO for *Construction in the Early 1980s* (HMSO, 1976) and to the Egyptian government for a World Bank project on their construction industry (1980-2). Among her publications are a research report on *Small Firms in the Construction Industry* for the Bolton Committee (HMSO, 1971) and *Economic Theory and the Construction Industry* (Macmillan, 1974).

ANALYSIS OF THE BRITISH CONSTRUCTION INDUSTRY

Patricia M. Hillebrandt
B.Sc. (Econ.), Ph.D.

M

MACMILLAN PUBLISHERS
LONDON

First published 1984 by
MACMILLAN PUBLISHERS LTD
(Journals Division)
and distributed by
Globe Book Services Ltd
Brunel Road, Houndmills,
Basingstoke, Hampshire RG21 2XS

ISBN 0 333 34688 2

Typeset in Great Britain by
RDL Artset Ltd, Sutton, Surrey

Printed in Hong Kong

To
my husband

Contents

x   *Contents*

Preface

This book grew out of my experience in the construction industry as economist to a contractor, at NEDO, as a teacher and as a consultant. It is about the industry as a whole rather than the firms that are part of the industry or the projects that represent its products. It describes the backcloth against which the component parts function and analyses their place. It is written for the people who work in the industry and are connected with it and those who will do so, especially those students who as part of their course are required to understand what the industry is and how it works.

The beginning of the 1980s is an appropriate time to write such a book. The statistics on the industry have developed over the post-war period to provide a comprehensive body of data and although they are now being reduced by government expenditure cuts, the late 1970s and early 1980s probably represent the peak of the supply of information. Moreover, in the early 1980s the industry is in a state of flux. It is a good moment to take stock to consider the present situation in relation to the recent past and, to some extent, the future.

The book is descriptive and analytical. It is not, however, theoretical in its approach and assumes no knowledge of economic theory or mathematics. It is sometimes controversial but is, I hope, impartial.

The organisation of the mass of data available inevitably presents problems, because of the tangled web of interrelationships that are part of any industry, but particularly the construction industry. The division into chapters and the order of their presentation must therefore be somewhat arbitrary. Broadly Chapters 1-9 deal with the industry overall and Chapters 11-17 with the inputs. Chapter 10 is a link chapter between the overall view and inputs.

In the book an attempt has been made to concentrate on matters of long-term rather than transitory interest and consequence, and often, as in the case of forecasts, to look at methodology rather than the actual results at any one time.

In general past statistics are given from 1970. This gives the advantage of a lead-in to the exceptional boom of 1973, and most series are readily available from 1970 to the present time. Tables of such data have spaces for readers to enter comparable statistics for later years as they become available.

It must be stressed that the coverage, even of a non-historical review, cannot be comprehensive. In writing the book there has been a constant trading-off process between reasonable length and complete coverage. To some extent the shortcomings are reduced by the list of references, the indications in notes as to where more detailed information is available, and the select bibliography. A subject well covered elsewhere has often been given a brief description here with appropriate references in order to save length. In this connection the comprehensive statistical source book by Fleming[1] must be mentioned as the first source of reference for statistical data on any aspect of the industry, including sources, their method of collection and interpretation. Since this work is in existence any other major statistical commentary seemed superfluous.

The geographical coverage presents a problem in that the statistics published are sometimes for the United Kingdom, particularly those produced by the Central Statistical Office; sometimes for Great Britain, especially the bulk of the statistics produced by the Department of the Environment on the industry; and occasionally for England and Wales or Scotland separately. Statistics on the construction industry in Northern Ireland are not comprehensive. The output of construction in Northern Ireland comprises about 3 per cent of that of the United Kingdom as a whole. The decision was taken wherever possible to give data for Great Britain, and where this has not been possible the coverage is clearly stated. Scotland presents some difficulties, too, since most of the practices described refer to England, Wales and Scotland but in some cases Scotland is quite different, for example in the traditional organisation of the contracting process. It has not been possible to deal with all these differences.

May 1983   P. M. H.

List of Figures

List of Tables

Acknowledgements

I am indebted to many statistical and other sources for the basic data in this book. The material from government publications, notably the Department of the Environment *Housing and Construction Statistics*, the Central Statistical Office *National Income and Expenditure* Blue Books, Marsh *et al.*, *Labour Mobility in the Construction Industry* (OPCS, 1981) and a series of NEDO publications, namely *The Public Client and the Construction Industry* (1975), *Construction into the Early 1980s* (1976), *How Flexible is Construction?* (1978), *Construction for Industrial Recovery* (1978) and *Faster Building for Industry* (1983) are used or reproduced with the permission of the Controller of Her Majesty's Stationery Office. The Statistics Construction Division of the Department of the Environment has provided me with series of statistics and other assistance. The Business Statistics Office of the Department of Industry has supplied me with some breakdowns of the gross domestic fixed capital formation figures. The Building Research Station has permitted me to use some research data on resource use. The National Economic Development Office has permitted me to quote from a paper *Overseas Capital Projects: A Report by Sir Archie Lamb* (1982). The National House Building Council has allowed me to quote data from *Private House Building Statistics* and the National Home Improvement Council a table from a *Report on the Market for Home Improvement, Repair and Maintenance and DIY 1977-80*. The National Council of Building Material Producers has given permission to adapt a graph from *The Need for Building Materials* (1978) and the House-Builders Federation to quote from a report underaken for them by Specialist Research Unit (1981). I am indebted to the Chartered Institute of Building for permission to reproduce diagrams from *Project Management in Building* (1982) and from their *Yearbook*, to the Royal Institute of British Architects to quote from the *Census of Private Architectural Practices 1980* (1981) and the Building Cost Information Service of the Royal Institute of Chartered Surveyors for permission to use cost and price indices and other data. Savory Milln & Co. has kindly allowed me to quote and use their building books and Green & Co. their books on investment in plant hire and in construction. Mr Michael Ball of Birkbeck College has allowed me to quote from tables in *Mergers and Accumulation in the British Construction Industry 1960-79*. Mr Michael R. Denison-Pender of Gira UK Ltd has allowed me to quote data based on work in *The Changing Structures of Stockholding and Distribution of Building Products and Materials in the UK* (1982).

I have been encouraged by the willingness of so many persons and organisations to give information and comment on ideas. I have had contact with all parts of the industry: contractors, trade unions, employers' and trade organisations, government departments, professional institutions, research organisations, universities and others. Their help ranges from long discussions and comments on passages in the book to chance conversations that have thrown light on some aspect of the industry. They are too numerous to mention individually but I thank them all.

Finally, to the three friends and colleagues, Mrs Margaret Bloom, Mrs Jacqueline Cannon and Mr Jim Meikle, who undertook the onerous task of reading the whole book in draft and commenting on it, I send my very special thanks. For any remaining errors and for all opinions expressed I am solely responsible.

P. M. H.

List of Abbreviations and Acronyms

ACE	Association of Consulting Engineers
APTC	Administrative, Professional, Technical, and Clerical
ARCUK	Architects Registration Council of the United Kingdom
BAS	Building Advisory Service (of the NFBTE)
BATJIC	Building and Allied Trades Joint Industrial Council
BCIS	Building Cost Information Service (of the RICS)
BICS	Building Industry Careers Service
BDA	Brick Development Association
BMF	Builders Merchants Federation
BPF	British Property Federation
BRE	Building Research Establishment
BRS	Building Research Station (now part of BRE)
BSA	Building Societies Association
BSI	British Standards Institution
BSO	Business Statistics Office
BSRIA	Building Services Research and Information Association
CABIN	Campaign Against Building Industry Nationalisation
CASEC	Committee of Associations of Specialist Engineering Contractors
CBI	Confederation of British Industry
C & CA	Cement and Concrete Association
CE	Civil Engineering
CECCB	Civil Engineering Construction Conciliation Board
CEI	Council of Engineering Institutions
CEOTS	Civil Engineering Operative Training Scheme
CIBS	Chartered Institute of Building Services
CIOB	Chartered Institute of Building
C & CA	Cement & Concrete Association

*See also Notes and Abbreviations used in Table, p. xxiv.

CIPFA	Chartered Institute of Public Finance and Accountancy
CIRIA	Construction Industry Research and Information Association
CITB	Construction Industry Training Board
Cmnd	Command (paper)
CNAA	Council for National Academic Awards
CPD	Continuing Professional Development
CPDC	Continuing Professional Development in Construction Group
CSO	Central Statistical Office
DB & E	Davis, Belfield & Everest
DE	Department of Employment
DIY	Do-it-Yourself
DLO	Direct Labour Organisation
DoE	Department of the Environment
DOT	Department of Trade
DQSD	Directorate of Quantity Surveying Development (now DQSS)
DQSS	Directorate of Quantity Surveying Services
ECGD	Export Credits Guarantee Department
EDC	Economic Development Committee
EIU	Economist Intelligence Unit
EETPU	Electrical, Electronic, Telecommunications and Plumbing Union
FAS	Faculty of Architects and Surveyors
FASS	Federation of Associations of Specialists and Subcontractors
FIDIC	Federation Internationale des Ingenieurs Conseils
FMB	Federation of Master Builders
FTAT	Furniture Timber and Allied Trades Union
GDFCF	Gross Domestic Fixed Capital Formation
GDP	Gross Domestic Product
GLC	Greater London Council
GMBATU	General, Municipal, Boilermakers and Allied Trades Union
HBF	House-Builders Federation
HMSO	Her Majesty's Stationery Office
H of L	House of Lords
HSE	Health and Safety Executive
HVCA	Heating and Ventilating Contractors Association
IAAS	Incorporated Association of Architects and Surveyors
ICE	Institution of Civil Engineers
ILEA	Inner London Education Authority
IOB	Institute of Building (now CIOB)
IQS	Institute of Quantity Surveyors

I. Struct. E.	Institution of Structural Engineers
JCT	Joint Contracts Tribunal
JIBECI	Joint Industry Board for the Electrical Contracting Industry
JIBPMES	Joint Industry Board for Plumbing, Mechanical and Engineering Services
LOSC	Labour-only Subcontracting
MHLG	Ministry of Housing and Local Government
MOW	Ministry of Works
MPBW	Ministry of Public Building and Works
MSC	Manpower Services Commission
NAAS	National Agricultural Advisory Service
NCBMP	National Council of Building Material Producers
NFBPM	National Federation of Builders and Plumbers Merchants (now BMF)
NFBTE	National Federation of Building Trades Employers
NFBTO	National Federation of Building Trades Operatives
NHBC	National House-Builders Council (formerly NHBRC, National House Builders Registration Council)
NHIC	National Home Improvement Council
NIESR	National Institute for Economic and Social Research
NJCBI	National Joint Council for the Building Industry
NJCC	National Joint Consultative Council of Architects, Quantity Surveyors and Builders
OECD	Organisation for Economic Co-operation and Development
OPCS	Office of Population Census and Surveys
PCUE	Presidents Committee for the Urban Environment
PESC	Public Expenditure Survey Committee
PIB	Prices and Incomes Board
PSA	Property Services Agency
PSBR	Public Sector Borrowing Requirement
RAF	Royal Air Force
RIAS	Royal Incorporation of Architects in Scotland
RIBA	Royal Institute of British Architects
RICS	Royal Institution of Chartered Surveyors
RTPI	Royal Town Planning Institute
SERC	Science and Engineering Research Council
SIC	Standard Industrial Classification
SMM	Standard Method of Measurement
TGWU	Transport and General Workers Union
TOPS	Training Opportunities Scheme
TRADA	Timber Research and Development Association

TUC	Trades Union Congress
UCATT	Union of Construction, Allied Trades and Technicians
UK	United Kingdom
VAT	Value Added Tax
WRC	Water Research Council
YTS	Youth Training Scheme

Notes and Abbreviations used in Tables

av.	average
E	estimate
est.	estimate
excl.	excluding
m	million
n.a.	not available
n.c.	no change
neg.	negligible
no.	number
nss	not separately specified
P	provisional
th	thousand
Totals	do not always equal sum of components due to rounding
...	not applicable
-	nil
——	break in the series

1 The Construction Industry

DEFINITION

The product area covered in this book is that of the Standard Industrial Classification 1968[1] for construction as follows:

> Erecting and repairing buildings of all types. constructing and repairing roads and bridges: erecting steel and reinforced concrete structures; other civil engineering work such as laying sewers, gas or water mains, and electricity cables, erecting overhead lines and line supports and aerial masts, extracting coal from opencast workings, etc. The building and civil engineering establishments of government departments, local authorities and New Town Corporations and Commissions are included. On-site industrialised building is also included.
>
> Establishments specialising in demolition work or in sections of construction work such as asphalting, electrical wiring, flooring, glazing, installing heating and ventilation apparatus, painting, plastering, plumbing, roofing. The hiring of contractors' plant and scaffolding is included.

However for purposes of this book the construction industry is defined somewhat wider to cover all those parties involved in the construction process including the professions, the contracting industry (as above) and to some extent the suppliers of inputs who jointly respond to the needs of the clients of the industry.

CHARACTERISTICS

The construction industry has characteristics that separately are shared by other industries but in combination appear in construction alone.

First the physical nature of the product is important; the final pro-

1

duct of the industry is for new work, large, heavy and expensive. Generally speaking, it is immovable so that once built it is fixed in location. Moreover, most of the output is custom-built to a unique specification and geographically widely distributed. The products, especially buildings, include in their production a great variety of materials and components supplied by a number of other industries. There is a great range of buildings and works supplied by the industry from dams to piped water, from multi-storey office blocks to houses, from a new factory complex to repair and maintenance on a house.

New buildings and works may have an ultimate use as

(a) a means of further production, e.g. factory building
(b) an addition to or improvement of the infrastructure of the economy, e.g. roads
(c) social investment, e.g. hospitals
(d) direct enjoyment, e.g. housing.

They are investment goods in the sense that they are generally required not for their own sake but to produce a flow of production of goods, services or amenities over a long period. They generally have a long life which means that the size of the stock is large in relation to the annual production.

The determinants of demand for these and for improvement and repair are different and need separate analysis. But since investment as opposed to consumption is often postponable and the perceived need for investment is dependent on the state of the economy and government policies, the construction industry is subject to substantial fluctuations in the demand for its products.

The physical nature of the product, its diversity and often complexity, as well as the wide geographical spread of demand for it and the fluctuations in demand, have together moulded the structure of the industry and determined the process of creating a construction good from the client's need to the production on site.

The structure of the industry is complex in the large range of types of contractors and professional firms, including main contractors and sub-contractors, one-man firms and international companies, low-technology firms and sophisticated specialists, builders and civil engineers and a whole range of professionals connected with the industry.

The construction process is long and involves a large number of separate organisations in design, costing, pricing and production of each product often with a client, private or corporate, who has never or rarely before been involved in a major construction operation and for whom the expenditure involved is among the largest he has ever made. Not only is the new building or works normally designed by a separate organisation from that which will construct it, but, since it must usually be priced before it is produced, there are great uncertainties for the contractor in that pricing process. Furthermore each product tends to be large in relation to the size of the contractor undertaking its construction so that the risks for that firm are considerable. The physical process of production is often a messy one carried out substantially in the open and subjected to the vagaries of the weather. Conditions of work are generally inferior to those in factories. Partly as a consequence of this the public image of the industry is poor and this poor image means that the standard of entrants to the industry is low, which in turn perpetuates poor management and workmanship and the image of the industry. This affects investment and the view of the industry taken by politicians and the general public.

The industry may be classified in many ways of which the principal ones, with the chapters in which they are dealt with, are as follows:

(a) the way in which demand reaches the industry from the client, the method of finance, and the method of organising the construction process (Chapters 2 and 3)
(b) the use to which the product is to be put, for example, education, water supply, housing (Chapters 2 and 4)
(c) the type of construction, for example, heavy civil engineering, timber-frame housing or repair and maintenance (Chapter 4)
(d) the type of organisation involved in construction, for example, large international contractors or small local contractors, general contractors or specialist subcontractors, builders or civil engineers, a full professional team or design on-the-job by the local builder (Chapters 7 and 8).

A division of the industry that to some extent spans these four categories is that into building and civil engineering. The differences between them are considerable. Civil engineering is often concerned with particularly large projects and the basic infrastructure of the economy. Hence it is more subject to the uncertainties of ground and weather conditions. It derives its demand mainly from the public sector and is more active in export markets. Building is a fragmented industry with many professions and contractors and subcontractors and a wider range of project size. Clients are diverse including the public sector and a large number of individual firms and persons. Yet there is considerable overlap in, for example, the use of materials, labour and plant and many contractors operate in both the building and the civil engineering fields.

RELATION TO THE ECONOMY

It is arguable that the construction industry, through the products that it creates, has a greater effect on the environment than any other industry. In 1981 the value of the products of the industry in the stock of dwellings and other buildings and in civil engineering and other construction works was over 72 per cent of the total capital stock at current replacement cost.[2] It is so high because the products of the construction industry have a much longer life than most vehicles, ships, aircraft and plant and machinery and the accumulated stock constitutes the construction part of all the infrastructure of the country: harbours, docks, roads, railways, power-stations, water installations and so on, and the houses and other buildings in our towns and villages.

The very size of the construction industry means that it is of importance to the economy. There are several ways in which the size of the industry can be measured and expressed. The value of work done by the industry in Great Britain in 1981 was £21.3 thousand million.[3] To most this is a meaningless figure but, when it is expressed in relation to the total value of goods and services produced in the United Kingdom – the gross domestic product (GDP) – of £210.8 thousand million[4] or over 10 per cent of this total,[5] it can be seen to be formidable, even in a year of low output of construction. The 10 per cent represents the gross value of work done in the period of all buildings and works, including all the components and materials produced by other industries that are used in these buildings and works. If the net contribution of construction to GDP is taken, that is excluding all the inputs of these other industries and of the professions, then the figure of construction output, thus narrowly defined, in the United Kingdom is £13.5 thousand million[6] or 6.4 per cent of GDP. Even this output is twelve times that of the ship-building and marine engineering industry and over twice the size of the food, drink and tobacco industries. The construction industry narrowly defined has two and a half times the value of output of agriculture, forestry and fishing.[7]

Another measure of the vital role of construction in the economy is the contribution of the industry to investment measured by gross fixed capital formation. This of course excludes all repair and maintenance undertaken by the industry. In 1981 gross domestic fixed capital formation in dwellings and other new buildings and works was £17.5 thousand million out of a total of £39.4 thousand million or 44.4 per cent of the total. The other components are vehicles, ships and aircraft (11.7 per cent) and plant and machinery (39.6 per cent).[8] In addition there are transfer costs of land and buildings of stamp duties, legal fees, dealer margins, agents commissions, etc.[9] relevant to construction which are included in the total gross fixed capital formation figures. In 1981 they were £1.7 thousand million or 0.4 per cent of the total.[10]

A further indication of the importance of construction in the economy is the amount of manpower employed and this is high in construction since the industry is relatively labour-intensive. Manpower in construction in 1981, including most self-employed and employees in the private and public sectors, was about 1.5 million.[11] In addition there may be some 0.3 million extra self-employed[12] and even this may not include all. Taking the figure of 1.8 million and comparing it with the total employed labour force,[13] the percentage of construction is 6.9 per cent compared with the net contribution to GDP of 6.4 per cent.

The construction industry has as its customers virtually every industry and public- or private-sector organisation and many households in the country, if not for new work then for repair and maintenance. It draws its supplies from a more limited sector of the economy. In the 1974 input–output tables[14] 102 industry and commodity groups are listed of which 81 are manufacturing industry. Construction drew 83 per cent of its manufactured goods from just fifteen of these manufacturing commodity groups.

It is mainly a domestic industry. Imports of contracting and professional services are minimal, in spite of membership of the EEC, and exports of contractors' services in value of work done in 1980–1 were about 6 per cent of the total value of work done in Great Britain in 1981.[15] The contribution to the balance of payments by contractors is small but exports of professional services make a larger contribution, although still small in relation to the economy as a whole.[16] The total value of imports of goods and services purchased by the construction industry in 1974 was £546 million or 5.4 per cent of output,[17] although the total imports of construction materials were higher at about £950 million[18] but many of these will be sold by the Do-It-Yourself industry. The percentage used by the construction industry itself has probably changed little by the early 1980s. The industry is therefore of importance within the home economy rather than for the external position.

Three studies have recently been undertaken with the objective of persuading government to increase public expenditure on construction. As a by-product they provide data on the possible effect on the economy of various increases in construction expenditure. That by the Economist Intelligence Unit (EIU) commissioned by the Federation of Civil Engineering Contractors[19] simulates the effects of a £2000 million increase in capital expenditure annually for three years on various assumptions on money supply, current expenditure and other policies. The report by Cambridge Econometrics Ltd,[20] jointly commissioned by five construction industry organisations, examines the effects of a £500 million injection of capital over each of three years (but not increasing annually as in the EIU case) through public-sector housing investment (two-thirds on new dwellings, one-third for rehabilitation work) or increased civil engineering expenditure on roads, water and sewerage. Lastly, the TUC has prepared a document entitled *Reconstruction of Britain*[21] with a massive expenditure programme of £24 000 million over five years. Most but not all expenditure would benefit the construction industry. All three reports are reviewed by NEDO.[22]

Together these reports represent a considerable addition to the information on the relationship of certain types of construction spending to the economy. They are all agreed that the public sector borrowing requirement (PSBR) per job created is about half or considerably less than half of the gross expenditure per job because of the reduction in payments such as unemployment and social security benefits, the increase in receipts from taxation, etc. Furthermore, the net PSBR cost per job created by the various forms of construction investment is not high by the standards of many other public programmes. The detailed effect of the construction programmes is very dependent on assumptions about methods of financing, and policies in relation to the money supply and other public expenditure. For all assumptions, however, the direct and indirect effects of the construction expenditure postulated on manufacturing output and GDP and on the level of employment is favourable and considerable. The unfavourable effects on the balance of payments and inflation are not as high as sometimes implied.

ROLE OF GOVERNMENT

Government plays a substantial part in all aspects of the industry. It must be interested in the industry by reason of its contribution to gross domestic product, to investment, and its share of employment and unemployment. Government should be concerned that the level of investment in the economy is adequate and construction provides investment goods. Moreover, the public sector is the client for around half of the output of the industry, the exact proportion depending on the economic climate and the policies of the government in power (see Chapter 4). It is able therefore to affect the industry, not only as a government in its functions of managing the economy and setting and maintaining standards, but also directly as a client.

The government affects demand (as is described in Chapter 2) indirectly by acting on the level of overall demand in the economy, on taxation, on interest rates, and the supply of credit, and directly by determining the level of public-sector spending on construction. It is argued in Chapter 4, in commenting on the pattern of output over the last twenty-five years or so, that the government has from time to time directly used the construction industry as a regulator of the economy, that is, it has increased or decreased demand on the industry with the intention of affecting the overall level of activity in the economy. The problem with trying to use the industry as a regulator is that it is an ineffective tool because it is too slow to act. One of the features of the construction process is its duration and the expenditure on projects builds up slowly. There is therefore at any time a large amount of work already underway and a change in the rate of starts of projects will make little impact on the total work-load for a long time. At the same time to stop the construction process once underway is disruptive, inefficient and costly to the client.

The demand for construction is subject to considerable fluctuations. At times government has reduced these fluctuations in its management of the economy but has also often exacerbated them. Their existence and the uncertainties created by them makes the industry one where the participants have to give great emphasis in their method of operation to risk reduction and this affects the level of investment, the method of employment, technologies used and structure of the industry. These matters are referred to again, notably in Chapters 7, 11 and 15.

In setting standards the government acts on the types of buildings and works created through the planning laws, on the standard of construction, now mainly through building regulations, but in the past through regulations for local authorities on standards, for example the now abandoned Parker Morris standards for public housing.[23] It also gives recognition and support to organisations to uphold standards of the professions, for example the Architects Registration Council of the United Kingdom, and, by granting royal charters to professional bodies, places them under the aegis of the Privy Council.

It affects the methods of construction by laying down and enforcing safety regulations on sites and on its own contracts has insisted on certain minimum welfare provisions and on precautions on site to ensure that building could proceed during bad winter weather. Lastly, through the courts and other means contracts are enforced and arbitration machinery exists.

Government plays a substantial part in innovation and it is interesting that for a period in the early 1960s the sponsor department, then the Ministry of Public Buildings and Works, was given special responsibility for improving the efficiency of the industry – a brief not shared by other sponsor departments. In the sixties government was very active in attempting to improve efficiency and the Directorate General of Research and Development was established in 1962 with organisations looking at improvements in methods of building, management, research, and collection and dissemination of economic and statistical data. The Department of the Environment is now sponsor department of the industry. It represents the industry in government as a whole, and to this end liaises with the industry through, for example, the Group of 'Eight', the Economic Development Committees for Building and Civil Engineering and through numerous specialised committees and groups.

Government has a substantial role in research and development (described in Chapter 17).

Lastly, government gives assistance to exports as described in Chapter 5 through diplomatic posts abroad, through the Export Credits Guarantee Department (ECGD) and the Department of Trade generally and on specific projects.

2 Determinants of Demand

INTRODUCTION

Demand is regarded by economists as the requirement for goods and services that the customer is able and willing to pay for. It must not be confused with need which, for buildings and works, may be defined as the difference between an accepted standard of provision and the extent to which the stock reaches this standard. However the two are clearly interrelated and both will be referred to in this chapter.

The determination of demand for construction is a very complex process. This stems partly from the characteristics of the products of the industry referred to in Chapter 1, especially their size and high cost, their long life, the investment nature of the products and the complexity of the process. There are five major requirements that must be favourable before demand can be created:

(a) that there is a user or potential user for the building or works in the short run or in the long run
(b) that some person or organisation is prepared to own the building or works
(c) that a person or organisation is prepared to provide finance for the construction of the product and for its ultimate ownership
(d) that some person or organisation is prepared to initiate the process
(e) that the environment and external conditions in which items (a)–(d) above operate are favourable.

There are thus potentially four persons or institutions involved: the user, the owner, the financier and the initiator and to these one might add government, since government in one form or another has a substantial influence on the environment in which the demand creation must take place. In practice two or more roles may be combined but the combinations vary from one building type to another and the situation may be complicated by advisers. Need is felt by the user or by the owner, although it may be assessed by the community as represented by government or some other organisation as outlined in Chapter 6.

The process of demand creation will be examined separately for each main type of construction but, since many of the environmental factors are common, they will first be reviewed. The construction types separately examined are private housing; private new work other than housing; public new work including housing; rehabilitation improvement, repair and maintenance. In each case the factors influencing the demand and the persons or organisations performing each role will be considered. The methods that are used to forecast demand will be considered in Chapter 6 where comments on factors affecting demand for more specific work types are included.

Although there are some indicators of demand, there are no statistics of demand – only of output. Thus, although the concept is clear, there are no hard data to evaluate the level of demand separately from output. Over considerable periods of time the level of demand and the level of output have probably been more or less the same. However, when the industry is regarded as not meeting demand or working at over-full capacity, this implies that what people are able and willing to pay for is not being provided and that demand is greater than output. Evidence suggests that this situation existed in 1964–5 and in 1973. However, since there are no demand data the evidence is based on the way the supply side of the industry behaved – material shortages and prices, for example. In Chapter 4 is a broad description of the history of output since 1955 and it is there and in the discussion in Chapter 10 that this excess demand is discussed.

THE ENVIRONMENT FOR DEMAND CREATION

The first and most obvious aspect of the environment that affects all construction demand is the general economic situation and expectations about how this will change. In a buoyant economy with high and growing gross domestic product, a satisfactory balance of payments position and a reasonable level of employment and with expectations of a continuation of this situation, then generally standards of living will be rising, consumer expenditure increasing and government will feel able to spend on improving services for the community. The rate of interest can, subject to international constraints, be kept low in real terms and finance will generally be readily available. In a depressed situation such as obtains in the early 1980s, the whole position is reversed and while expectations of improvement remain low very little demand for construction will be created.

The rate of inflation alone does not have such a clear effect on the level of construction activity partly because property ownership is regarded as a hedge against inflation and indeed property values over a long period of time have kept up with inflation. Table 2.1 shows indices of commercial and industrial rents which partly determine property values and also indices of house prices. These are compared with the retail price index and it is seen that the increase in both rents and house prices have for long periods exceeded the general level of inflation. It is when the level of prices rises so much that the general economic environment is affected and government takes action to deflate, that the dampening effect of inflation on construction is felt.

The second group of environmental factors that affect all areas of construction is the cost of construction in relation to the cost of other products and services on which persons and organisations can spend money. Over the last decade or so the cost of new construction has risen rather faster (over five times 1970–81) than either the Retail Price Index or plant and machinery index (between three and four times 1970–80) and considerably faster than durable consumer goods.[1] Further information is contained in Chapter 9, Table 9.2. This means that individuals or organisations will, because of price increases, prefer to spend their income on other things – for example, durable consumer goods or cars – and industrialists may consider putting new plant and machinery into old buildings. Repair and maintenance has increased considerably in price and this will deter spending in this sector.

Subsidies and grants, however, influence the effective price paid by purchasers of construction products. For housing, for example, there are grants for renovations and the tax concessions on capital expenditure by industry reduce the real cost of new construction. Furthermore, although the detailed situation changes, VAT is not payable on new building but is on repair and maintenance and this distorts the pattern of choice of consumers. They should be treated the same.

It also favours the very small builder, who does not charge VAT, compared with the larger firm.

Incentives to locate businesses in areas of high unemployment go back to before the Second World War and, in the recession of the early 1980s, there is a multiplicity of schemes, including cash grants for capital investment, provision of government factories, and loans on advantageous

TABLE 2.1   *Indices of rents, house prices and retail prices from 1962 (1975 = 100)*

| Year | Rents[a] | | | House prices | | Retail prices[d] |
	All offices	All shops	Factories	New[b]	Existing[c]	
1962	23	n.a.	n.a.	24	n.a.	39
1963	26	n.a.	n.a.	25	n.a.	40
1964	26	n.a.	n.a.	28	n.a.	41
1965	29	44	n.a.	31	n.a.	43
1966	31	46	n.a.	33	n.a.	45
1967	31	49	n.a.	35	n.a.	46
1968	37	50	n.a.	37	n.a.	48
1969	46	54	54	39	n.a.	51
1970	57	56	61	42	n.a.	54
1971	63	60	60	48	n.a.	59
1972	71	66	64	63	n.a.	64
1973	91	77	78	86	n.a.	69
1974	106	90	88	91	n.a.	80
1975	100	100	100	100	100	100
1976	94	111	124	108	107	117
1977	103	n.a.	125	119	114	135
1978	120	n.a.	150	143	133	135
1979	140	n.a.	175	183	172	166
1980	n.a.	n.a.	n.a.	220	198	196
1981	n.a.	n.a.	n.a.	225	202	219
1982						238
1983						
1984						

Notes and sources:

[a] DoE, *Commercial and Industrial Property Statistics 1979* (HMSO, 1980) Table 24 converted to 1975 = 100. England and Wales. Series discontinued.
[b] DoE, *Housing and Construction Statistics 1971–1981* (HMSO, 1982) Table 1, average price of new dwellings for which building society advances approved. UK.
[c] DoE, *Housing and Construction Statistics 1971–1981* (HMSO, 1982) Table 108 converted to index 1975 = 100. Average price other than new dwellings for which building society mortgages approved.
[d] CSO, *Annual Abstract of Statistics 1968* (HMSO, 1968) Table 379. UK.
CSO, *Annual Abstract of Statistics 1982* (HMSO, 1982) Table 18.1. UK.
DE, *Employment Gazette*, vol. 91, no. 3 Mar 1983 (HMSO, 1983) Table 6.4. UK.

terms. Some are available only for specific areas, or specific industries or for small firms. They all, however, affect demand decisions.

The third and last group of environmental factors affecting whether the demand can become effective is the operation of the rules and

regulations governing land use and construction. Clearly the environment needs protection and there must be regulation of the use of agricultural land and countryside for building. Proper planning involves achieving the correct balance between the claims on land resources and this is
the objective of the planning system that determines the availability of
land for particular use.

A study by the University of Aston relating to the period 1968-73
found that the stock of land with permission for building has at times
been used up faster than it has been replenished by the planning laws.
The effects of this depend partly, however, on landholdings about which
relatively little is known and on planning delays.[2] Certainly landholdings
by developers create a buffer against any short-term deficiency of land
with planning permission becoming available. Developers may, however,
be less willing and able to provide this buffer if the price of land for
building is expected to fall or fluctuate in price as has happened over the
last ten years.

Much of the discussion about the availability of land for building is
concentrated on the supply for housing. If insufficient land is allocated
for new housing, then the planning system can become a brake on the
demand for construction because there is an absolute shortage, because
purchasers expect a shortage or they expect to be able to make a profit
out of increasing prices. The overall rate of increase in the price of land
for private housebuilding has been in the last ten years or so higher than
the Retail Price Index. In the earlier period of 1963-72 'when the Retail
Price Index rose at a rate of 5 per cent a year, both agricultural and residential land rose at between 16 and 17 per cent a year although not
always in step'.[3] The period 1970-4 is of particular interest. There was a
surge in prices in the boom years of 1973 and 1974 followed by a dramatic fall. The NEDO report states[4]

A DoE study on the reasons for the land price boom in 1971–73
found it difficult to produce evidence to attribute it to any major
cause.[5] It suspected the main factor was the public's optimistic
anticipation of future housing price rises. Other factors could have
been legislation changes, population rises, a change in the cost of
finance and of more significance, possibly, the increase at the time in
the percentage of refusals on the increased number of planning
applications. The report also points out, however, that land owners
may have been motivated to make more and more speculative applications in response to the price rises.

In the early 1980s it has been suggested that the stock of land for new
housing may be inadequate. The land provision for new housing in the

Structure Plans of local authorities was quoted by Shaw, in answer to a parliamentary question, in broad terms as 180 000–190 000 new houses a year in England in both private and public sectors.[6] This compares with projections of dwelling output for Great Britain of around 300 000 in the Green Paper on Housing[7] and lower more recent estimates of land requirements by the Joint Land Requirements Committee[8] from 160 000 to over 250 000 dwellings a year depending on the scenario adopted. Even allowing that these figures included Wales and Scotland there would seem to be a potential problem.

There have separately from the town and country planning system been controls from time to time on the location of industrial and office building. Until January 1982 Industrial Development Certificates were required for industrial development over a certain size and for some years there were similar controls on office development. In addition for a brief period in the 1960s, licences were required for private work other than housing and industrial building. It is not known how far these controls restricted the demand for construction. Few applications were formally refused but clients of the industry may have been inhibited from attempting to build because of the existence of the restrictions.

Delays in the processing of applications for planning may reduce demand. The Building and Civil Engineering EDCs reported that[9]

> Many clients and developers claim that they experience significant delays in obtaining planning permission for projects and that these delays not only postpone development but also lead to increases in costs – in some cases even making projects no longer financially viable.

Since that was written there have been changes in the procedures dealt with in Chapter 3, but the preoccupation with delays remains. Similarly the building control system - mainly for the enforcement of the building regulations – is a potential constraint and is dealt with in more detail in Chapter 3.

NEW PRIVATE HOUSING

The demand for private housing is to a substantial extent determined by the need for new housing as a whole. Since the end of the war, when there was an acute shortage of housing, the situation has undergone a dramatic change, for the numbers constructed each year have exceeded

the demolitions and the requirements of new households by a considerable margin. A DoE report[10] showed that whereas in 1951 in England
and Wales there was a surplus of households over dwellings of about
730 000, by 1961, using census enumerated households, the dwellings
and households were more or less in balance and by 1971 there was a
surplus of dwellings over the households enumerated in the census of
about 500 000 (although if DoE estimates of households are taken that
include households absent on census night and undercounting of one-
person households, the surplus was only about 250 000). By 1981
provisional census data showed the surplus of dwellings over households
had risen to about 1.6 million.[11]

These dwellings include many that are unsuitable because they do not
have proper amenities or are in need of repair or are just unsuitable for
modern conditions and living standards (see section on rehabilitation,
improvement, repair and maintenance below). They also include a small
number of second homes. Nevertheless it means that factors to create a
demand for private housing need to be more favourable than hitherto if
that demand is to be substantial.

The provision of private housing to rent has dwindled so that by the
1981 Census only 13.2 per cent of the private households in Great Britain
lived in accommodation to rent from a private landlord or housing
association, compared with 21.6 per cent in 1971.[12] Thus most of the
new private housing is built for sale so that owners and users are the
same.

There have been great changes in user requirements and, since dwellings
built before 1919 still constitute nearly 30 per cent of the stock in Great
Britain and those from 1919 to 1944 another 21 per cent,[13] the changes
in requirements have to be met by adaptation of existing dwellings and
by appropriate additions to the stock. There is the change in the size of
household including a reduction from pre-1914 in the numbers of children
in the family; there is the virtual disappearance of living-in domestic help;
large kitchens were regarded as unnecessary in the inter-war and immedi-
ate post-war period until the change in eating habits and the increased
space required for durable consumer goods again led to a demand for
large kitchens. The changes in household size in the last two decades
alone have been dramatic, with an increase in families with children
but a decrease in large families and a sharp rise in married couples without children and in one-person households.

The decision of the owner/user to try to obtain a new dwelling is
dependent on a number of factors, including the advantages of a new
dwelling compared with existing dwellings available for his existing and

projected requirements; his ability to pay for a new dwelling, which in turn depends largely on income and the availability of capital to him and his expectations of change in income or capital; the cost of the dwelling; the charge for borrowing money and the cost of alternative assets or other goods and services on which he can spend his money. These are some of the factors that determine the demand for housing although there are others. A research report for the House-Builders Federation[14] found that people buy new, *inter alia*, because it is easier to arrange, because repair bills are likely to be less and because there is an attraction in a house in pristine condition, untouched by others.

Finance of private-sector housing is undertaken to a large extent by building societies. Other institutional sources are insurance companies, banks and local authorities. Table 2.2 shows advances for new dwellings by building societies, insurance companies and local authorities accounting for 76 per cent of all new dwellings in 1981. There are no statistics of advances by banks for new dwellings alone. However, the banks entered the housing market in style in 1978 and by 1981 the value of their net advances for new and existing dwellings had risen to over a quarter of the total of new lending.[15] Thereafter, the rise continued but at a lower rate.[16] The pension funds are now also entering the field, notably through the Building Trust.[17] Other lenders are new towns and the Housing Corporation;[18] friendly societies, relatives and friends, and in some cases the existing owner.[19] The major housebuilders are also now increasingly supplying some form of finance for housing. The banks and these other sources, as well as the buyers' own resources, would have financed in 1981 the remaining 24 per cent of all new houses bought and this implies that the banks' share of the new housing market is lower than their share of the total market.

The lenders operate in different but overlapping markets. Generally, local authorities have concentrated on the lower end of the market in cities, in which building societies were not very interested because of the risks of price depreciation; banks, apart from their traditional role of providing bridging loans, have been at the top end of the market. Insurance companies have also been at the upper end of the market, partly because their mortgages are usually linked to endowment insurance which benefits higher taxpayers most. Competition for building societies in the 1980s is greater than in previous periods because of the increased role of the banks but it still is not so great that the societies cannot operate as a cartel as put forward by, for example, Gough.[20] They have an official body recommending prices – the Building Societies Association – and this has had the effect, he says, of stabilising building society lending and

TABLE 2.2 Institutional finance for new dwellings compared with private dwellings completed from 1970, UK

Year	Private dwellings	Building societies		Insurance companies		Local authorities	
	completed^a th	Number of advances^b th	% of private completions %	Number of advances^c th	% of private completions %	Number of advances^d th	% of private completions %
1970	174	133	76	9	5	3	1
1971	196	165	84	8	4	3	1
1972	201	164	82	7	3	2	1
1973	191	142	74	7	4	3	1
1974	146	102	70	6	4	5	3
1975	155	121	78	4	3	6	4
1976	155	129	83	3	2	1	neg.
1977	144	122	85	2	2	neg.	neg.
1978	152	134	88	3	2	neg.	neg.
1979	144	117	81	3	2	neg.	neg.
1980	130	94	72	2	2	n.a.	n.a.
1981	118	87	74	2	1	n.a.	n.a.
1982	124P	94P	76	2P	1	n.a.	n.a.
1983							
1984							

Notes and sources:

a DoE, *Housing and Construction Statistics 1970–1980* (HMSO, 1981) Table 72; DoE, *Housing and Construction Statistics 1971–1981* (HMSO, 1982) Table 70; DoE, *Housing and Construction Statistics December Quarter 1982*, no. 12 (HMSO, 1983) Table 1.3.

b DoE, *Housing and Construction Statistics 1970–1980* (HMSO, 1981) Table 112; DoE, *Housing and Construction Statistics 1971–1981* (HMSO, 1982) Table 106; DoE, *Housing and Construction Statistics December Quarter 1982*, no. 12 (HMSO, 1983) Table 1.6; return and coverage revised January 1975 and January 1981.

c DoE, *Housing and Construction Statistics 1970–1980* (HMSO, 1981) Table 125; DoE, *Housing and Construction Statistics 1971–1981* (HMSO, 1982) Table 119; DoE, *Housing and Construction Statistics December Quarter 1982* (HMSO, 1983) Table 1.9; return revised Jan 1976.

d DoE, *Housing and Construction Statistics* no. 12, 4th quarter 1974 (HMSO, 1975) Table 40, DoE, *Housing and Construction Statistics*, no. 32, 4th quarter 1979 (HMSO, 1980) Table 41; series discontinued.

borrowing rates in an environment of increasingly fluctuating rates elsewhere in the economy. He goes on to say that this has resulted in periods of competitive advantage to the societies being followed by competitive disadvantage with house prices following changes in net receipts after a lag of just over a year. This conclusion is largely supported by work done by Mayes on the house property boom of the early 1970s.[21] The increase in demand backed by the increase in the supply of mortgages led to an increase in the price of houses because new building does not and cannot, because of the lags, respond quickly to changes in demand.

Gough also argues that the volatility of the mortgage market has been the main reason for the variation in output of the private house-building industry.[22] It has led to variations in the sizes and types of houses constructed, for example with larger houses for those trading-up in the market and smaller houses for first-time buyers in periods of sluggish markets. Gough also thinks that mortgage availability affects the construction time for dwellings, being long in periods of mortgage scarcity.

The privileges given to house owners in the form of taxation advantages through the building societies, tax relief on mortgage interest and exemption from capital gains tax has led to the conclusion by some[23] that the favourable treatment has gone too far and that the result has been a diversion of funds into the housing market which would otherwise have gone into private enterprise and industry.

If that was the conclusion at the end of the 1970s, it may be even more telling in the next decades, for the level of demand for new housing is likely to fluctuate around a lower level. Lending by building societies for new housing has declined over the last decade from over 25 per cent of total loans to about 12 per cent in 1981.[24] The danger that house prices will fluctuate widely is to some extent reduced by the willingness of building societies to alter the interest rates more frequently largely in response to the banks' entry into the market, but they still change less often than those of banks, and if the banks retreat from the market they may try to maintain rates longer. Other steps may need to be taken to allow building societies to use their funds in other directions than housing – perhaps for the financing of construction of other buildings and works, and this could be part of reforms of a more sweeping nature advocated by some, for example Mabey and Tillett.[25] The past situation where in thirty-two years, 1946–78, retail prices increased seven times, house prices twelve and a half times, and share values five times[26] needs to be avoided.

The initiators of the dwelling construction process in the private sector for the great majority of the output are developers who buy land, plan the site, obtain planning permission, organise construction of the dwellings and sell them to the new owner. Above all, they assess the markets and take risks. There has been substantial change in the structure of the house-development business in the last few years with a much greater concentration of output in the hands of a few builders. This is described in Chapter 7.

PRIVATE NEW WORK OTHER THAN HOUSING

This group of building covers all industrial buildings, including factories and warehouses, and commercial buildings, including offices and shops which accounted in 1981 for about 70 per cent of the commercial sector. It is on these three types of property – industrial, offices and shops – that the analysis in this section is concentrated.

The users are the whole range of companies, partnerships and individuals undertaking any form of business enterprise. Particularly in the case of industrial building, the user requires the building as a means of production of some other goods. His demand for construction is dependent on the demand for the goods or services which will be produced in the building and is known as derived demand. Thus the expectations of the manufacturer for future demand for the goods or services he produces are vital to the decision to seek to use a new building. Equally important are his expectations of future costs, since he is concerned to make a profit out of his investment in new buildings and works.

Demand for new industrial buildings is created by an increase in demand for products or the development of new processes that cannot be housed in the existing buildings. Table 2.3 analyses the returns of 299 firms in the survey undertaken by NEDO.[27] However, the building itself is but a small part of the total investment required for production – plant and machinery being normally more costly. Indeed the need for investment in buildings may be less obvious and the advantages more difficult to quantify partly because the life of the building is long. Plant and machinery have a shorter pay-back period producing a less risky investment.

Offices and shops are also required for the goods and services they help to produce but the link is sometimes less obvious. Hillebrandt[28] undertook an analysis of the factors affecting the demand for industrial and commercial building, one of which is technological change which is perhaps understated in the NEDO analysis.

TABLE 2.3 *Reasons for investment in new industrial buildings*

Stated reason	% of firms	No. of firms concerned
To meet additional demand	57	170
To achieve a better process lay-out	34	103
To accommodate new machinery	36	109
To overcome labour supply problems	5	15
To reduce maintenance costs	9	26
To improve conditions in an old factory	31	93
Necessitated by outside factors	5	14
Unable to expand on previous site	13	40
To take advantage of government grants	9	27
To achieve better links with markets by road	4	13
To achieve better links with markets by sea	2	5
To provide other facilities	4	12
As part of an investment programme	20	61
Other	6	18

Notes:

Firms gave a number of reasons in each case. The need solely to meet additional demand came in 29 cases; a combination of this and the need to accommodate new machinery came in 18 cases.

Source:

EDC, for Building and Civil Engineering, *Construction for Industrial Recovery*, NEDO (HMSO, 1978).

Many of the new private construction projects are owned and initiated by their users. Table 2.4. shows that over 60 per cent of buildings and works other than dwellings in the private sector are bought by industrial and commercial companies other than property companies. The importance of financial companies and institutions as spenders on new buildings and works has grown over the last decade at the expense of the personal sector which as investors in new buildings and works other than housing is mainly professional persons, farmers and other sole traders and partnerships.[29] This trend seems to have been going on a long time as indicated by the ownership of the capital stock. In 1970 financial companies and institutions owned just over 6 per cent of the net capital stock whereas by 1981 it was over 10 per cent. Industrial and commerical companies in 1981 owned 73 per cent of other buildings and works – about the same as in 1970.[30]

Within the financial sector the 'other' residual category has increased dramatically. Property companies have, however, decreased in importance. The importance of the pension funds is now considerable.

TABLE 2.4 Gross domestic fixed capital formation in buildings and works other than dwellings by the private sector from 1970, UK, (current prices)

Year	Personal sector[a] £m	%	Industrial and commercial companies Total[a] £m	%	of which property owning[b] £m	%	Financial companies and institutions Total[a] £m	%	of which insurance[b] £m	of which banking[b] £m	of which other[b] £m	Overall total £m
1970	278	23	802	67	126	10	125	10	70	43	12	1 205
1971	306	23	878	66	143	11	151	11	93	41	19	1 335
1972	330	23	944	66	168	12	160	11	94	39	27	1 434
1973	400	21	1 228	64	197	10	279	15	182	50	50	1 907
1974	465	17	1 874	68	313	11	399	15	269	82	50	2 738
1975	437	14	2 349	73	213	7	441	14	264	117	60	3 227
1976	450	13	2 533	72	235	7	521	15	312	138	72	3 504
1977	495	13	2 663	73	175	5	515	14	243	179	93	3 673
1978	572	14	2 934	72	178	4	541	13	267	174	102	4 047
1979	712	15	3 403	71	250	5	668	14	376	180	114	4 783
1980	908	16	3 983P	69	445	6	879	15	531	206	144	5 770P
1981P	957	15	4 269	69	535	6	994	16	583	235	180	6 220
1982												
1983												
1984												

Notes and sources:

[a] CSO, *National Income and Expenditure 1981 Edition* (HMSO, 1981) Table 10.3; CSO, *National Income and Expenditure 1982 Edition* (HMSO, 1982) Table 10.3; with revisions provided by BSO.

[b] Information provided by the Business Statistics Office. The figures for insurance are different in definition but similar to those published for new buildings in BSO, *Insurance Companies and Pension Fund Investments*, 4th quarter 1981, Business Monitor MO5 (HMSO, 1982) for the years 1979–81. That publication also shows the investment in new buildings for the three years of various types of pension funds. For 1981 the figures with revision provided by BSO were: private pension funds, £50m; local authority pension funds, £16m; other public pension funds, £43m. These are not included in the above table.

It is likely that much of the stock of industrial buildings is owned by the industrial companies themselves. Insurance companies and pension funds have concentrated their investment on offices and shops and may be responsible for financing about a third of the new buildings of this type. The attraction of this type of investment to long-term investors is that, unlike much industrial investment, it is not specific to one type of user. The report by the Property Advisory Group – the Pilcher Report – (DoE 1975) states that 'Most long term development finance comes from insurance companies and pension funds'[31] Most of the other investment in offices and shops is therefore probably provided by owner-occupiers including a substantial share in retail distribution.

The initiator of construction may be the same as the owner, that is, the owner-occupier, or the financial institution; he may be the user, for example a large company that wishes to occupy a new office block or shop development but does not wish to lock up its capital in its ownership; or it may be the developer. The Pilcher Report[32] lists the tasks involved in development and stresses the need continually to monitor economic feasibility and assess risks. Developers must estimate demand, identify and secure appropriate sites, arrange for short- and long-term finance to fund site acquisition and construction, arrange for and manage design and construction, let and manage the completed buildings.

The large firms of chartered surveyors acting as property agents and building surveyors play an important role in the early stages of projects as initiators in the sense that they conceive a scheme and bring together the various participants in the process. They also advise various funding organisations.

The great majority of commercial developments has been undertaken by private development companies alone or in co-operation with local authorities. The amount of profit to be obtained from developing and from owning offices, shops or industrial premises depends largely on the level of rents now and in the future. In Table 2.1 it will be seen that the level of office rents multiplied six times in 1962–79 while the Retail Price Index multiplied about five times. However, what it does not show is that office rents in the City in the same period multiplied by eight, in the West End by six and in decentralised areas of London by eleven times. Provincial rents were more moderate in their behaviour multiplying by less than five times or rather less than the Retail Price Index.[33] Developers made very large profits during this period. The system has many critics and there is little doubt that the interests of users, owners, financiers and developers do not always coincide and they are certainly not always at one with community interests. Ambrose and Colenutt[34] criticise the extensive office development for its effects on employment opportunities, for the creation of greater irregularities of wealth and for its 'misuse of national resources'. Some of this criticism is reduced by the introduction of the Development Land Tax in 1976 on realisation of development value. There is, however, considerable doubt as to whether profit is a good measure of the desirability from the point of view of the economy of so large amounts of resources going into offices and shops and less into industrial buildings and infrastructure.

One other development in this area must be mentioned and that is the increasing role of the local authority as owner, developer and initiator of development linked to the more traditional role of planner. The Pilcher Report discusses this at some length but in the light of the Community Land Act, now repealed. There is, however, a clear role for local authorities to act in the development process often in partnership with the private sector.

PUBLIC NEW WORK INCLUDING HOUSING

The demand for this work may be divided into several categories. The first is the demand of the public authorities run more or less as commercial or industrial enterprises, even if they receive some form of government subsidy, such as the British Steel Corporation, the National Coal Board and British Rail. Their freedom to operate on a profit-maximising basis or on one to meet public need varies over time partly in sympathy with the nature of the government in power but normal commercial principles, such as those affecting the private industrial sector, are clearly important. Second, there is the whole range of capital expenditure for goods that are used by the community as a whole without specific payment for use. They constitute most of the infrastructure of roads, harbours, hospitals, libraries, schools, defence, prisons, police stations, etc. In between these two is a grey area where commercial principles apply to some extent in that consumers pay for use but do not necessarily pay the full economic price on a commercial pricing basis, such as water supply and sewerage, some housing and, more recently, some services for small firms. It depends on the policy of the government how great a proportion is paid for by users.

There are no hard and fast divisions between these categories. For example, parts of housing owned by the public sector are run on commercial principles, while other housing is more of a social service to the individual who cannot afford the full commercial price. To a large extent, however, this problem is dealt with by giving income to those who cannot afford services regarded as essential by the community, so that they may be able to purchase them.

There is no comprehensive assessment of need for public-sector construction, although most long-term forecasts contain some discussion of need (see Chapter 6). One reason is that there is no general agreement on the standards by which need can be measured. What, for example, should be the standard for provision of roads? It depends on provision of other transport forms, of energy policy of the government, of the value put on the benefits of pleasure motoring, etc. Moreover, every need assessment has for practical purposes to be tempered by the knowledge of conflicting claims of other sectors and the economic health of the country. Thus there can be said to be an urgent need to replace hospitals of which the average age is somewhere in the region of seventy years. Yet some governments have not seen that as an urgent matter requiring substantial resources. It is, however, generally agreed that there is a need for replacement or relining of much of the infrastructure of pipes and other installations of water supply and sewerage,[35] the prison stock is in urgent need of replacement and probably extension; there would seem to be a need for some extra airport facility. Unfortunately need as judged by users or owners falls short of provision to such an extent that the resources cannot be made available to meet need and the government must decide on priorities.

For public-sector housing the users are individuals and families. They take the decision to apply for a local authority dwelling and the normal procedure is that they are put on a waiting list and then in due course are offered accommodation to accept or reject. If they reject the accommodation offered a number of times they return to the waiting list. Thus the decision to occupy a new dwelling as opposed to an existing dwelling is only partially theirs. In the case of housing associations the user may have more control on what the association is providing since he is a member of the association or will choose to join one that meets his needs.

Often the owner and initiator of demand for buildings and works are the same, namely the public authority, central or local, and they may also be the financier. In these cases the process of initiating the development should be less complex than, say, in private or commercial development, although the multiplicity of departments and elected committees, each with separate interests within large public organisations, may mitigate against ease in the decision-making process. In the specific case of housing associations the owner of the dwelling is a semi-private association or, in the case of shared ownership, initially the user and the association. The association is the initiator of construction but the finance is provided by the housing corporation or local authorities.

No analysis is available on the ultimate source of funds for capital expenditure on construction because the data on gross domestic fixed capital formation relate to expenditure by actual owners of the assets. Central government gives grants to local authorities but the expenditure appears as the authorities' own. Nevertheless, the ownership of new capital projects is of relevance especially since these spenders are usually also the initiators. Table 2.5 shows the gross domestic fixed capital formation on buildings and works, other than dwellings and is comparable to Table 2.4.

The overall financial situation is to a large extent controlled by central government. Government publishes annually in a White Paper estimates of public expenditure both central and local up to four years ahead.[36] These are prepared by the Public Expenditure Survey Committee (PESC) and agreed by the Cabinet. What is published represents the departmental, public authority and local authority allowed and expected expenditure, after all the negotiations have taken place between the various spending organisations and the Treasury. They are therefore a compromise of what the various spending authorities would like to spend and what resources they can achieve in relation to overall government plans. There have in the past been abrupt changes in government expenditure plans that have necessitated drastic revision of the PESC figures so that although the White Paper is couched in terms of reasonable expectation that the programme will be adhered to, they rarely are. It is not easy to compare figures in one White Paper with those in another because of the past method of using 'survey prices' for the basis of projection. These survey prices are usually prices ruling in the autumn of the year previous to the spring in which they are published and the data is not necessarily the same for each sector. The Thatcher government has altered these to cash terms starting with the White Paper published in 1981. However, it is clear that in the past the public expenditure Whtie Paper figures have been a poor indication of future expenditure. The analysis reported in a study by the National Council for the Building Material Producers of the change in plans for expenditure in the years 1976/77 and 1977/78 show that the expenditure in real terms was a third to a half of that originally projected for education and roads and very substantially less for water and sewerage.[37]

According to the Local Government Planning and Land Act, government from 1981/82 set up a new system for local authority capital

26

TABLE 2.5 *Gross domestic fixed capital formation in buildings and works other than dwellings by the public sector from 1970, UK (current prices)*

Year	Public corporation		Central government		Local authorities		Total
	£m	% of total	£m	% of total	£m	% of total	£m
1970	408	24	465	27	843	49	1 716
1971	456	24	467	24	995	52	1 918
1972	445	21	504	24	1 147	55	2 096
1973	447	17	598	23	1 514	59	2 559
1974	906	31	700	24	1 325	45	2 931
1975	1 477	40	929	25	1 302	35	3 708
1976	1 645	40	1 029	25	1 416	35	4 090
1977	1 717	44	914	24	1 255	32	3 886
1978	1 883	46	917	23	1 272	31	4 072
1979	2 072	44	1 108	24	1 530	32	4 710
1980	2 587	45	1 319	23	1 869	32	5 775
1981	2 685	44	1 435	24	1 973	32	6 093
1982							
1983							
1984							

Notes:

The figures can be affected by change in the scope of the sectors as well as by the rate of capital formation.

Sources:

CSO, *National Income and Expenditure 1981 Edition* (HMSO, 1981) Table 10.3; CSO, *National Income and Expenditure 1982 Edition* (HMSO, 1982) Table 10.3.

expenditure in England and Wales explained in Public Expenditure White Paper March 1981:[38]

> Separate controls will apply in England and Wales with a cash limit on aggregate local capital expenditure in each case. Except for expenditure on police, probation and magistrates courts, and certain projects of national or regional importance, local authorities will be able to decide their own priorities for expenditure within the cash limits.
>
> In Scotland the formal grant distribution arrangements remain unchanged and the control of local authority capital expenditure under the financial and planning system will continue. . . [This] new capital control scheme represents a significant increase in the discretion of local authorities to allocate their capital programmes in line with their local priorities whilst strengthening substantially central government's control over the aggregate of capital expenditure.

However the system has had considerable practical problems. In the years 1981/82 and 1982/83 there has been a substantial shortfall of actual capital expenditure compared with allocations. In all sectors including nationalised industries, under the present system almost all allocations for particular spending programmes have to be spent in the year for which they are allocated or else revert to the Treasury. There are difficulties in doing this. The present system penalises over-spenders as well as under-spenders so that the authorities can maximise their receipts only by spending precisely their allocation. On capital projects where the gestation period is long and the actual expenditure in any one year determined by many parties to the process, many of them outside the direct control of the public authorities as clients, this is very difficult to arrange. For example, an authority that has signed a contract with a private contractor to underake a construction project, say over three years, will have written a final completion date into the contract and a total contract sum but the rate at which the contractor undertakes the work is variable. Yet it is this which, through the professional's certificates of value of work done, determines the bill in any one year for the client to pay. The construction process works best with an even planned programme of work. In October 1980 the government imposed a moratorium on housing starts by local authorities, and lifted it at the end of the financial year. Housing associations have, during the 1980s, had a series of cutbacks and moratoria, one lifted only a month after it was imposed. It is perhaps not surprising that authorities are finding planning of their capital programmes as difficult as ever. Each time there is a change in direction adjustment of the systems take weeks or months. The construction process in particular cannot be switched on and switched off at will without disruption.

The situation is exacerbated by the substantial receipts of local authorities from the sale of dwellings to their tenants. The Thatcher government has encouraged and indeed insisted on local authorities offering dwellings for sale to their tenants and although this has been taking place for some years, the rate of sales has increased dramatically in the last few years. Table 2.6 shows the growth of disposals by local authorities as well as those built for disposal. In 1970–82 nearly 590 000 local authority dwellings were sold. Disposals by new towns are a maxi-

TABLE 2.6 *Disposal of local authority dwellings from 1970, England and Wales*

Year	Total number of dwellings	Built for disposal (full ownership sales)
	Number of dwellings th	
1970	6.8	0.6
1971	17.2	0.4
1972	45.9	0.8
1973	34.3	0.6
1974	4.7	0.5
1975	2.7	0.6
1976	5.8	0.9
1977	13.0	0.5
1978	30.0	0.5
1979	41.7	0.6
1980	81.5	1.2
1981	102.8	0.6
1982	200.7P	0.6P
1983		
1984		

Notes:

Up to the 1st quarter 1977 local authority figures relate to sales reported in the period, thereafter they are rounded estimates of sales in the period including adjustments for returns not received.

Sources:

DoE, *Housing and Construction Statistics 1970–1980* (HMSO, 1981) Table 82; DoE, *Housing and Construction Statistics 1971–1981* (HMSO, 1982) Table 80; DoE, *Housing and Construction Statistics December Quarter 1982*, no. 12 (HMSO, 1983) Table 2.12.

mum of about 5 per cent of those by local authorities. Clearly these sales add considerably to the funds of local authorities and these funds, unlike the annual allocations from government, can be carried forward to the following years. It is estimated that by the end of 1982/83 councils will have sold houses worth £2000 million of which they can keep half.[39]

> Councils are prohibited from using cash receipts to keep rates down, increase staff pay or any other current spending. They may, however, use them for capital investment other than on housing: public amenities, commercial development, even local roads. Less happily Councils are not prohibited from putting the money on deposit and using the interest to pay older debts. And it would appear that this is exactly what is happening.

The Association of Metropolitan Authorities thinks that authorities are trying to build up cash reserves to ensure some longer-term continuity of capital investment programmes and that the underspending is partly a consequence of government's failure to allow local authorities to plan ahead.[40]

There are other reasons too for the underspend. Local authorities have often overestimated the likely increases in tender prices and have then had extra money to spend for which they had not planned. Moreover, the recession has meant that jobs were completed more quickly than expected.

There have been a number of investigations into the planning of public-sector demand on the construction industry. In 1962 Emmerson said that[41]

> There is real substance in the view that greater efficiency will result if the Government can adopt as a main feature in its policies a steady and expanding construction programme for some years ahead, to keep pace with a steady rate of growth in the economy.

Many reports by the Building and Civil Engineering EDCs have stressed the need for longer-term programmes and in particular that on the public client and the construction industries.[42] The need for steady programmes does not diminish just because the underlying trend is not upwards. Apart from the overall long-term fluctuations, short-term fluctuations in the industry are induced by the rigid annual accounting system. Within programmes this leads to the bunching of tenders with consequent increases of costs towards the end of the financial year.[43]

As well as the inefficiencies within the contracting and supplying organisations, the National Joint Consultative Committee for Building (NJCC) has reviewed fifty local authorities and found that over 40 per cent of the annual capital issue was put out to tender in the last quarter of the financial year. It is now discussing proposals for rolling programmes.[44]

What is required is a new consideration of an alternative to annual budgets or a scheme to overcome their deficiencies with more emphasis on longer-term planning of programmes. This has been said so often but must be said again. Second, investigation is required into the types of capital expenditure which necessarily or potentially generate greater current expenditure and those that can reduce it. This is important because some authorities report that they cannot spend capital allocations because they are not allowed to increase current spending. There are stories of new hospitals and other buildings standing empty because the authority cannot afford to run them. At the same time some replacement of building by modern ones should reduce current expenditure, not increase it.

There are under consideration various innovative approaches to the provision of private finance for public projects and an EDC working party is considering the matter. An example is roads where the owners would be private and the government would pay for usage on a royalty basis. There are great difficulties in working out such schemes because the risks are very difficult to quantify, and private financiers may well not be prepared to undertake them at a economic price. However, there may well be publicly used buildings where some system could be devised. Over all, however, it seems that government is sometimes attempting to keep public borrowing down at the expense of efficiency in the allocation of funds and of risks in the community as a whole.

REHABILITATION, IMPROVEMENT, REPAIR AND MAINTENANCE

Rehabilitation may be regarded as the process of changing a building or area previously unusable or unsuitable to a state where it becomes usable at a standard acceptable to the community. It may involve substantial change of use. Improvement is less dramatic and does not usually involve change of use, while repair and maintenance implies continuing upkeep of the stock to existing standards. There is no hard and fast line between these three categories. However, from the point of view of statistics of the industry, rehabilitation and improvement are classed as new work, except in the case of housing where they are included with repair and maintenance. There is therefore very little statistical data for the whole group.

The sector as a whole has become of increased importance in recent years. Repair and maintenance including housing improvement alone has increased its proportion of the work-load from about 25 per cent in the 1950s to over 40 per cent in 1982. In absolute terms too it has increased but to a lesser extent (see Figure 4.2). However, in a period of recession this is itself remarkable. In addition there is the considerable but unknown amount of non-housing rehabilitation and improvement.

There are several reasons for this situation. In a mature economy, once there are sufficient buildings and works, there will inevitably be more emphasis on repair and maintenance and improvement rather than on new construction. At the same time the long life of construction products implies a long interval between new construction and replacement. There was a severe shortage of buildings and works as a result of the Second World War but by the mid-1970s the urgent demands for additional stock had been met. The demand for new buildings is low, leaving repair and maintenance and improvement with a higher proportion of the total.

On the other hand, the age and condition of some stock and the fact that some is no longer suitable or required for the purpose for which it was originally intended means that there is a demand for rehabilitation and improvement. In addition there has been a reaction against new building and in favour of rehabilitation for aesthetic reasons and because of the defects and failures caused by the new buildings in the 1960s and early 1970s. Lastly, there is usually a cost advantage – albeit often small – in rehabilitation as opposed to new building.

Rehabilitation of Whole Areas

There has been recent impetus given to schemes to rehabilitate substantial geographical areas particularly in inner cities, many of which have under-utilised, wrongly utilised and dilapidated buildings. The run-down buildings and poor environment in these areas tend to generate or exacerbate social problems which, in their turn, cause misuse and vandalism of buildings and neighbourhoods. A number of organisations have for some time been concerned with grants for the regeneration of cities, for examples the Scottish and Welsh Development Agencies. In the early 1980s a number of new initiatives have been taken. These are interesting partly for the different forms of finance and partly for the new relationships between the public and the private sector. They were reviewed in 'Finding the Funds'.[45]

The Urban Programme was launched by government in July 1981 under which local authorities were asked to develop schemes for securing economic regeneration, improving the physical environment and ensuring that local services and amenities are geared to the particular social needs of the local communities in urban areas. Under this programme the government grants 75 per cent of expenditure by local authorities and voluntary bodies which they support.

Private-sector involvement is encouraged in these schemes and partnership and programme authorities under the Urban Programme are required to consult local industry. Government gives urban development grants to projects with a significant private-sector involvement to allow such schemes to go ahead with the help of some public contribution. Enterprise Zones have been set up with special encouragement for industrial and commercial activities. For Development Areas and Special Development Areas where there is very high unemployment, Regional Development Grants of up to 22 per cent are available for the provision of buildings, plant, equipment and works in manufacturing sector and are also available from the European Community. There are also grants for derelict land clearance and conservation.

Three basically private groups are particularly interesting: Business in the Community was established by a group of leading companies and aims to encourage and assist in the extension of the involvement of industrial and commercial concerns with local economic and social development.[46] Local Enterprise Agencies have been set up partly in conjunction with Business in the Community and DoE regional offices. Lastly, there is Inner City Enterprise Ltd, funded by the financial institutions to seek out schemes for urban regeneration for finance from the institutions. This is the successor body to a sort of inner-city financial 'Think Tank' set up by government – the Financial Institutions Group – which examined these problems over a year from 1981–2.[47]

These institutional changes are interesting in that they are trying to look at the problem of regeneration as a whole; that they are combining expertise of various sectors of the economy which have previously not considered this problem together; and lastly, that they are innovative in their approach. The basic philosophy behind these groups could well be applied to areas that need regeneration but are not yet so run down to qualify for grants. If this is not done they will fall behind the areas that have special asssistance and become the Development Areas of the future.

Housing

The need for improvement and repair and maintenance in housing is documented in the English House Condition Survey 1981.[48] It deals with three categories of unsuitability: dwellings unfit to be lived in of which there were 1.1 million; dwellings lacking one of five basic amenities of which there were 0.9 million, and dwellings requiring repairs in excess of over £7000 of which there were 1 million. However, the three categories overlap and 2 million dwellings fell into one or more categories. If the threshold of disrepair is extended to include dwellings needing more than £2500 spent on them, then the number in total increases to 4.3 million dwellings. Over the ten years 1971–81 there has been a substantial decline in the dwellings lacking one or more amenities, but the number of unfit dwellings is about the same and the number with high repair cost has increased, particularly in the owner-occupied sector. In part the last is due to the high average age of persons living in pre-1919 dwellings who tend to have low incomes.

Government encouragement has been given since 1949, but with many changes in the system since then, to the rehabilitation of housing under schemes financed through local authorities. The dwellings receiving grants in England in 1981 were between six and seven times the number demolished under slum clearance in 1980-1, although ten years earlier the number was just over double.[49] The cost of improvement and repair and maintenance grants in 1979 was about £650 million in England and, making estimates for Scotland and Wales for which no value figures are available, probably nearer £850 million for Great Britain.[50]

The initiator of the grant-aided improvement process is, in the case of local authority dwellings, usually the local authority itself. In the private sector it is normally the owner, although in the case of rented property may be the owner or the tenant or user. The financier is usually partly the local authority, supported by a government grant, and partly the owner.

However, the grant-aided work is small in comparison to the work financed by householders themselves with the help of loans from banks, building societies or others. Table 2.7 gives an estimate of the expenditure on housing improvements and repairs, excluding apparently private non-occupier expenditure which is small. The total spending without the occupiers' material purchases is shown as rather higher than the output figures of repair and maintenance on housing but is of the same order. Including an estimate for Wales and Scotland, the improvement and repair grants to private owners were 3-4 per cent of the total occupier spending on improvement and maintenance in 1979 and 1980 but local authority and housing association grant-aided expenditure accounted for over 40 per cent of public-sector spending in 1979 - the latest year for which figures are available.[51]

TABLE 2.7 *The market for rehabilitation, improvement, repair and maintenance of dwellings, 1977–80, UK*

	1977	1978	1979	1980	1977	1978		1979		1980	
	£m	£m	£m	£m	£m	£m	% change	£m	% change	£m	% change
		(current prices)						*(1975 prices)*			
Occupier spending:											
Material purchases	897	1 090	1 374	1 687	636	703	+10	761	+8	862	+13
Payments to contractors											
– non-structural work	514	494	735	856	389	348	–11	449	+29	394	–12
– structural work	668	555	1 807	1 690	506	390	–23	1 104	+183	784	–29
Total occupier spending	2 079	2 139	3 917	4 233	1 531	1 441	–6	2 314	+61	2 040	–12
Public-sector spending:											
Local authority dwellings											
– repair and maintenance	553	679	662	1 117	419	478	+14	404	–15	571	+41
– improvement and rehabilitation	480	642	771	697	364	452	+24	470	+4	356	–24
Housing association dwellings											
– improvement and rehabilitation	76	167	277	159	58	118	+103	169	+43	81	–52
Total public-sector spending:	1 110	1 488	1 710	1 973	841	1 048	+25	1 043	nc	1 009	–3
All spending:	3 189	3 627	5 627	6 206	2 372	2 489	+5	3 357	+35	3 049	–9

Source:

National Home Improvement Council, *Report on the Market for Home Improvement, Repair and Maintenance and DIY 1977–80* (NHIC, June 1982) Table 1. Table 1 consists of Housing and Construction Research Associates estimates based on the Family Expenditure Survey, Government Expenditure Plans and CIPFA Housing Revenue a/c (revised).

Table 2.7 also shows the volatility of some of the expenditure on housing, particularly owner-occupied spending on structural work. It is this work that is often most easily postponable and therefore subject to fluctuations in the light of real incomes, future expectations and rates of interest, all of which deteriorated between 1979 and 1980. Whereas for most repair and maintenance work by owner-occupiers, where the expenditure will normally come out of income, the owner, the financier and the initiator are usually the same, for more major works a bank or other financial institution may also need to be willing for the expenditure to take place.

About 90 per cent of expenditure by occupiers is by owner-occupiers, the remainder being by the private rented and public rented sector where the owners and user are different.[52] In the case of public authorities the authority determines the expenditure at a 'reasonable' level. A problem with the private rented sector is that the owner has often inadequate income under the Rent Acts to undertake work.

In addition there is a different approach being developed to the problem of run-down council estates, some of them multi-storey blocks. Private-sector developers have purchased local authority housing estates for rehabilitation and sale sometimes on an outright purchase but sometimes with part of the proceeds of sale to be paid to the local authority as a second stage payment of the purchase price.

Other Sectors

There is a need for rehabilitation, improvement and repair and maintenance for other types of buildings and works. In the case of most of the infrastructure the stock is under public-sector ownership and is subject to the usual factors determining public expenditure. There is some information on the state of the stock which indicates deterioration of standards, in particular in the water and sewerage system referred to earlier.[53] The state of the roads is monitored annually in the National Road Maintenance Condition Survey[54] and the House of Commons Transport Select Committee has recently completed a study of road maintenance.[55] Concern at standards is expressed in both these documents.

In the private sector, because the expenditure on existing building is likely to be internally financed, the user, the owner, the initiator and the financier are likely to be the same or, if different, to be along the same lines as for comparable new work. Many under-utilised or empty warehouses and factories are decaying and although some can be rehabilitated for industrial or other uses, others are not suitable for modern industry because, for example, of inadequate office accommodation, low quality, too many storeys or wrong location. There is a substantial amount of rehabilitation of existing offices under way. However it would be expected that in a recession some maintenance would be postponed and the changes in the state of the stock are probably very varied from one area and type of building to another.

THE INFLUENCE OF THE CONSTRUCTION INDUSTRY

With the multiplicity of partners concerned before demand is even created there is little reason why the demand that is put to the construction industry should follow a smooth, even path. Indeed it does not do so, as the fluctuations in the level of output shown in Chapter 4, and particularly Figure 4.1, demonstrate. Government has undoubtedly the greatest single influence on the level of demand on the construction industry, but even government is not able quickly to change the level of demand largely because of the long time lags in construction (dealt with in Chapter 3).

Most industry can influence the level of demand for its product by its pricing policies, publicity and effective marketing. The construction industry would like to have more influence over the demand for its products. One way of doing this is to influence government to act in a way that directly or indirectly will affect the level of construction demand. Ever since the boom of 1973 it has been trying to do this through a number of meetings between government and parts of the industry, through the EDCs for Building and Civil Engineering and most recently since 1977 through the Group of Eight which is a group consisting of the Presidents of RIBA, RICS, ICE, NFBTE, FCEC, NCBMP, and the General Secretaries of UCATT and TGWU. Their efforts have been successful in improving liaison between government and the industry and in obtaining more information of government spending plans for construction.

More recently they were instrumental in persuading government to press for the reduction in the underspending of public-sector allocations. However, over all they appear to have failed to affect the general level of output except that, as always in these situations, one will never know how different it might have been had there been no lobbying by the group.

Another area to which the industry has turned its attention is marketing. It is important to distinguish between marketing that is going to increase the work of the industry as a whole, in which case it is competing against other goods and services, and that which increases the market share of one firm. It is quite possible for imaginative marketing by one firm to increase its output without diminishing that of others. It depends whether it persuades a client to build who would otherwise not have done so (or in the case of speculative housing whether it persuades a household to buy).

The marketing by the industry as a whole has not been very impressive. Probably the most important in recent years has been the attempts to 'sell' new industrial buildings by the NFBTE and the Building EDC.[56] The totality of marketing by construction companies may well be more fruitful because they are better able to reach the individual decision-maker and influence him positively in favour of undertaking a specific project rather than his being subjected to general publicity that does not really impinge upon him.

In view of the complexities of the processes of demand formation and the number of roles involved, one of the ways in which the industry might be able to increase demand is by acting as a catalyst to get the parties to the process together in new ways – to help to create the demand for the products which it wishes to construct.

Probably more important than general marketing operations is the need for the industry to find out more about the needs of the client in terms of the service he requires in matters of time, cost and organisation and to change the packages that it offers to meet these client requirements (see Chapter 3).

However much the industry tries to influence demand and even if it has some measure of success, the forces that affect demand will often be too strong for it to change except in a very marginal way. It will continue to be at the receiving end of government measures that affect the industry, and continue to be affected more than many industries by the general level of economic activity and the expectations of change in that level. While not abrogating its right to put its case to government and potential clients, it should accept that it must continue to live with an uncertain fluctuating work-load and, so far as possible, plan its actions accordingly.

3 The Process

INTRODUCTION

The construction process is long, involved and often cumbersome and inefficient. Its success depends on having the right relationships between the parties to the process. There is a great range of possible methods of organising the process each with its different contractual relationships and procedures. Matters to be dealt with include the determination of exactly what is required by the client, financial and operational viability and conformity to legal requirements of the scheme, the design of the building or works required and its construction within cost and time targets.

RELATIONSHIPS OF THE PARTIES TO THE PROCESS

Figure 3.1 shows in diagrammatic form the traditional process for new building and civil engineering works. Even if this process is not used, almost all the activities in this diagram have to be underaken.

In view of the large number of participants in the construction process, the complexity of the relationships and the large number of functions to be performed, it is not surprising that there has been concern in the industry itself and in government that the process does not always work smoothly. A whole number of investigations and reports have since 1944 reviewed the situation and proposed improvements, most of which have been implemented only slowly, if at all. The most important of these are listed in the select bibliography of this chapter. The theme of all is expressed in the words of the Banwell Report: 'We consider that the most urgent problem that confronts the construction industry is the necessity of thinking and acting as a whole.'[1]

40

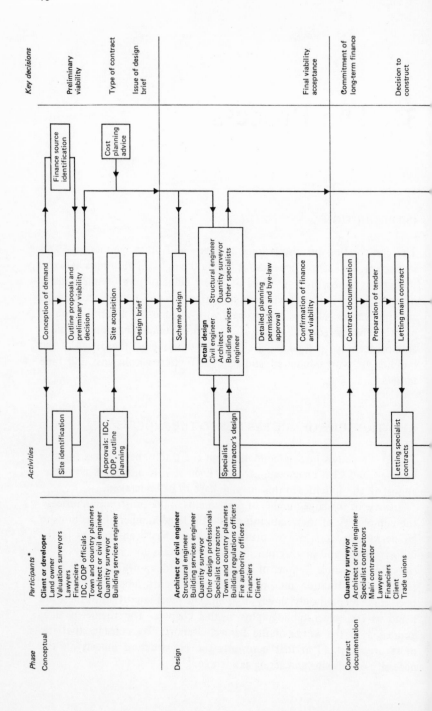

41

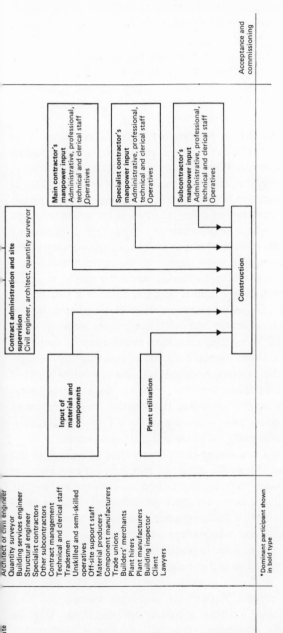

FIGURE 3.1 *Traditional construction process for new building and civil engineering works*

Notes:

1. This is intended only to demonstrate an outline of the traditional construction process without attempting to detail the many activities, duties and relationships involved. These may be found in other publications such as the RIBA plan of work for design.

2. Many variations are possible on the traditional construction process:
some activities may be omitted, e.g. in private housing where the developer is also the contractor
the order of activities may be different, e.g. the site may already be owned before the project is conceived; the contract may be let before design is started, for some types of contract.

3. Although the flows between activities are all shown as one-way, many of them will be two-way.

Source:

EDCs for Building and Civil Engineering, *How Flexible Is Construction?* NEDO (HMSO, 1978) pp. 4–5.

This is true twenty years later and the industry is still seeking ways in the organisation and management of the process to achieve a unification of purpose and efficiency in achieving it. In part it is doing this by variations on the relationships between the parties; in part by improving the traditional mechanisms. One of the problems is that the professional institutions often work against one another and that the educational process does not span the traditional disciplines except at postgraduate level (see Chapter 13).

The traditional approach in building is that the client appoints his principal designer who becomes the main client adviser. In most building projects he will be the architect but sometimes he could be the structural, chemical or services engineer, especially in the case of specific industrial buildings. The main designer becomes the leader of the team and advises the client on the appointment of other members of the design team and the quantity surveyor who is responsible for cost advice and for drawing up contract documents. The designer, and often the quantity surveyor, advises on the selection and appointment of the contractor and may decide to nominate some subcontractors. However the only contractual relationship of the professional team is with the client as is that also of the main contractor. The subcontractors, whether nominated by the architect or not, have a contractual relationship only with the main contractor. Figure 3.2 shows this traditional relationship in simplified form, distinguishing between management and contractual relationships. In civil engineering the position is similar with the consulting engineer in the main design and leadership role. However there is usually no quantity surveyor in civil engineering, the function being performed by the consulting engineer who, according to the ICE form of contract, is responsible for measurement, valuation and cost management.

Where the client is a continuing client in any field of work, and this applies particularly in the public sector, he may have his own in-house design team and possibly construction team too. Thus the architect in Figure 3.2 may be the in-house architect but other relationships could remain the same. Similarly if the contractor is the direct labour department, strictly speaking the relationships should be as in Figure 3.2, although it may become confused in practice.

A variant on this method is the design and construct project, sometimes called package deal or a turnkey project. In this case the client calls in a general contractor first and the contractor arranges and leads the team. The contractor has then a contractual relationship with the client and with all the professional organisations. This is illustrated in Figure 3.3. The design and construct method is valuable where, for

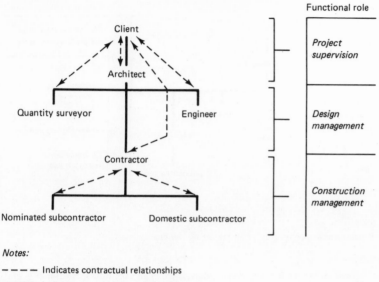

Notes:

– – – – Indicates contractual relationships

▬▬▬▬ Indicates management relationships

Source:

Chartered Institute of Building, *Project Management in Building* (CIOB, 1982) p. 8.

FIGURE 3.2 *Traditional management structure of a project*

example, there is a need for the contractor to be involved at a very early stage of the process, and especially where a saving of time is particularly important. Unfortunately there is very little up-to-date information on the extent of the use of package dealing, but about 30 per cent of the case studies in the NEDO study of industrial building were design and build.[2] Commercial building also has a high proportion. In local authority housing design and build projects have not, since about 1966 when they were 15 per cent of schemes,[3] accounted for more than 10 per cent of the schemes and were in 1980 only 0.2 per cent of schemes.[4] In 1965, apart from housing there were no local authority package deals, whereas in the private sector for factories from 1968-72 package deals were estimated to account for 28 per cent of schemes and in offices 19 per cent.[5] Design and construct projects are comparatively rare in civil engineering.

Largely because of the difficulties of managing large complex projects,

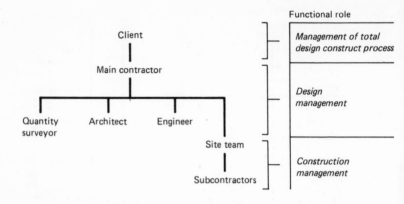

Note:
Management and contractual relationships are identical.

Source:
Chartered Institute of Building, *Project Management in Building* (CIOB, 1982) p. 8.

FIGURE 3.3   *Management structure for design construct*

variations of approaches in Figures 3.2 and 3.3 have been developed. One of these is project management defined in the Chartered Institute of Building publication as[6]

> The overall planning, control and co-ordination of a project from inception to completion aimed at meeting a clients requirements and ensuring completion on time within cost and to required quality standards.

The project manager may be an extension of the client with a co-ordinating role or he may be the executive manager of the process taking this role over from the chief designer. The latter is illustrated in Figure 3.4. The qualifications for a project manager are first, that he should have considerable experience of the construction industry and second, that he should have personal qualities of leadership. The original discipline of the project manager is not so important. A study for the National Economic Development Office found:[7]

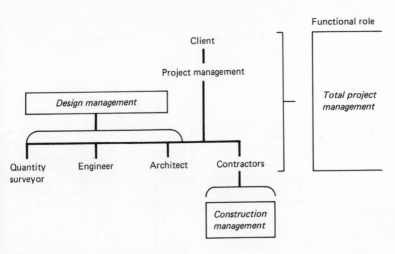

Note:
Functional roles are in italics.

Source:
Chartered Institute of Building, *Project Management in Building* (CIOB, 1982) p. 11.

FIGURE 3.4 *Management structure for executive project management*

Some form of unified project management becomes necessary when projects have some or all of the following characteristics: high value, a short time scale, high complexity (high cost per sq. ft.), novelty, resource scarcity, high intensity (high value per unit of time), geographical dispersion of site and/or parties to the process, large number of participants.

Another development is that of management contracting whereby the construction process is managed by a contractor's team on a fee basis but with the management contractor having the contractual relationship with the subcontractors. It has the merit that the construction manager can be called in at an early stage while still enabling the construction work on site to be let on a competitive basis. He is concerned to liaise with the design team and to ensure that the construction on site can proceed smoothly. He arranges contracts with a number of subcontractors and manages the construction on site. This was to some extent a logical development from the main contractor having a contract with the client to produce a building but in fact subcontracting almost all the work to others. A typical management contracting situation is illutated in Figure 3.5.

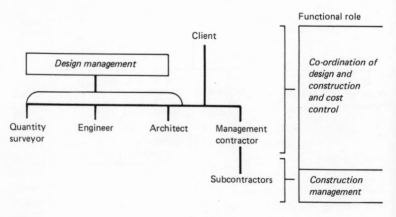

Notes:

Management and contractual structure are identical. Functional roles in italics.

Source:

Chartered Institute of Building, *Project Management in Building* (CIOB, 1982) p. 9.

FIGURE 3.5   *Management structure for management contracting*

If the role of management of construction is taken on by a purely professional firm, the firm usually arranges a number of contracts for specialist trades and general construction direct with the client. If this firm is also undertaking the design in a professional capacity, it links on to the concept of project management although in the ideal case the project manager does not undertake any of the functions of the other professions. It is also similar to the traditional Scottish separate trades system whereby the architect, instead of letting the contract to a main contractor, lets each trade contract separately and manages the project on behalf of the client. This system in Scotland is, however, largely being replaced.

It is difficult to establish firm lines between the great variety of arrangements practised. In the public sector the person in the authority responsible for the project may be performing many of the functions of the independent project manager and has done so for a considerable time. There does seem to be a movement towards project management and the role is undertaken by construction industry professions and also increasingly by professional firms peripheral to the construction industry, such as those who are primarily estate agents or management consultants. This challenge to the established organisations in the industry is good and could provide innovative solutions provided the employees of these firms have the necessary construction industry experience, in which case the professional firm to which they belong is a matter of marketing convenience. But if they have inadequate construction industry experience, then it is likely to be an unsatisfactory venture.

The EDC study on time for industrial building found that project managers performed a wide range of tasks on projects between £0.25 and £2.5 million. They were used more by experienced clients than by first-time customers.[8] There is no hard data on the extent to which management contracting and project managers are used in this country. About half the very large contractors have a separate management contracting organisation. The value of output on projects using project management and management contracting may have been of the order of £200 million or more in 1982 mainly in large projects in private industrial and commercial work compared with about £600 million total work in these types of work, but also in some public-sector work, notably Terminal 4 at Heathrow. The evidence is that this method accounts for a significant proportion of large private industrial and commercial work.

Project management by professional firms hits the headlines from time to time but the total average annual value of work done in this area is probably a small fraction of that done by management contractors. It sometimes includes a design service.

The EDC study found that management contracting with an integrated design service was used in industrial building mostly where there was a high process plant element.[9]

There are great difficulties in a client's decision as to which method of approach to use. If he is a continuing client of the industry he will have past experience to go on and may be able to afford some experimentation. For a one-off client, however, the problem is a major one and he will need to consult other clients who have similar buildings and many of the persons and organisations who have experience of various roles in the industry. Here the client may be in difficulty because each person consulted may tend to advocate the method of organisation where his role is important, if only because that is the type of which he has most experience. This view is supported by the EDC study[10] which found that the customers of the industry 'lacked sources of information or impartial advice about the options or alternative courses of action open to them', and that, 'projects were often organised traditionally by default rather than as a result of conscious decision', often with unsatisfactory consequences. What is needed, but exists only in an informal way, is an independent adviser who has knowledge of the process and of the advantages and disadvantages of various methods of organisation but who will have no part in the process and is therefore completely impartial.

The choice of method should depend on the objectives and priorities of the client, the strength of his ability to mount, from within his own organisation, a client's management team, his past experience as a client of the industry and of course the nature of the project.

The public client tends to be concerned to obtain the lowest cost of the project provided that the objectives are achieved and that the process be seen as fair. This means that the traditional process is favoured because the work accounting for the greater part of the cost can then be let in competition. This is less easy with package deals and management contracting, although some limited competition for these is possible. The public client is more likely to have his own expert in-house staff to form a competent team to manage the project. The Wood Report[11] suggested that the traditional approach did not always obtain value for money when time and cost are considered together but time is often insufficiently weighted in decisions of many public-sector clients.

The private client is often more concerned with time, particularly for industrial buildings, and may place more emphasis on certainty of cost at an early stage in the process than on the lowest cost. Thus risk reduction on these two matters of time and cost may be paramount. There is, however, no reason why there should not be speedy construction without any sacrifice of cost or quality.[12] The client may favour a package deal where he can obtain a firm price well before design is completed, rather than wait till tenders come in by the traditional method. He may also prefer to deal with one organisation, especially if he is unable or not qualified to produce a good management team of his own. On the other hand, he may prefer to keep nearer to the traditional process with more choice of designers and contractors and strengthen the management of the project by employing a project manager, who will in turn choose the design team and the contractor using either the traditional tendering process, negotiation or a construction management team.

The nature of the project will have a substantial bearing on the decision on which system to use both for the private and public client. The more important the design characteristics of the project, the more important it is for the client to have a wide choice of designers, whether architects or engineers, sometimes resorting to design competitions. On the other hand, the greater the complexity of the construction process, the more the need for a system whereby the contractor can contribute to the design by a package deal or by early appointment by negotiation or non-traditional limited tender.

THE CLIENT'S ROLE

Assuming that the client has taken a decision as to which method of organisation to adopt for his construction he then has to choose the first appointee, whether he be designer or other professional – notably project manager of whatever background or quantity surveyor or contractor. Most professional organisations have some advisory service that assists in the choice of the firm with the appropriate experience and the client should visit the offices of a short list as well as investigate other clients' satisfaction with past performance of firms not only on their technical competence but especially on their ability to manage the project. This is particularly important because the emphasis given to management by many professional organisations and firms is inadequate (see Chapter 13). The criteria that should be considered to assess the suitability of a firm are listed in *Before You Build*[13] as size of firm, experience, work-load, the senior persons in charge, business efficiency, practices, quality of past work and location.

Surveys undertaken by NEDO[14] investigated the use made of various designers by public and private clients as shown in Tabel 3.1. In terms of value, external consultants were more important, because the projects designed by consultants were larger than those by in-house teams or by contractors. For private-sector projects, *Before You Build* showed that for projects under 300 square metres there would usually be an architect only, for large projects up to 2000 square metres an architect and quantity surveyor, and over 2000 square metres architect, quantity surveyors and other specialist designers.[15]

The exact stage at which the main client adviser is appointed varies. The client may, for example, already have the site and have determined the viability of the project or he may need a feasibility study and/or to find and purchase land. In any case the first task of the principal adviser or manager is to obtain a clear brief from the client to include the function and the range of cost and timing of the proposed construction. This may appear obvious but there are often very considerable difficulties at

TABLE 3.1 *Agencies employed to provide detailed design services*

Type of designer	Public client	Private client[a]
	% of number of projects	
In-house design teams	71	9
External consultants	21	51
Design and construct firms or suppliers of standard buildings	7	26
Others/not stated	1	14
	100	100

Notes:

[a] Based on a NEDO survey of 1250 private-sector clients of factory and office developments.

Source:

EDCs for Building and Civil Engineering, *The Public Client and the Construction Industries* (The Wood Report) NEDO (HMSO, 1975) Table 4.1.

this stage, especially if the client is a multiple and complex one and where the project is also complicated. Hospital building, for example, is a type of work on which problems tend to arise because the administrators, doctors and nursing staff have different views on how various conflicting objectives should be reconciled. Sometimes the client has prejudged the issue. He may want more usable space but this may be achievable by a rearrangement of existing spaces rather than by an extension of the premises.

Producing a brief is not by any means the only function of the client. He must also be involved in approval of design at various stages and ensuring that the design is proceeding smoothly. He must take speedy decisions on many matters submitted to him at the design stage and then try to limit the variations to the agreed design to a minimum. The loss of time and increase in costs through a client's indecision and change of mind can be considerable and some of the costs may or may not be appropriately reflected in the price the client pays thus increasing the uncertainty of the contractors. The client must also be concerned in the selection of the contractor and keep a watching brief on progress.

STATUTORY CONSENTS

Once the preliminary brief is obtained, the designer can proceed with obtaining some of the necessary statutory consents. Others come after the design has been completed. Statutory requirements vary over time and are now probably fewer than at any time in the post-war period but those that remain are complex and time-consuming. The main consents now required are planning permission and building regulations approval. Planning regulation is intended to ensure that development takes place in a coherent manner according to local authority development plans and is in keeping with the area as a whole, in order that the often conflicting interests of the client or developer and the community shall be reconciled in the best way possible. There is a need to strike a balance in this process between the interests of efficiency and the interests of democracy. The basic procedure is that outline planning permission is sought, followed at the design stage by detailed permission. However, if it is a controversial scheme there follow appeals, often with public inquiries, and the whole process can take many years, with a resultant great cost in work by all parties and in loss of development which often affects whole communities. The planning system has been investigated on a number of occasions, notably in the Dobry Report[16] and the House of Commons Expenditure Committee Report on Planning Procedures.[17] Many alterations have been made over the last few years and most recently, following a consultation paper, that in the appeals procedure, by which appeals decisions are made by inspectors instead of by the relevant minister. This and other streamlining helped by a reduction in activity levels, have significantly speeded up the planning system. From the second quarter of 1981 to the second quarter of 1982 the percentage decided within the statutory period of eight weeks increased from 62 to 70 per cent in England. Some 88 per cent of applications were granted.[18] In 1981 the number of appeals grew but the processing times of appeals was reduced. Those determined by the Secretary of State took an average of forty-four weeks, but those determined by inspectors with an inquiry twenty-six weeks and eighteen weeks with written representations only by inspectors.[19]

Extreme durations apply to the large public cases such as airport terminals and motorways and to smaller cases often complicated by listed building consent and drawn out by attempts to get settlement by negotiation.

Building regulations are also administered locally and are concerned with the structural, health and fire safety as well as with energy conservation. Consequently approval for building regulations can be given only after detailed design stage. The regulations and procedures are in the process of change.

New regulations should be shorter and more logical and readable which should in turn facilitate their administration. Discussions are proceeding on ways of involving the design team themselves certifying that a building conforms to regulations. Of particular concern to the industry is the time taken and inconsistencies, especially from one part of the country to another, of the fire officers' interpretation of the fire regulations. These, according to the study of industrial building by the EDC, caused several weeks' delay on some sites.[20] There are in addition other consents needed in special situations, for example listed buildings consents.

Becoming ever more important are the grants and other concessions for industrial and other building for special industries or special locations (see Chapter 2). These must be considered where relevant at a very early stage of the process as they may affect decision on, for example, site location.

Lastly, in a different but related category, it is necessary to have the co-operation of the statutory undertakers supplying gas, water, electricity and drainage. They can cause considerable delay and additional unnecessary cost.[21]

THE DESIGN

The design of the project is generally regarded as the principal function of the preconstruction phase and the chief designer has the main role. Design in fact covers more than one stage. There is first the definition of a broad outline design culminating in a sketch design. This is usually done by a senior person in the firm of consultants who is in direct touch with the client. Then there is the translation and development of the sketch design to a workable project and finally there is the production of the detailed working drawings that enable the designers' ideas to be communicated to the contractor in a way that enables him to produce the building or civil works. This last part is usually undertaken by relatively junior personnel. It is important to the efficient functioning of the process that the drawings be produced at the time they are required. In the case of the traditional process all the main drawings should be ready before the bill of quantities and other tender documents are produced. If they are not so available the bill of quantities may not represent the true quantities and there will be claims and delay in settling the final account. Alternatively in a departure from the strict traditional system a bill of approximate quantities can be used as a basis for tenders and this saves time. If the detailed working drawings are not available when the contractor requires them there will be similar problems and the contractor will claim against the client for the disruption so caused.

In other than the traditional process, it is often possible to save time by the more detailed drawings wanted at a later stage of the process being produced concurrently with the construction work on site of the early stages of the work. The schedules of drawing production must then be very carefully worked out and the dates adhered to.

The design team and the quantity surveyors are paid by the client normally on the basis of fees related to the total cost of the building. Thus they have no direct financial incentive to keep the overall cost of the building low, and it may be more expensive in time to design a cheap than an expensive building. It is argued in Chapter 8 that there is something wrong with a system that relies on professional integrity to place the interests of the client above the financial interest of a participant to the process. There are quite sufficient difficulties in the construction team acting as a team, without having inbuilt divergence of interest between the client and his team.

One of the problems of design is the extent to which the client may change his mind during the design process or more critically during the construction process. It is costly in terms of abortive work for the client to alter his mind, but clearly the client's needs are paramount, and a system sometimes advocated and nearer to that used in the USA (whereby the variations are penalised) is undesirable because it leads sometimes to a client having a building that is not exactly what he wants. However, clearly the variations should be kept to a minimum. It is important that they are properly costed and this is dealt with under contracts on pp. 58–60.

SELECTING THE MAIN CONTRACTOR

While the design for the building project is going on the chief designer and the quantity surveyor may be advising the client on the best method of appointing the contractor and the type of contract to use. How the contractor is chosen is clearly partly dependent on which pattern of relationships outlined in the earlier part of this chapter is to be followed. However, the variants that can be used with the traditional process will first be discussed.

The method with the most potential contenders for a job is that of open competitive tender whereby through advertisement tenders are invited from any contractor and in general the lowest tender is accepted.

The advantages of this sytem are its apparent fairness and low initial cost to the client. Its disadvantages, however, generally outweigh the advantages. These are, first, that there is no guarantee that the contractor who puts in the lowest tender is technically, managerially or financially capable of doing the job. If he is not, the costs of remedial work may far outweigh the gain by the lower initial price. Second, the costs of tendering to the would-be contractor are high and have to be recouped so that they will be reflected in higher overhead costs. Successive reports from the Simon Report[22] to the Wood Report[23] have recommended against its use. The Wood Report states:[24]

> We cannot, however, endorse the continued use of open competition. It has little to offer over some form of selection prior to invitation to tender, and we cannot entertain any justification for its continued use in the face of repeated condemnation in past reports, and the poor performance on such contracts in our statistical survey.

Open tendering was used quite substantially in public-sector work and in 1965 more than a quarter of each of local authority housing, schools, roads, water and sewage schemes were let by open tender, although since with the exception of water, most of these were smaller projects, the proportion of the total value was less. Hardly any private-sector projects were then or now let by open competition.[25] The position in the public sector in 1974 was much improved but still unsatisfactory. Table 3.2

TABLE 3.2 *Procedures used by public clients in the selection of main contractors for contracts over £50 000*

	Building	Civil engineering
	% by number of contracts	
Open competition	16	17
Select competition	65	77
Negotiation	14	4
Two-stage tender	3	1
Serial/continuity tender	1	—
Other	—	1
	100	100

Source:

NEDO Survey reported in EDCs for Building and Civil Engineering, *The Public Client and the Construction Industries* (The Wood Report) NEDO (HMSO, 1975) Table 5.1.

shows that for projects over £50 000 in value in 1974, 16 per cent of building and 17 per cent of civil engineering projects were let by open competition. The same survey[26] found that open tendering was most prevalent in housing, very small road schemes and other civil engineering work and less used in education and other building. In all types of work it was used more on small schemes than on large, and more by smaller district authorities. It is rarely used by central government, universities and new towns. Since 1974 local authority practice for housing schemes has been to move increasingly away from open tendering to selective tendering so that whereas in 1974 17.8 per cent of tenders were in open competitive tender, by 1980 the figure had fallen to 6.3 per cent of schemes and furthermore these schemes had a smaller average number of dwellings of twenty in 1980 compared with twenty-nine in 1974.[27] In local authority work generally a survey by Newcombe[28] suggested that in 1977 there had been little improvement, with the exception of London Boroughs which seemed to have abandoned open tendering.

Selective tendering is the system whereby a number of contractors are invited to tender for a particular job. The National Joint Consultative Council of Architects, Quantity Surveyors and Builders (NJCC) has recommended the number of contractors who should be invited to tender[29] and the number has been selected to balance the advantages of competition with the high cost of tendering. However, especially in periods of low work-load on the industry the number invited is often far in excess of these recommendations. Moreover, sometimes in a buyers' market the client decides to ask contractors to re-tender and in this way to obtain lower tenders all round.[30] This procedure is very wasteful of resources. Tender costs average for civil engineering projects $\frac{1}{2}$ per cent of company turnover and, if design is involved, as much as 1 per cent or more.[31] In such cases the process of selective tendering is very little different from open tendering. In periods of high work-load on the industry, however – for example in 1973 – there has been difficulty in clients obtaining more than one or two tenders for work, especially for public-sector building work.

Selective tendering has generally been recommended by the various committees investigating the matter as the most desirable usual method of contractor selection.

Table 3.2 shows that selective tendering has become the dominant method of selecting the contractor for the public sector. For the private sector there is no up-to-date information. Already in the period 1968–72 negotiation, two-stage selective tendering and package dealing accounted for well over half the projects[32] and this is probably still the situation leaving selective tendering in less than half the total private work.

There are a number of variants of selective tendering, each of which has merits. Serial tendering or continuity tendering is an arrangement whereby a contractor, having won a contract on one job, continues on the same or similar basis for a number of related projects. He thus obtains continuity of work and should be able to put in a lower price as he can expect to gain by experience as work progresses. There are, however, few types of projects of appropriate size and similarity where such methods are possible. Telephone exchanges are one where the method has been tried.

Two-stage tender is another method of choosing a contractor early and of choosing a contractor on matters of expertise, resources and site organisation as well as of price. There are various ways of obtaining rough tenders before design is complete. One is by the use of a bill of approximate quantities so that rates can be determined. The second stage is not strictly a tender but a determination of final price. These methods of tendering are assessed in some detail in the Wood Report and for the private sector in the Wilson Report.

Lastly, contracts may be negotiated, usually on the basis of past experience of working with a contractor or by strong recommendation, coupled with need to involve the contractor in design or to save time, or because of the inherent uncertainties in the project. There are various methods of price determination once the contractor is chosen. This may, for example, be a prime cost plus fixed fee contract or a target cost, in which the savings in or excess over the target cost are divided as pre-arranged between client and contractor.

There are, however, difficulties in relation to EEC directives in negotiating public-sector projects over a certain size. They have first to be open to competition from firms of all member states.

Table 3.2 shows that for the public sector, apart from negotiation, there is very little of use of more unusual methods of selecting the contractor. This is partly because of the requirement for public accountability. The Wood Report criticises the interpretation of public accountability as least cost and considers that the public interest may be better served by stimulating the search for value for money in a wide range of practices and procedures, including less traditional means of contract selection, such as those mentioned above.

TENDER DOCUMENTS AND CONTRACTS

In the traditional process when the design is substantially complete, the quantity surveyor will draw up a bill of quantities in which each of the components in a building is itemised so that the contractor can price each item when he puts in his tender. This is the main tender document and the procedure is different from a number of other countries where tenders are based on drawings and specifications or on a simpler bill. The bill of quantities is used as a basis for tendering, measuring work done and assessing final accounts, including claims. Attempts are being made by the Standard Method of Measurement (SMM) Development Group to simplify the bill and to find ways to support it by drawings and specification preambles. Research was undertaken into an alternative form of bill – the Operational Bill – by the Building Research Establishment in the 1960s. This bill separates the work into work tasks by gangs of men and then into the labour, materials and plant requirements for each task. The tasks are grouped in the order in which they are likely to occur. It thus facilitates material ordering and project planning and also the control of costs and the feedback of cost information for later projects. Although it has been used on a few projects it has not been adopted by the industry for reasons discussed in work by Lansley.[33] For civil engineering work the consulting engineer is responsible for 'taking off' the quantities and the civil engineering bill is considerably simpler than that for building. It also gives greater flexibility for dealing with uncertainty in a project since greater emphasis is given to quoting rates or lump sums for certain operations based on approximations as to how much of each operation will be involved.

The basis for price determination on contracts in the public sector is shown in Table 3.3. The 'other' category will include cost reimbursement (prime cost plus percentage or plus fixed fee), target cost and varying arrangements under package deal and management contracts.

The type of contract is related to the way in which the contractor is selected and the type of tender documentation used. The standard form of contract for building is that prepared by the Joint Contracts Tribunal (JCT)[34] but published by the RIBA. Hence it is sometimes called the JCT form and sometimes the RIBA form. It is issued in several varieties, for firm quantities, approximate quantities and without quantities, each for local authority and private projects. In addition, separate contract forms are available for simpler types of work and for subcontractors, as well as an increasing number of the less traditional contractual arrangements. The contract document deals with the role of architects and quantity surveyors and the clerk of works, who is the client's representative on site, with measurement and certification and payment for the work done on a monthly basis subject to a retention, normally of 5 per cent, to be paid over at the end of the retention period

TABLE 3.3　*Basis for price determination of contract used by public clients in the selection of main contractors*

	Building	Civil engineering
	% of number of contracts	
Lump sum with full bills of quantities	87	36
Lump sum with drawings and specifications	8	1
Lump sum with bills of approximate quantities	2	33
Schedule of rates with approximate quantities	1	27
Schedule of rates without quantities	1	1
Other	1	2
	100	100

Source:

NEDO Survey reported in EDCs for Building and Civil Engineering, *The Public Client and the Construction Industries* (The Wood Report) NEDO (HMSO, 1975) Table 5.2.

if the work is certified as satisfactory. It provides for the way in which the contract value is to be increased for extra work and by the way in which the contractor shall be recompensed for delays in provision of drawings etc. and for payment of liquidated damages by the contractor for delays caused by him. Each contract is available with three alternative clauses for the way in which adjustments are to be made for increased costs, namely a firm price contract, a fluctuating cost clause, where reimbursement is made for changes in material prices and wage rates, and a cost of building formula adjustment whereby national indices are used.

The latest edition of the JCT forms of contract produced in 1980 has been much criticised because of its length and complexity. However, it clarifies many matters that had previously been subject to dispute and is a thorough document agreed by all members of the JCT. The 1963 form is still in use but the use of the JCT 80 form is spreading. Moreover, other forms of contract have been issued by other bodies which purport to overcome some of the difficulties of the JCT form. They do not, however, contain means to avoid as many potential disputes as the new JCT form.

The standard civil engineering contract is the ICE form. This is produced by the Institution of Civil Engineers (ICE), the Federation of
Civil Engineering Contractors (FCEC) and the Association of Consulting
Engineers (ACE). In addition, there is a separate international form for
civil engineering by the International Federation of national associations
of independent consulting engineers (FIDIC) which is largely a development of the ICE Form. This FIDIC contract is also used for some international building contracts. The engineering forms are generally simpler
than the JCT contracts and make provision for more uncertainty in
projects. In addition there are separate contracts produced by DoE for
certain government contracts in building and in civil engineering – the
GC Works 1 Edition 2 Contract. Contractors dislike this form of contract
because it is so drafted that it does not cater for contractors experiencing
unforeseen ground conditions and it does not include any right to go to
arbitration in a dispute. There are also complaints that the PSA claims
procedure is too slow.

In general many of the contractors' problems on the practical aspects
of contracts were concerned with the slowness of settling of claims
including those that go to arbitration.

The use of various forms of contract is not well documented except
for local authority housing where, since 1979, all housing schemes have
been let by the JCT form.[35] Not surprisingly, in view of inflation, the
percentage of contracts let under firm price conditions has declined from
93.5 per cent in 1970 to 18 per cent in 1980.[36]

There have been difficulties in projects keeping to time and cost
targets. In the NEDO survey of public-sector contracts,[37] fewer than
40 per cent of projects were completed within the time in the contract
plus 5 per cent. Over 30 per cent overran by more than 20 per cent.
There were similar problems with costs. The percentage of contracts in
the same survey that cost within 5 per cent of the contract price ranged
from less than 60 per cent with open and select competition to over 80
per cent with two-stage tendering.

There are a number of reasons for the uncertainties in time and cost.
The first is that the client may alter his mind and introduce variations.
These, if substantial, will understandably affect performance. One problem is that it is very difficult for a client to find out in advance what
the effect of a variation will be. Some experienced clients make substantial allowances in their budgets for cost overruns.

Then there are the whole range of reasons why the contractor may be
granted an extension of time and cost – such as unforeseen ground conditions, bad weather, late drawings, etc. This means that the risk of

these events occurring is borne by the client. The difficulty is that there is little incentive under this system for the contractor to deal with the causes of time and cost overrun or to compensate for their effects by, for example, better liaison with the architects' office on provision of drawings, winter building precautions and catching up on lost time. At the present time, from the moment a contract is signed the contractor keeps careful record of the evidence on which he is to base his claim for increased cost. He should have an incentive to ensure that this is unnecessary. If the contractor accepts the risks in some of these matters, the contract price would be higher but increased certainty would probably be worth the extra cost to a significant proportion of clients. Clients should at least have a choice with a contract form designed for minimum client risk of time and cost.

Some clients, especially in the public sector and in international work, required performance bonds under which a financial institution guarantees that the contractor will fulfil the contract. This should be unnecessary if the client has taken sufficient trouble to investigate the credentials and financial position of the contractor and should be disappearing with the increasing use of selective as opposed to open tendering. There is no up-to-date information on the extent of the practice of requiring performance bonds. However in 1976, thirty-two out of forty-five local authorities in a survey of all London Boroughs and thirteen other authorities required bonds in local authority housing work.[38] In 1978 it was reported that approximately half UK construction work was bonded at a cost up to 3 per cent of the contract value.[39]

CHOICE OF SUBCONTRACTORS AND THE CONTRACT CONDITIONS

There are two main ways in which a subcontractor can be appointed. The first is known as nomination, that is, he is selected by the client through his chief designer but his contractual relationship is with the main contractor. Client control of selection may be advantageous where the technical ability of the subcontractor or his ability to undertake detailed design work for the project is important, or where the subcontractor has a very substantial or critical role in the contract. It has great advantages to the subcontractor in many other ways also. The procedure is that the architect or other client's designer asks for tenders from a selected list. Then the selected subcontractor, under the JCT 80 contract arrangements, negotiates his programme of work and certain other conditions with the main contractor and, when this has been completed to the satisfaction of both parties, signs the subcontract. Under this it is said that many sources of friction between the main contractor and subcontractor are dealt with in advance.

The other type of subcontractor is that selected by the main contractor without the intervention of the client or his adviser. Domestic subcontracting is clearly appropriate for fairly simple subcontracts or where requirements for specialist skills are less rigorous. The advantage to the main contractor is that he can choose the subcontractor he wishes – perhaps one he regularly works with – and may be able to obtain his services at a lower price than those of the nominated subcontractor. Since it is the main contractor who is responsible for the total job, it is arguable that he should be allowed to choose his own subcontractors. The main contractor is responsible for all operations on site and should have control over all aspects of them. However, the subcontractors normally prefer nomination, partly because the tendering process is seen to be fairer with no opportunity for the contractor to conduct a 'Dutch auction' either at his tender stage or after he has obtained the contract but before the contract with the subcontractor is signed. The subcontractor particularly objects to a 'Dutch auction' at the second of these stages and there is no benefit to the client because any reduction in price is retained by the main contractor.

The other reason that the subcontractors prefer nomination is that the contract conditions normally are more equitable, not only for themselves but for all parties involved. In particular, under a JCT 80 subcontract (mandatory if the nomination is under the main JCT 80 form) the architect informs the nominated subcontractor of how much work has been certified and the date, so that the subcontractor is in a position to ask the main contractor for payment; the subcontractor has redress direct to the client for payment if the main contractor does not pay him and the client has redress to the subcontractor if the latter causes delay or extra cost on the contract. (The main contractor is not liable for this in the case of a nominated subcontractor if he has taken all reasonable steps to prevent the delay.) The contract arrangements can be very unsatisfactory for domestic subcontractors, that is, those chosen directly by the main contractor. The principal agreed form is that negotiated by the National Federation of Building Trades Employers (NFBTE) (the principal main contractors' federation although it also has subcontractor members), the Federation of Associations of Specialists and Subcontractors (FASS) and the Committee of Associations of Specialist Engineering Contractors (CASEC), but there are numerous other forms of contract in use, often produced *ad hoc* by the main contractor, or the main contractor amends the agreed form. Subcontractors are not infrequently employed without any contract which, in a situation of mutual trust, is satisfactory but can lead to problems. None of these domestic contract forms gives the subcontractor any claim on the client if the main contractor does not pay him and, in addition, they often contain a clause that states that the subcontractor will get paid only when the main contractor is paid. During a period of recession the subcontractor's payment is often long delayed and if he is dependent for future work on the contractor concerned then his effective redress is small. The most seriously affected are the sub-subcontractors who are often kept waiting months after the due time for their payments.

In civil engineering the principles of selection are similar. The subcontract form used is one prepared by the Institution of Civil Engineers (ICE). Negotiations on a new form have been going on for some years between the Federation of Civil Engineering Contractors (FCEC) and the subcontractors' organisations. One of the main stumbling blocks is the 'pay when paid' clause.

The use of nomination has tended to decrease during the recession of the early 1980s and its wide use is undesirable on management grounds. However, the subcontractors are hit particularly hard during a recession. The main contractor tries to reduce the payments he makes to subcontractors but the subcontractor may have no similar bargaining position with his supplier of materials who is usually a much larger organisation than he is. Thus the margins get squeezed from the top but the subcontractor has less ability to squeeze. If, in addition, due payments are delayed he will be in a very difficult financial position indeed. In a situation where the amount of work subcontracted on any one job can be up to 100 per cent and where the average for large main contractors is about 40 per cent, there is a case for strengthening the contractual position of the subcontractor in non-nominated work.

WORK ON SITE

As soon as work on site commences the main contractor takes over from the designer the principal role in the process. It is his responsibility to organise all the site operations by his own team and by subcontractors, whether nominated by the designer or chosen by himself, and whether providing a full service or employed on labour-only basis. The professional team, however, still has a very important role to play. The designers are responsible for seeing that what is built is what has been agreed and the quantity surveyor or engineer, as the case may be, with measuring the work so that the contractor may be paid for work done during each month. The client on larger projects will have a clerk of works on site whose task is basically to inspect the work on behalf of the client to ensure that it conforms to the architect's drawings, and he will also undertake a number of other functions including, for example, measuring work that will be covered up before the quantity surveyor is on site again. He works under the direction of the architect. His formal role has been eroded over time. In practice, however, it is often greater than the formal position suggests and the investigation by BRE into quality on public non-housing sites found that his role is often crucial to the construction of satisfactory buildings.[40] Similarly a comprehensive research report on the clerk of works in the National Health Service[41] sees a need for an improved educational programme for clerks of works in the Health Service because he is regarded as being in a unique position to contribute to performance.

THE OVERALL DURATION OF THE PROCESS

It is not surprising in view of the complexity of the process illustrated in Figure 3.1 (which is after all a very simplified version) that the duration of the total construction process is long. Indeed it is almost surprising that anything gets built at all!

The information on the length of time required for various work types is extremely scattered, but Table 3.4 substantially prepared by NEDO draws it together. It is generally thought, and there is some evidence, that the duration is longer than in most developed countries.[42] The range of duration of the conceptual stage is very broad owing partly to the varying sizes of projects. In the case of new road construction, notably motorways for example, the determination of the line of the road with public inquiries and the necessary compulsory purchase procedures, etc. will, in general, be longer the longer the stretch of road involved.

The causes, apart from sheer size of project and complexities of the procedures to be adopted, for the long duration of preconstruction time may be divided into those determined outside the construction team and those from within the team. Those outside the influence of the team are statutory approvals, grants, and to some extent finance and land purchase. This does not mean that the industry cannot press for improvement. Indeed it is doing so all the time.

TABLE 3.4 *Characteristic times involved in the various phases of the construction process for some types of new work*

	Conceptual phase	Design and contract documentation phases	Construction on site phases
	Years	Years	Years
Public sector:			
Housing	1–4	1–3	½–2 (1–4)
Health	1–5	½–4	½–5
Education	1–4	½–3	½–2½
Other large buildings (e.g. lawcourts, civic buildings)	1–7	1–3	1½–2½
Other small and medium buildings (e.g. general offices, telephone exchanges, public libraries)	½–3	½–2	½–1½
Roads and harbours	1½–10	1–4	½–3
Water and sewerage	1–4	½–3	½–2½
Private sector:			
Housing	½–6	½–4	½–1½
Industrial	½–2	½–2½	½–2
Commercial	1–10	1–4	½–3

Notes and Sources:

EDCs for Building and Civil Engineering, *How Flexible Is Construction?* NEDO (HMSO, 1978) Table 2.1 which gives the following main sources: *Housing Land Availability in South East* (DoE); *Fifth Report of Action Group on London Housing; The Public Client and the Construction Industries* (HMSO); *Scottish Construction into the 1980s* (HMSO); *Study of the Building Timetable* (University College Environmental Research Group); *Industrial Investment* (Slough Estates); unpublished NEDO case studies on private housing; NEDO discussions with industrialists and developers.

For the final column of construction on-site phase, the figure for public-sector housing has been amended in line with new data on expected duration of contracts. The reduction is probably due to a decrease in multi-storey construction and to smaller schemes. (DoE, *Housing and Construction Statistics 1971–1981* (HMSO, 1982) Table 81; DoE, *Housing and Construction Statistics* no. 2, 2nd quarter 1972 (HMSO, 1972) Table 83.)

Much of the duration of the preconstruction phase is, however, in control of the team. To some extent it is determined by the clients' expectations of how long it will take and therefore the time he allows for and is prepared to accept. If the client has planned for a certain duration and his estimate of time is correct that at least gives him certainty. On the other hand there are always uncertainties, for example as to whether planning permission or government assistance will be obtained, whether finance will be available and at what price. The greater these uncertainties, the greater the likelihood that the client will postpone commencing other activities, such as further design work, until the outcome is clear in order to avoid abortive work, even though the duration is longer. Lastly, there may be a long duration because of inadequate performance on the part of any member of the team (including the client), for example, delays in finalising the brief, in acquiring the site or unacceptable sketch designs. There are many reasons why time schedules are not met. Sometimes extra work is required or designs are changed. It may be something that is within the field of the contractor to organise better or anticipate – such as shortages of inputs, bad industrial relations or arrangements with subcontractors, plain bad management, or, of course, his business may fail. It may be bad luck, for example – the weather, or a strike in some other industry, such as railways.

A study on construction times for industrial building by the Building Research Establishment on behalf of the EDC for Building funded by DoE and referred to earlier in this chapter comprises a very valuable piece of research. The reasons for delays according to their survey are shown in Table 3.5.

An important conclusion is that[43]

> it is not the form of contract which primarily determines whether targets are met but the attitude of the parties to which the form of contract may contribute. The standard form of contract offers penalties for delays but not incentives for speed. Industry and customer should look for ways of sharing the benefits from improved performance.

The costs of delay are of two main types. The first is the costs of money paid on which interest has to be met but which, until the project is used, brings no return. Clearly the longer the duration, the larger the interest charges but, since the expenditure in the early stages is small, the relationship is far from linear.

The second is that a project that is not ready when required may cause

TABLE 3.5   *Reasons for delay in industrial building*

Cause of hold-up and delay	Case studies % projects
Subcontracting	49
Tenant/client variations	45
Ground problems – water, rock, etc.	37
Bad weather	27
Components/equipment delivery	25
Sewer/drains obstruction or re-routing	20
Information late	20
Poor supervision	18
Steel strike	16
Statutory undertakers	14
Labour supply	10
Design complexity	6

Source:

EDC for Building, *Faster Building for Industry*, NEDO (HMSO, 1983) para 14.17.

the client to lose money. This is particularly clear in factory building where if goods cannot be produced when required, a market may be lost. At the same time it is often impossible to forecast as far ahead as the combined duration of preconstruction and construction phases when that will be. Similar costs arise owing to the non-availability of other projects when required, for example, schools for the start of the year on 1 September.

Often, to get over some of these problems the preliminary work is done in advance and then the work started on site when conditions are right. A pool of public-sector projects ready to go ahead is advocated and does to some extent exist, especially in a period of cut-back because some projects that were nearly ready to start on site have been postponed. Sometimes this results in putting the effect and cost of uncertainty on to other parties. For example, the study by Construction Industry Research and Information Association (CIRIA) on Pre-Contract Delays in Civil Engineering Projects[44] found that there were many instances of unduly long tender adjudication periods or schemes being shelved after tendering or re-tendering that cause high costs to contractors and they proposed that the tender costs should in such cases be reimbursed to contractors by the client.

The other matter to be borne in mind in all this is that the duration periods quoted in Table 3.4 are 'typical'. This does not mean that when a client is in a hurry for a project he cannot obtain his building quickly. He can do this, for example, by undertaking many of the activities simultaneously, and by letting the contract so that this can happen. Generally speaking, the private client gives more emphasis to time than the public client. However, this may be because the value of time saved and the cost of delays are not properly assessed in the public sector.

4 Output in Great Britain

It is difficult to understand the situation of the construction industry in the seventies and eighties without a look back at the period since the Second World War. During the war there was virtually no civilian new building and only essential stop-gap repairs were undertaken. In 1945, therefore, the stock of all types of buildings and works was badly depleted in terms of accommodation and facilities provided compared with requirements, and in terms of the standard of repair. There was a long period of slow reconstruction during which a system of building permits was in operation so that essential work had priority. In 1954 the permit system was discontinued and the industry began to have the freedom to develop in its own way. There was still, however, a very substantial backlog of demand especially for housing and the industry was mostly fully occupied and often stretched to meet the demands upon it.

Figure 4.1 shows in terms of an index growth of construction output from 1955–73 when it reached its peak. It is in retrospect a fairly smooth curve and although there were falls in output for particular quarters, there was no calendar year in which output was lower than the previous year until 1969. The sharp fall in the first quarter of 1963 was due to the very severe weather conditions. It was in fact a period of growth and reasonable stability. At the time, however, it was not seen by the industry in this light. The fifties and sixties were periods of recurrent balance of payments crises and the government of whatever colour was committed to managing the economy to try to balance the often conflicting objectives of a satisfactory balance of payments position, full employment and, especially since 1962 when the National Economic Development Council was established, growth of gross domestic product. The construction industry was at the receiving end of measures taken by successive

69

FIGURE 4.1 *Economic events related to construction output by all agencies from 1955, Great Britain (indices 1975 = 100 approximately indicated)*

governments in the management of the economy. When the balance of payments was in deficit they reduced demand at home by increased taxation, higher interest rates and lower public spending. Since it is always much easier to postpone or cut capital expenditure than to reduce current expenditure, public construction programmes were cut back. Private industrialists postponed investment because they could not see the demand for their products increasing as originally anticipated and because capital would cost more. Householders decreased their demand for new housing because of lower income expectations and higher mortgage costs. Once the crisis was over the whole process was reversed and the go-ahead was given. Some major measures are indicated in Figure 4.1 to show the type and frequency of events. This was known as 'stop-go' and the construction industry complained bitterly to government of its effects. It is true that it made forecasting and planning difficult and therefore contractors and others in the industry needed to be flexible to cope with fluctuations. For while the output of the whole country did not greatly waver there were much greater fluctuations in orders received by contractors, in separate types of work and in separate areas. But a study of twenty-three firms by Ashridge Management College[1] found that in spite of substantial fluctuations in demand many of the individual firms had managed to increase their turnover and efficiency. Not only were there complaints about 'stop-go' but government was accused of using the industry as a regulator of the economy. It did so perhaps in the **Building Control Act of 1966** to provide for the licensing of private-sector projects other than housing and industrial building. In 1971 the government introduced an emergency programme of public works in areas of high unemployment to help to increase the level of employment. In May 1973 the government cuts in expenditure had a high construction component and in the measures of December 1973 the cuts on the construction sector were so severe that it is difficult to doubt that the industry was being used as a regulator of the economy.

The fall in output in 1969 and the falter in growth to the end of 1972 were due in a considerable measure to housing which had reached its peak in 1968, both in terms of value of output and of numbers completed. This was partly the result of the growing surplus of dwellings over households that is described in Chapter 2. Although many of the existing dwellings were far from satisfactory, the urgency of building large numbers was decreasing and other factors were beginning to play a greater part in determining the level of housing in any one year. In the period 1969–73 when overall output was still rising year by year, public housing output was falling and so was other public work and private industrial building.

Commercial building was beginning to falter. However, private housing was buoyant and so was repair and maintenance. The year 1973 was one of record output in the industry, but it was not an entirely unmixed blessing for there were strong signs that the industry was operating above its proper capacity level, and part of the reason for the government measures of December 1973 in which the largest ever cuts on government construction expenditure were imposed was to reduce the overheating in the industry. In fact, as so often happens when trying to act on construction industry output levels, the output was already falling rapidly by the time the curbs were introduced and the industry knew this although it was not understood by government until the statistics were produced some weeks later. The year 1973 marks the end of the post-war building boom. By this time stocks of buildings and works had recovered from the depletions of the war and economic conditions, and more recently political decisions, began to play a large part in determining the level of output.

Until the mid to late seventies, which government was in power made virtually no difference to the level of construction output and relatively little difference in its composition. Political parties vied with one another to increase the number of houses constructed. They all saw the need for strengthening the infrastructure in motorways, ports, etc. and in providing more satisfactory facilities for education and health. Writing in the first half of the eighties the situation seems very different and, for the first time since the war, there is little doubt that politics will substantially affect the construction industry output. The economic constraints on the government of the day may mean that in the long run the overall level of output may not change much, but the composition of output between public and private sectors and within sectors will change substantially. The period of consensus politics in construction, as in broader matters, is over and has perhaps been replaced by one of instability and fluctuation depending on the government in power.

TYPES OF WORK

Figure 4.2 shows construction output in the main categories of work at constant 1975 prices in 1963–82. From this it is clear that from 1973 there were substantial falls in all types of work – except repair and maintenance which remained buoyant. From 1964, when the share of repair and maintenance was at its lowest point in this period of 27.7 per cent of total output, it increased in 1982 to 41.4 per cent. The share of

73

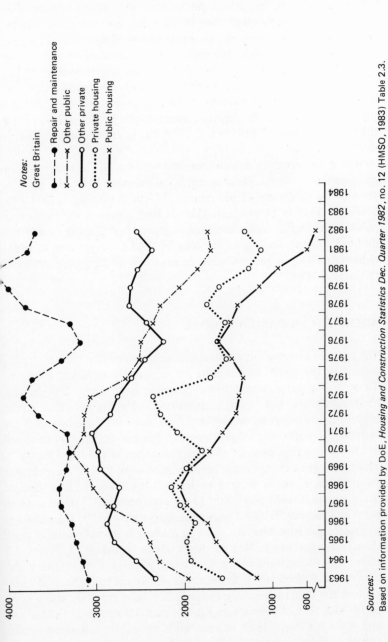

Notes:
Great Britain
●——— Repair and maintenance
×—··—× Other public
○——— Other private
○········○ Private housing
×——— × Public housing

Sources:
Based on information provided by DoE, *Housing and Construction Statistics Dec. Quarter 1982*, no. 12 (HMSO, 1983) Table 2.3.

FIGURE 4.2 *Construction output, 1975 prices, all agencies, from 1963*

housing in the total has fallen, particularly public-sector housing. The share of public work other than housing has also fallen but not by as much as might be expected in the light of government policies because of the overall fall in work. The share of private commercial and private industrial work has remained remarkably consistent: they were 23 per cent of the total in 1963 and 24 per cent in 1981. There has been a substantial change in the proportion of public to private new work. In 1963 the public sector was the client for about 45 per cent of new work and this rose to nearly 52 per cent in 1976 but by 1981 had declined to under 40 per cent.

Within the repair and maintenance total, data are available on the composition of output. Housing repair and maintenance has increased its share of the total from 42 per cent in 1963 to 48 per cent in 1981 with a peak in 1973 of 50 per cent. This has been mainly at the expense of public-sector repair and maintenance other than housing which has declined from 41 per cent of the total in 1963 to 35 per cent in 1981. Other private repair and maintenance work was 17 per cent in 1963 and the same in 1981.

AGENCIES CARRYING OUT WORK

The agencies carrying out construction work are contractors and organisations in the public sector using labour directly employed by them. These public-sector organisations comprise government departments, local authorities, new towns, nationalised industries and other public corporations. Output by employees of gas and water undertakings is not included in construction industry output.[2] Further details of the structure of the contracting parts of these organisations is given in Chapter 7. There has been a change in the proportion of work done by direct labour departments of public authorities. In 1963 it was about 12 per cent of the total and in 1981 was nearly 13 per cent, but in 1973 it was at a low point of 9 per cent. Table 4.1 shows the change since 1970. These changes in percentages have been due more to changes in the volume of all work than to fluctuations in that by direct labour organisations. Figure 4.3 shows the fluctuations in the new work, repair and maintenance and total work of direct labour departments and contractors. The total work-load of the direct labour organisations has been relatively stable compared with that of contractors but this conceals very large fluctuations and a decline since 1968 in new work by public authorities – much greater than by contractors – and a stable repair and maintenance work-

TABLE 4.1 *Proportion of industry's work-load done by public authorities' direct labour departments by type of work from 1970, Great Britain*

| Year | % of total public- and private-sector work | | | | % of public-sector work[a] | | | |
| | All work % | New work % | Repair and maintenance | | New work | | | Repair and maintenance other than housing % |
			Housing %	Other %	Total %	Housing %	Other %	
1970	10.5	3.5	17.6	37.1	6.8	6.4	6.9	54.0
1971	10.4	3.3	18.0	38.0	6.8	6.1	7.1	54.5
1972	10.4	3.2	18.2	37.7	6.8	5.6	7.4	52.8
1973	9.1	2.3	16.4	34.4	6.1	5.3	6.4	49.3
1974	9.2	2.5	16.4	33.9	5.4	5.1	5.6	50.6
1975	11.3	2.7	22.7	39.2	5.5	5.3	5.6	56.2
1976	11.8	3.1	20.8	39.0	6.1	5.7	6.3	56.8
1977	12.1	3.0	24.0	38.2	6.0	6.1	6.1	56.8
1978	11.4	2.7	21.3	35.7	6.2	5.9	6.3	54.4
1979	11.4	2.3	20.2	35.2	5.6	5.6	5.6	53.7
1980	11.1	2.3	19.7	32.6	5.6	5.8	5.5	49.5
1981	12.8	2.3	20.8	35.2	5.8	6.1	5.8	52.5
1982								
1983								
1984								

Note:
[a]No figures are available from the DoE for total housing repair and maintenance undertaken for the public sector. This means that no figures can be given for this nor for 'all work'.

Sources:
Based on DoE, *Housing and Construction Statistics 1970–1980* (HMSO, 1981) Tables 9 and 11; DoE, *Housing and Construction Statistics 1971–1981* (HMSO, 1982) Tables 9 and 11.

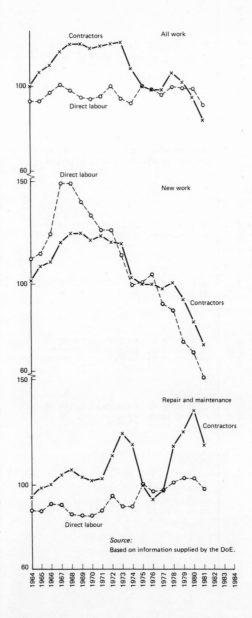

FIGURE 4.3 *Fluctuations in work of direct labour organisations and contractors from 1964, Great Britain - indices 1975 = 100 from 1964*

load. Because, as is shown in Table 4.2, the proportion of new work in the total work done by direct labour organisations is small – only about 11 per cent in 1981 – the effect of the fluctuations in new work is hardly seen in the total work-load. Contractors, by contrast, have experienced fluctuations both in new work and in repair and maintenance and the rise in repair and maintenance since 1976 has to some extent compensated for the fall in new work.

TABLE 4.2 *Proportion of work of various types in work-load of direct labour organisations of public authorities, 1970 and 1981, Great Britain (current prices)*

Type of work	1970	1981
	% of total	
New work:		
Housing	7.6	2.8
Other new work	16.4	8.0
Repair and maintenance:		
Housing	20.8	31.7
Other work	55.2	57.6
Total	100.0	100.0

Sources:
Based on DoE, *Housing and Construction Statistics 1970–1980* (HMSO, 1981) Table 11; DoE, *Housing and Construction Statistics 1971–1981* (HMSO, 1982) Table 11.

It is unfortunate that there is no breakdown of the housing repair and maintenance output figures into that for the public and that for the private sectors. This means that it is not known what proportion of public housing repair and maintenance is done by direct labour organisations to complete the data in Table 4.1. However, it is known that the direct labour organisations undertake about 20 per cent of all housing maintenance – public and private. Since the public sector owns about 40 per cent of the net capital stock at current replacement cost in dwellings[3] the picture may be much the same in housing as in other public-sector work. A further estimate is possible from the data in the National Home Improvement Council Report[4] and this suggests a range of 38–46 per cent in the years 1977–80.

Construction is also undertaken by householders on a Do-It-Yourself (DIY) basis. This construction activity is not included in the output figures but it is nevertheless important because it represents a contribution to the maintenance of the stock of buildings, generates demand for materials and tools and is work some of which might otherwise be done by the industry although much also might remain undone. In addition, there is work done by the 'black' economy, that is, work undertaken on a cash basis avoiding payment of VAT and tax by persons who may be registered as self-employed, be employed on some other job or be unemployed. Some idea of the volume of these two categories, that is, the genuine DIY and the 'black' economy operators, may be gained from estimates of materials sold direct to the public which in 1980 were approaching £1700 million in value. It is unlikely to have increased between 1980 and 1982 because of the fall in real disposable income and consumer expenditure. If the commercial price of the labour involved in repair and maintenance and improvements is about twice the value of materials, the value of work would be one and a half times the total value of housing repair and maintenance and improvement work done by contractors of about £3300 in 1980. The range of types of DIY work is considerable from small repairs and decoration to construction of new houses of which over 7000 were completed in 1981 on a DIY basis (verbally, Customs and Excise, 1982).

If expenditure by households only is considered, that is, excluding landlord payments to contractors, the gross value of DIY including an allowance for labour would be nearly double that of the work by contractors.[5]

OUTPUT BY CONTRACTORS

Types of Work

More information has been available about the type of work done by contractors since 1980 when the method of collection of output data was changed.[6] Table 4.3 shows the types of work undertaken for the public and private sectors. This table shows too an approximate division into building and civil engineering work. This probably understates the civil engineering component since there is a civil engineering element in building works, especially foundations and related roads and services, some oil work and part of the 'other' public relates to civil engineering work, including, for example, part of naval dockyards, UK Atomic

TABLE 4.3 *Value at current prices of contractors' output on new work by type of work, 1981, Great Britain*

Type of work	£m	% of total
For the public sector:		
Mainly building work:		
Housing	1 159	9.3
Education	311	2.5
Health	396	3.2
Factories, oil, steel, warehouses	282	2.3
Offices, garages, shops	320	2.6
Other (may be civil engineering too)	556	4.5
Total	3 024	24.4
Mainly civil engineering work:		
Gas, electricity, coal-mining	498	4.0
Railways, air transport	146	1.2
Roads	620	5.0
Harbours	130	1.0
Water	105	0.8
Sewerage	209	1.7
Total	1 708	13.8
All public work	4 731	38.2
For the private sector:		
Mainly building work:		
Housing	2 553	20.6
Industrial		
Factories	1 661	13.4
Warehouses	549	4.4
Other	207	1.7
Total	2 417	19.5
Commercial		
Offices	1 321	10.6
Shops	548	4.4
Entertainment	374	3.0
Garages	108	0.9
Schools and colleges	53	0.4
Agriculture	109	0.9
Others	186	1.5
Total	2 699	21.8
All private work	7 669	61.8
All work total	12 400	100.0

Source:
DoE, *Housing and Construction Statistics 1971-1981* (HMSO, 1982) Table 13.

Energy Authority work, RAF airfields and land drainage. In the private-sector work too there is a civil engineering element – for example, agricultural and fen drainage, runways on private airfields and private roads, as well as oil work, bridges, etc. In addition, much of the public new work other than housing by direct labour will be civil engineering work. On the other hand, some of the work under the civil engineering heading will be building such as power-stations, air terminals, railway stations, air terminals, railway stations, water works, etc. There is no hard and fast definition. Civil engineering probably accounts for about 20 per cent of total new construction and over 90 per cent of that work is for the public sector.

Trends in the amount of civil engineering work can be to some extent traced by the figures of gross domestic fixed capital formation at constant prices. These are figures of expenditure by types of organisation so that railway expenditure will include track, which is civil engineering, but also stations and offices which may be mainly building. Another way of assessing change over time is to look at figures of contractors' new orders by type of work. These are more volatile than output figures but give a good indication over a long period. Table 4.4 shows that the fluctuations in public-sector civil engineering work have been very great – more than in construction as a whole – with peak output in the period 1970-81 being well over double the lowest output. This is partly because of the substantial size of civil engineering works. This causes difficulties for the firms concerned with waste of resources. Similar fluctuations affect other types of work.

Size and Duration of Contract

Data on new orders received by contractors are broken down by size of contract and duration of contract. Table 4.5 shows the broad position in 1981 for the value of contracts. The figures are striking: about a third of the work in these contracts over £25 000 was in contracts exceeding £2 million but they accounted for only about 1 per cent of the number of contracts; most large contracts were in public work other than housing and private commercial work; 84 per cent of contracts were less than £250 000 (and more than £25 000) but they accounted for only 28 per cent of the work; a large proportion of these small contracts was in private housing; most public housing work was in contracts of £$\frac{1}{2}$-2 million.

It is very difficult to assess the trends in the size of contracts because the size ranges are at current prices and are discrete groups. Table 4.6

TABLE 4.4 *Public-sector civil engineering:*[a] *new orders for contractors from 1970, Great Britain*

Year	Index 1975 = 100	% of all contractors' new orders
1970	120	16.3
1971	139	17.6
1972	153	17.0
1973	140	14.9
1974	104	16.2
1975	100	18.3
1976	97	17.6
1977	86	16.2
1978	80	13.6
1979	70	12.9
1980	69	16.4
1981	76	18.6
1982	62	14.6
1983		
1984		

Note:
[a]Gas, electricity, coal-mining, railways, air transport, roads, harbours, water, sewerage.

Sources:
Based on DoE, *Housing and Construction Statistics 1970–1980* (HMSO, 1981) Tables 4 and 5; DoE, *Housing and Construction Statistics 1971–1981* (HMSO, 1982) Tables 4 and 5; DoE, *Housing and Construction Statistics Dec – Quarter 1982*, no. 12 (HMSO, 1983) Tables 2.6 and 2.7.

attempts an analysis of the large contracts of over £2 million at 1981 prices. Using the output price index for all new construction[7] £2 million in 1981 was equivalent to about £400 000 in 1971 and £1 million in 1976. Therefore the contracts in Table 4.6 are roughly of comparable physical size. Again the results are interesting. The number of large contracts has fallen dramatically so that in 1981 there were only about 550 compared with about double in earlier periods. The most important changes are in the public sector where there has been a dramatic fall in large non-housing contracts and in public housing, partly because these two types of work in total have fallen rapidly. It is convenient to take the years selected but the figures suggest that these years were fairly typical of those of their period.

Data on expected duration of contracts are shown in Table 4.7. Over

TABLE 4.5 New orders received by contractors by value,[a] – 1981, Great Britain

Value range	New housing				Other new work						Total new work	
	Public		Private		Public		Private industrial		Private commercial			
£ thousand	No. %	Value %	No. %	Value %	No. %	Value %	No. %	Value %	No. %	Value %	No. %	Value %
25–250	50	14	92	60	79	19	79	27	84	23	84	28
% of size range (figures in brackets)	(2)	(3)	(44)	(38)	(23)	(25)	(10)	(13)	(20)	(21)	(100)	(100)
250–500	23	21	5	16	10	11	11	17	7	9	8	13
% of size range (figures in brackets)	(11)	(11)	(26)	(22)	(31)	(31)	(15)	(19)	(17)	(18)	(100)	(100)
500–2000	26	55	3	20	9	24	8	32	6	21	6	26
% of size range (figures in brackets)	(16)	(14)	(17)	(14)	(33)	(33)	(14)	(18)	(19)	(21)	(100)	(100)
2000+	1	10	neg.	4	2	46	1	24	3	46	1	33
% of size range (figures in brackets)	(4)	(2)	(3)	(2)	(44)	(50)	(11)	(10)	(37)	(36)	(100)	(100)
	100	100	100	100	100	100	100	100	100	100	100	100

Note:
[a] All figures relate to contracts over £25 000.

Source:
Based on DoE, Housing and Construction Statistics 1971–1981 (HMSO, 1982), Table 7.

TABLE 4.6 *Estimated number of new orders received by contractors of value approximately equivalent to £2 million and over at 1981 prices, 1971, 1976 and 1981, Great Britain*

Value	New housing		Other new work			Total new work
	Public	Private	Public	Private industrial	Private commercial	
1971 equivalent £400th + at 1971 prices	270	few	650	150	235	1 300
1976 equivalent £1m + at 1976 prices	455	30	360	80	115	1 040
1981 £2m + at 1981 prices	25	15	240	65	205	550

Sources:
Based on DoE, *Housing and Construction Statistics no. 5*, 1st quarter 1973 (HMSO, 1973) Table V; DoE, *Housing and Construction Statistics no. 25*, 1st quarter 1978 (HMSO, 1978) Table V; DoE, *Housing and Construction Statistics 1971–1981* (HMSO, 1982) Table 7.

TABLE 4.7 New orders received by contractors by duration,[a] 1981, Great Britain

| Duration | New housing | | | | Other new work | | | | | | Total new work | |
| | Public | | Private | | Public | | Private industrial | | Private commercial | | | |
Months	No. %	Value %	No. %	Value %	No. %	Value %	No. %	Value %	No. %	Value %	No. %	Value %
0–6	21	5	75	55	61	16	75	33	73	23	69	26
7–12	44	28	22	28	25	19	21	43	21	25	23	26
13–18	28	44	2	9	9	17	3	18	5	22	5	19
19–24	7	18	1	6	3	17	neg.	6	1	14	2	13
25+	1	5	neg.	3	2	31	neg.	1	1	16	1	16

Note:
[a] Figures relate to contracts over £25 000 only.

Source:
Based on DoE, Housing and Construction Statistics 1971–1981 (HMSO, 1982) Table 8.

half the value of the contracts over £25 000 was in contracts expected to be completed in less than a year. This means, on the basis of a comparison with Table 4.5, that some of these must have been well over £500 000. It also shows that a significant proportion of contracts over £2 million must have had an expected duration of less than two years. The types of work having a high proportion of long contracts are public other than housing and private commercial. This would be expected because these sectors also have the largest contracts. Similarly, private housing has a high proportion of short contracts and of small contracts.

The number of contracts expected to take over three years let each year ranges from about fifty to over a hundred.[8]

Regional Distribution of Work

Data on the regional output of contractors is shown in Table 4.8. It compares the percentage of work done by contractors in each region with that region's share of population. The South East has considerably more than its fair share (on a population basis) with Greater London particularly high. Particularly low on construction output are the North West and West Midlands. The distribution of commercial building is very uneven. The South East has more than half the country's commercial building and much of this is in Greater London. Scotland does particularly well on industrial building and public work other than housing. It seems that the areas with high unemployment show a lower percentage of repair and maintenance compared with population share but it must be remembered that DIY expenditure, for which no reliable data are available, is not included.

CONSTRUCTION TYPES, TECHNIQUES AND STANDARDS

The type of output has changed in a number of ways. In the post-war period there was a swing towards industrialised construction. This took many forms broadly divided into industrialised systems and prefabrication. System building was most used in housing, school building but also in industrial building. Prefabrication of components has been developing continuously since the fifties.

The reasons for the growth of industrialised building were complex and include a general atmosphere favourable to innovation and experimentation in the 1950s and 1960s together with a shortage of manpower which made the industrialised techniques very attractive. Industrialised

TABLE 4.8 Share of each region in new work-load and of population, 1981, Great Britain

Region	New housing		Other new work			Total new work	Repair and maintenance[a]	Population (1980)
	Public	Private	Public	Private Industrial	Private Commercial			
	%	%	%	%	%	%	%	%
North	5	5	8	6	3	6	4	6
Yorkshire and Humberside	7	9	10	7	5	8	9	9
East Midlands	6	8	6	9	4	6	6	7
East Anglia	4	5	5	4	3	4	4	3
South East	37	32	29	32	55	37	37	31
(of which part Greater London)	(17)	(6)	(11)	(11)	(36)	(16)	(16)	(13)
South West	7	11	5	7	7	7	8	8
West Midlands	6	10	6	7	5	7	9	9
North West	11	9	11	10	7	9	10	12
Wales	5	4	8	6	3	6	4	5
Scotland	11	7	12	12	7	10	9	9
	100	100	100	100	100	100	100	100

Note:
[a]Repair and maintenance data are based on the region of registration of the contractor rather than the location of the work. However, since most contracts are undertaken by small local contractors the distortion would be slight.

Sources:
Based on DoE, Housing and Construction Statistics 1971–1981 (HMSO, 1982) Table 12; CSO, Regional Trends 1982 (HMSO, 1982) Table 2.1.

building saved site labour which was to some extent offset by an increase of factory labour but leaving a net saving of labour overall. Time of erection was reduced and there were benefits from operating under cover, unaffected by weather where working conditions were better, and production was more susceptible to planning and quality control. The reduction in industrialised building took place in housing because the most successful and economical use of industrialised systems was in multi-storey flat construction which, for social and environmental reasons, were becoming unacceptable and because some technical problems had not been adequately resolved. The decline was accelerated by the collapse of a block of flats known as Ronan Point in 1968. The quality and durability of the systems varied greatly with some of the revolutionary low-rise housing systems proving very satisfactory while many of the high-rise construction methods have brought failures and defects – some of which are only now coming to light.

However, the boost for prefabrication of components and for better planning of the site production process had effects more lasting than the industrialised systems and the very fact that there had been this period of innovative experimentation probably improved productivity and efficiency even on non-industrialised sites. Some systems, particularly in school building, have survived and led to a greater emphasis on standardisation of components. It is interesting that the latest development in the technology of dwelling construction – the large-scale use of timber-frame construction – represents a return to prefabrication, although in a different form.

The extent of the rise and fall of industrialised building may be seen from the figures of percentages of local authority and new town dwellings in England and Wales built by industrialised methods. The number approved rose through the sixties to a peak of 43 per cent in 1967, although completions did not reach their peak until 1970.[9] Then industrialised dwelling construction declined, with only a small rally in 1973-5, and by 1980 the percentage of industrialised dwellings in tenders approved was only 3.5 per cent.[10]

These figures may be related to the increase and decrease in high flats. In 1966 the number of dwellings built by local authorities and new towns in tenders approved in five storeys or more in England and Wales reached a peak in number and in percentage of the total at nearly 26 per cent.[11] By 1970 this had fallen to less than half that and by 1980 was less than $\frac{1}{2}$ per cent.[12]

In Scotland the change in the proportion of industrialised dwellings was less dramatic and, even in 1977, there were still about 14 per cent of the total public authority dwellings in industrialised systems.[13] However, although there were some minor differences in timing, the proportion of public-sector flats in five storeys or more followed much the same pattern as in England and Wales, dwindling to nil in 1980.[14]

Modern prefabrication for housing in the form of timber frame is affecting two-storey construction. It has been used for some time in public-sector housing and in 1976 – the peak year – various forms of timber industrialised methods of construction were used for over 13 000 dwellings in England and Wales.[15] Then there was a dramatic fall in public-sector demand and the producers turned their attention to the private housing market. In private housing timber-frame construction had been used for some time for higher-quality dwellings but was considered too expensive for cheaper housing. It may be more expensive in material components now, but the speed and flexibility of construction enables a reduction in capital locked up in speculative housing sites and this, together with other advantages, outweighs the possible higher costs. It has been estimated that 300–500 hours of on-site labour may be saved by use of a timber frame and once the frame is erected, using mechanical lifting equipment and a simple erection procedure, the interior trades can commence at once using dry methods that avoid drying-out time. Laying of cladding brickwork is less exacting than structural brickwork. The lighter structure also enables the use of lighter foundations. In addition high thermal and sound insulation properties are facilitated.[16] It is estimated by the National House-Builders Council (NHBC) that timber frames were used on about 20 per cent of private-sector housing in England and Wales in 1982 and about 50 per cent in Scotland.[17] They are increasingly used by many of the large developers and their use is expected to increase although some housebuilders are still unconvinced of their technical merit.

It is interesting that the position in Scotland with timber-frame construction is so far advanced. The construction industry in Scotland is different from that in England and Wales in many respects including its organisation (see Chapter 3) but also in its type of output. Housing illustrates this well. Private owner-occupied housing has taken a long time to become accepted in Scotland and is still far behind that in the rest of Great Britain. In 1981 it accounted for 36.8 per cent of dwellings compared with 56.4 in Great Britain as a whole.[18] But there are technical differences that are related to this. Scottish houses and those south of the border are traditionally constructed with the builder working from the inside, instead of the outside. This means that the outside finish is such that rendering is necessary but it also means that he can put the first floor in and work from that for the upper part, thus requiring only very simple scaffolding for the shell. The rendering on the outside needs separate additional scaffolding which, under the separate trades system, is provided by the renderer himself. The whole system is now changing, partly with the penetration of national contractors and partly with the increased complexity of modern building which is undermining the separate trades system. Bricks that are not indigenous are increasingly being used in Scotland as a facing, not only in housing but also for public buildings[19] and the use of timber-frame construction requiring only cladding may relate also to the use of brick and the pace of change in Scottish practice.

The Green Paper on Housing Policy[20] states that there has been a rise in public-sector housing standards since 1945. In part this is due to a policy of provision, regardless of ability to pay, and part through, for example, installation of central heating. The Green Paper is less certain about private-sector housing standards, where it is acknowledged that heating and electrical provision has improved, but space and plot sizes may have been reduced. This is perhaps not surprising in view of the increasing number of owner-occupiers, many of whom are first-time buyers and will have lower incomes.

More generally, there has been increasing concern in recent years at the standards of construction which have led to complaints of failures in parts of buildings. This is undoubtedly partly because many dwellings, especially high-rise local authority dwellings constructed in the fifties and sixties, are now found to be unsatisfactory and some are being demolished. For the rest it is difficult to judge whether it is a matter of increased awareness of and publicity for failures or an increase in their incidence. Whichever it is, it is leading to a consideration of measures to improve standards and alleviate the consequences of bad work for owners.

The Building Research Establishment has embarked on a series of research projects[21] to find out what quality problems arise in new construction, their causes and the action taken, and has recently set up a Housing Defects Unit. Moreover, papers on causes of failures and methods of avoiding them are numerous in the technical press.

Professional institutions are concerned to recommend standards as instanced by the report of the Institute of Housing and RIBA[22] on housing. One of the reasons for poor workmanship, particularly in the private-housing repair and maintenance and improvement field, is the apparently increasing numbers of unqualified, unskilled workers who are able to obtain work but carry it out badly. This is partly due to the 'black' economy referred to earlier.

One method of alleviating the effects of this and discouraging the employment of unskilled labour is by various forms of warranty schemes whereby the work of a builder who is a member of the scheme will, if it is unsatisfactory, be put right. The tested and successful example of such a scheme is that operated by the National House-Building Council. Most new houses are now built with their guarantee, required by building societies, and which is backed up by inspections and the resources from all the members of the scheme. More recently the Office of Fair Trading has been looking at the problem of poor workmanship and the other malpractices of many small operators and the contractors' trade asso-citions are in process of setting up their own schemes that would cover a broader range of types of work. The National Home Improvement Council is also taking action.

OUTPUT OF THE PROFESSIONS

The structure of the professions is dealt with in Chapter 8. There are, however, no comprehensive data for the professions that show their output or turnover. Estimates of how much construction work they design or for which they provide other professional services have to be obtained indirectly. This is attempted below for the primary designers – architects and civil engineers. If they are engaged on a project, other specialist designers or professionals may also be involved. In addition, other specialists such as chemical engineers may sometimes be the primary designers.

Architects

The main fields of employment of full-time architects are shown in Chapter 8, Table 8.1. According to this table, about 54 per cent of architects were employed as principals or employees in private practice and there are data on the value of new commissions, work entering the working drawing stage and work certified, going back some years. In 1982 6.8 per cent of architects were in other private-sector employment in industry, commerce, housing associations and freelance. These would include architects employed by contractors, on whom the DoE collected data until 1974.[23] The estimated proportion of private new housing work certified by private architectural practices in 1981 was about 10 per cent.[24] In addition, they will often have some involvement in the design of housing even if not providing a complete service. Some private housing is designed by architects in the employ of developers but the great majority of private housing work is designed for developers by non-architects.

Architects in private practice certified about 45 per cent of non-housing private new building work in 1981.[25] They are responsible for a large part of offices and other commercial building,[26] much of the remainder being designed by architects in the client organisations or by contractors. For industrial building, while about a third is designed by architects in private practice,[27] design by contractors' architects is also important as industrial building is a type of work for which standard designs are often available; for which speed may be vital; and where various non-traditional methods of organising the building process, such as package deals, are used.

Work certified excludes the partial service given by architects and, when this is included, private practice is thought to be involved in about half all new private work and the involvement of other private-sector architects, especially in work other than housing, will bring the total private work designed by architects to well over half.

In the public sector virtually all new work is architect designed but the proportions designed by private-practice architects and local-authority or other public-sector architects varies. Probably over half is done by private-practice architects. In particular, private architects do most of the housing association work and a substantial share of local authority housing and of hospitals and other health work.[28] Public-sector architects do most of the school work (but not universities) and also probably undertake a large part of the work on industrial schemes for local authority trading estates and nationalised industries. About a fifth of new work commissioned from private architects in 1982 was in rehabilitation work.[29]

Civil Engineers

There are no statistics of the value of work designed by private consulting engineers in Great Britain. The only indication available is that of the DoE figures of local authority work for 1978.[30] Civil engineering work carried out by and for local authorities at the working drawing stage was £1106 million and this represented an estimated 60 per cent of the civil-engineering component of output of new work. In addition a fairly high proportion – probably over 30 per cent – of civil engineers and other professional design staff connected with construction are employed in central government and national boards. Thus the private consulting engineers and directly employed engineers probably design virtually all the public-sector new civil engineering work.

5 Output Abroad

CONTRACTORS

United Kingdom contractors in the construction industry or associated with it undertook work abroad to the value of £1478 million in 1981-2 or some 7.4 per cent of their construction output in Great Britain and overseas combined.[1] This represents a check to the declining percentage since 1977-8, partly due to a rise in work abroad but also because of a further decline in work in Great Britain. Table 5.1 shows fluctuations in percentages since 1970. The actual figures cannot properly be corrected for inflation because work takes place all over the world and only a small part of the inputs are supplied from Great Britain. Most countries have no satisfactory construction price or cost indices and there is certainly no world construction price or cost index. Figure 5.1 shows the value of work done abroad at current prices. In order that some idea of real value may be obtained the output price index for Great Britain for all new construction is also shown. The value of contracts obtained and to a lesser extent the value of work outstanding fluctuate from year to year much more wildly than that of the value of work done which smooths the very large contracts over the period of the work. Growth in work abroad was sluggish until 1974-5 and after that year it increased faster than the price index until 1976-7. Since then the position has been less satisfactory until the more hopeful performance in 1981-2. Thus if contractors had a desire to offset the fall in output in the home market by going overseas, they did not succeed after 1977-8. One of the reasons for the fall in UK output abroad may have been the rapid increase in UK inflation which was not matched by all competitors and although this affects only the UK component, it, coupled with an often unfavourable exchange rate, could have been sufficient to make British contractors uncompetitive. At the same time there has been an increase in foreign

94

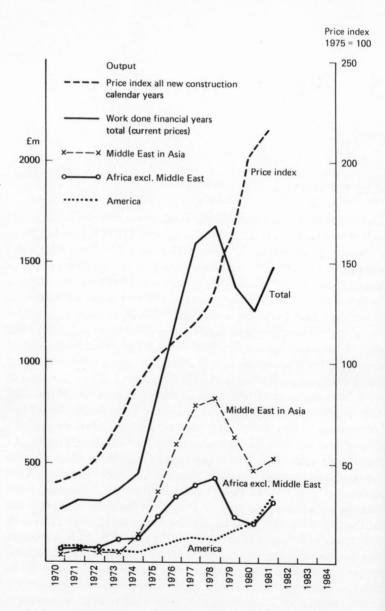

FIGURE 5.1 *Work done by British contractors abroad compared with price index for Great Britain from 1970*

TABLE 5.1   *Value of work done by contractors abroad from 1970 (current prices)*

Year	Value of work done £m	% of contractors' work in Great Britain and abroad
1970 or 1970–1	268	5.1
1971 or 1971–2	317	5.5
1972 or 1972–3	312	4.8
1973 or 1973–4	363	4.3
1974 or 1974–5	458	4.8
1975 or 1975–6	859	7.8
1976 or 1976–7	1 253	10.2
1977 or 1977–8	1 597	11.7
1978 or 1978–9	1 678	10.5
1979 or 1979–80	1 384	7.7
1980 or 1980–1	1 287	6.1
1981 or 1981–2	1 478	7.4
1982 or 1982–3		
1983 or 1983–4		
1984 or 1984–5		

Note:

These percentages are rather exaggerated because they include some overseas work which is not construction according to the Standard Industrial Classification.

Sources:

DoE, *Housing and Construction Statistics 1970–1980* (HMSO, 1981) Tables 10 and 66; DoE, *Housing and Construction Statistics 1971–1981* (HMSO, 1982) Tables 10 and 62; 'Building Up: The Work of UK Construction Firms Overseas', *British Business*, vol. 9, no. 6, 15–21 Oct 1982, pp. 256–61.

competition, especially from the Far East including Japan. Korea is now a major international competitor but other countries, some of whom earlier were simply suppliers of labour, are now increasing their participation and tendering for main contracts – especially housing and other technically relatively simple projects. These include Taiwan, India, Pakistan, Thailand, the Philippines and Turkey.[2] It is also possible that because of the world recession the total world market has shrunk so that the fall in British contractors' output abroad may partly reflect the total market situation.

There have been quite substantial changes in the importance of various markets with the great rise in significance of the Middle East and its recent decline to lower, but still high, levels. Figure 5.1 shows the value of work done in current prices for the three most important regions. It is clear that much of the change in British construction work is attributable to the Middle East which is broadly in line with the overall situation. Table 5.2 shows the changes in the proportion of work in each region at four-year intervals. There are few clear trends as would be expected in view of the preponderance of very large projects. Expected growth areas are the Far East and Africa and possibly South America.

TABLE 5.2 *Percentage of value of work done abroad by contractors[b]*
by region in three selected years, Great Britain

Region	1973-4 %	1977-8 %	1981-2P %
European Community[a]	3.0	0.5	2.6
Rest of Europe	11.8	6.8	1.2
Middle East in Asia	16.0	49.3	35.3
Middle East in Africa	0.3	1.7	3.4
Rest of Asia	4.4	2.9	6.6
Rest of Africa	31.7	24.9	20.6
America	17.1	8.0	22.9
Oceania	15.7	5.9	7.6
Total	100.0	100.0	100.0

Notes:

[a] Includes Greece throughout.
[b] British construction companies and their overseas branches and subsidiaries.

Sources:

DoE, *Housing and Construction Statistics 1971-1981* (HMSO, 1982) Table 62; 'Building Up: The Work of UK Construction Firms Overseas', *British Business*, vol. 9, no. 6, 15-21 Oct 1982, pp. 256-61.

Increasing competition from Far East contractors will however make the Far East a difficult market for British contractors to operate in profitably and they are likely to be more successful the higher the degree of technical competence required. The value of work done by British contractors in the European Community continues to be small in spite of the requirement that contracts in excess of a certain figure be advertised throughout the Community. Conversely, it must be said, the operations of European contractors in Great Britain are very small.

About 100 firms of various types engage in work abroad from time to time, but the top twenty British construction firms active overseas between them obtained about 90 per cent of new orders reported in

1980-1 and in 1981-2. In 1981-2 the top five contractors won nearly 70 per cent of the new British orders.[3] The construction industry contractors undertaking a large amount of work abroad include George Wimpey, Costain Group, Taylor Woodrow, Trafalgar House, Tarmac and John Mowlem & Co. Of these Wimpey undertakes the largest volume abroad but Costain has a higher percentage of work abroad – in excess of 50 per cent.[4] An idea of the importance of work abroad by the large firms may be obtained by comparing it with the value of work done in Great Britain by the thirty-nine firms which in 1981 employed over 1200 persons. The output of these firms was about £2500 million.[5] This compares with the value of work done abroad of about £1500 million, a large part of which would be done by these thirty-nine firms. The top half-dozen contractors probably, on average, do between a quarter and a third of their work abroad.

The number of contractors operating abroad is unlikely to increase significantly because of the high turnover in Great Britain needed to meet the costs of initial research on overseas markets and the costs of entry. It is essential to establish a presence well in advance of tendering. It has been stated that in order to gain entry to a market it may be necessary to spend £1 million.[6] The cost of one visit was put in 1979 at about £2000 and of a branch office about £50 000 a year. Even with a branch office it may take twelve to fifteen months to gain the first small contract and three to four years to gain a larger one.[7] The costs of tendering are very high and many tenders will be abortive in the early stages. Thus the risks of failure are great and the potential losses are very high.

It is often a legal requirement of operation in a country to have a local partner and, where this is not so, it may well be advantageous to do so to enable knowledge of the local conditions to be obtained and to have a short cut to appropriate introductions. In addition, once work has been obtained, local knowledge on the spot is invaluable. However there are difficulties in finding the appropriate partner and some British firms prefer to have only informal connections with local firms. Nevertheless, a satisfactory partner can substantially reduce risks. A way of sharing risks usually used for a one-off project is a joint venture with another international contractor, whereby both firms act together for the purpose of one project.

Some of the risks are lessened by the Export Credits Guarantee Department (ECGD). Its main function is to insure against non-payment by the client for commercial or political reasons and it also assists with guarantees for credit. However the main risks of operating in a country where the environment – economic, political and, above all, construction – is imperfectly understood, remain and can only be reduced by extensive and intensive preliminary research. Government has tried over a number of years to assist exports of construction. First there is the general assistance given to exporters through the British Overseas Trade Board and other government agencies. The Board gives financial assistance, for example, for exhibitors at overseas trade fairs and this is particularly relevant to building material producers. As part of the policy to assist in market research abroad and with a contribution to the funding of overhead costs for breaking into overseas markets, it assists contractors and consultants in this area – largely through the Overseas Projects Board (mentioned in more detail on p. 101). Second, government provides information on overseas markets through diplomatic posts abroad and through the Export Intelligence Service. Not all initiatives have been successful; for example the Construction Exports Advisory Board established in 1975 was wound up in 1978.[8]

One difficulty from the national point of view is that British contractors compete against each other on an individualistic basis instead of making a concerted effort to win against intense foreign competition. There are now a number of very large 'Jumbo' contracts which are too large for any one organisation to be able to bear all the risks. Moreover, the client government may wish to deal only with another government and often the client requires a total package deal contract including design and construction, provision of equipment and management of the operation of the building or works and, in some cases, finance.[9] This problem was examined as long ago as 1968 by Lord Cromer who much commended the ability to mount a total package as a means of getting work. He examined various types of consortia and came to the conclusion then that an *ad hoc* consortium is the most appropriate.[10]

However, the Civil Engineering EDC, ten years later, found that the success of UK contractors in these types of projects is limited compared with separate more traditional approaches and that even on smaller projects there is a failure of all parties including government to act together to obtain work. The EDC went on to recommend *inter alia* the establishment of a national marketing organisation.[11]

Sir Archie Lamb was asked by the EDC for Civil Engineering to investigate improvements that might be made towards winning contracts for overseas capital projects. His report goes into considerable detail on such matters as provision of finance, risks and risk insurance of overseas business and the development of continuing involvement in particular sectors. One of his major themes, however, is that export of capital projects requires a healthy home industry, and while government is consistently cutting the home industry and home expenditure on capital projects it cannot expect a healthy export sector. Another major theme is that the duration of the period for obtaining and carrying out projects is often equal to the span of several Parliaments and continual change in policies from one administration to the next must add to the difficulties of operation.[12]

CONSULTING ENGINEERS

The capital value of projects abroad undertaken by consulting engineers has increased dramatically since 1974 in money terms, as is shown in Figure 5.2. As with contractors, what is really required is an index of world inflation, but the price index indicates that the value of the capital projects has about kept pace with inflation in the UK in recent years.

The consulting engineers undertaking these projects are construction industry in a broader sense than the usual definition of construction activity. They include electrical and mechanical engineers, and the projects include, for example, electrical and mechanical services, power transmission lines and desalination plants. However, many of the practices involved are multidisciplinary and it is virtually impossible to separate the 'pure' construction element from the remainder.

The value of work in hand abroad by consulting engineers started to rise sharply in 1974. This was a period of falling work-load in Great Britain so that to some extent the rise in exports may have been the result of an attempt on the part of consultants to offset the decline in the home market. At the same time the rise in oil prices was giving countries with oil increased spending power.

The types of work being designed by British consulting engineers reflect the types of work being undertaken generally. Each type fluctuates as a percentage of the total because individual projects are often very large. Both in 1980 and 1981 over 40 per cent of work was connected with transport, that is, airports, harbours and docks, roads, bridges and tunnels (the largest item) and railways but this fell in 1982 to about 33 per cent. Structural work on commercial and industrial buildings is important in the total as is also water supply and drainage and sewerage together.[13]

The geographical spread of the activities of consulting engineers is very similar to that of contractors with a high proportion in the Middle East and Africa, and important work in the Far East and Amercia.[14]

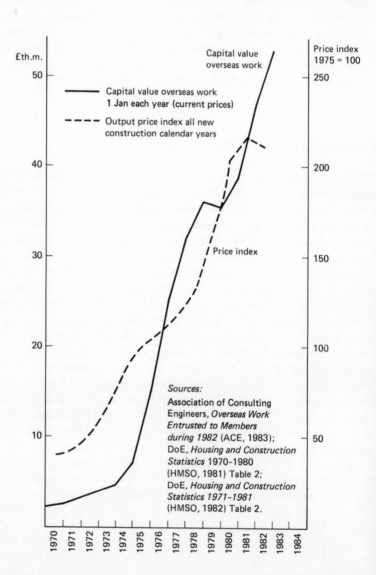

£th.m.

Price index
1975 = 100

Capital value
overseas work

—— Capital value overseas work
1 Jan each year (current prices)

––– Output price index all new
construction calendar years

Price index

Sources:
Association of Consulting
Engineers, *Overseas Work
Entrusted to Members
during 1982* (ACE, 1983);
DoE, *Housing and Construction
Statistics 1970-1980*
(HMSO, 1981) Table 2;
DoE, *Housing and Construction
Statistics 1971-1981*
(HMSO, 1982) Table 2.

FIGURE 5.2 *Total estimated capital values of overseas work in hand by ACE members compared with price index for Great Britain from 1970*

Well over a hundred distinct practices of consulting engineers are engaged in export work of whom many have separate partnerships in a number of countries.[15] It is the rule rather than the exception of larger firms to be engaged on consultancy abroad and some of the large firms in Great Britain have under 10 per cent of their turnover in Great Britain, while most of the larger firms have a high proportion of their work abroad. Over all, probably over three-quarters of the fee income comes from abroad.

The consulting engineers are affected as much as contractors by the increasing competition in overseas markets and by the trend towards large package work. Generally, less-developed countries rely entirely on expatriate consultants for planning and design of capital projects. As their level of competence rises, they use a mixture of local and foreign consultants often in a partnership arrangement and, at the final stage of development, foreign consultants for specialist work only.

Beardall, speaking at a conference, outlined the situation in obtaining work. As with contractors, to become established in a local market it is important to have some local representation and a continuing UK presence. At least a year must be assumed before getting a job in a new market, during which it will probably be necessary to register with each ministry concerned, make contacts with potential clients and become very well acquainted with local conditions and problems. Then the firm may get on a shortlist of bidders, with or without formal prequalification, which for large projects may involve a presentation. Tender documents for consulting engineers are now almost like contractors' documentation rather than the more gentlemanly agreement of the past. They may include provision for bid bonds, performance bonds, advance payments bonds, retentions, penalties for delay and are termed in very precise legal language. The price is a fixed lump sum not a scale fee.[16]

Assistance is available for very large projects from the Overseas Projects Fund administered by the Department of Trade on the advice of the Overseas Projects Board. The fund is intended to assist with the costs of bidding for major capital projects overseas and also for consultancies and feasibility studies. The potential contracts will normally be expected to have a potential UK content of £50 million and would usually be package contracts. Consultancies are eligible if they are valued at more than £5 million in their own right or as a forerunner to other contracts. Similar conditions apply to feasibility studies.[17]

ECGD insures consultants for fees, financing bonds and other export risks.

ARCHITECTS, PLANNERS AND QUANTITY SURVEYORS

Architects and planning firms undertake work abroad and the geographical distribution of their work is probably similar to that of contractors and consulting engineers.

There is very little information on work abroad by surveyors but this may be included in the results of a survey by the RICS to become available in 1983.

CONTRIBUTION TO BALANCE OF PAYMENTS

The proportion of the value of contracts, in which British designers and contractors are involved, brought back to this country varies considerably.

In the case of contractors, most materials and labour are obtained in the country in which the work is carried out or, in the case of labour, often from a low labour-cost country such as Pakistan, Egypt or Sri Lanka. Manufactured components of high value and low weight may be bought in Great Britain. Plant may be bought from Great Britain but, in view of the high cost of transport, it may be cheaper to purchase in, say, North America or another developed country. Thus often the contribution to the balance of payments consists of the UK-based management components and UK overheads and profit. The official balance of payments figure represents only 10–15 per cent of the value of work done.

For designers the fee income will, to a large extent, be brought back to this country as a large part of the design work is undertaken in Great Britain.

Table 5.3 shows the contribution to the balance of payments of construction, contractors, consulting engineers and architects and quantity surveyors. Whereas since 1971 contractors' contribution has just over doubled at current prices, both consulting engineers and architects and quantity surveyors have multiplied about ten times.

TABLE 5.3 *Contribution of construction to the balance of payments from 1971, UK (current prices)*

Year	Contractors	Consulting engineers	Architects and quantity surveyors
	£m	£m	£m
1971	52	48	8
1972	58	65	11
1973	71	84	14
1974	94	108	18
1975	130	136	23
1976	174	214	36
1977	201	305	51
1978	213	370	63
1979	151	401	64
1980	126	423	79
1981	124	487	88
1982			
1983			
1984			

Source:

CSO, *United Kingdom Balance of Payments*, 1982 Edition (HMSO, 1982) Table 3.9.

6 Forecasting and Forecasts of Demand and Output

Forecasting is the process of using data about the past and present to predict the future. Some assumptions about the future are necessary as a basis for almost any type of decision. The assumptions may be based on a 'hunch' or on a systematic use of whatever data are relevant. The 'hunch' forecaster may produce a better prognostication than the formal forecaster because he is more observant, more experienced or just luckier. In general, however, a systematic approach yields better results than a 'hunch' approach. Furthermore, if the assumptions are clearly stated, then it should be relatively easy to determine when and for which reasons the forecast should be updated.

The approach in Chapter 2 to analysis of demand through consideration of the roles of potential users, owners, financiers and initiators as well as a favourable environment is difficult to apply in detail in forecasting. The reason is that there are insufficient data on the intentions of all the persons or organisations involved, especially for forecasting beyond a very limited period of a year or so. Thus for short-term forecasting reliance has to be placed on whatever indicators are available. For long-term forecasts it is necessary to consider the very factors that influence the actions of the participants in the process of demand creation, notably need and the extent to which it is likely that it will be turned into economic demand. The participants in demand creation will often themselves be concerned with such forecasts.

Short-term forecasts of demand and output are based on a number of indicators and are fundamentally a prediction of how much work in the earlier stage of the pipeline will get translated into output and at what rate, helped by prediction of how other factors such as underlying economic conditions will affect this. These forecasts are needed, for example, by contractors and material producers to forecast their likely work-load. These short-term forecasts may be made up to a period of two to three years ahead. Beyond this there are no data on the 'pipe-line'.

Longer-term forecasts must be based on much more fundamental factors – basically a forecast of need and the rate at which this is likely to be met – to arrive at economic demand. These forecasts are needed by a number of organisations for any decision likely to have consequences several years ahead, for example, new plant for material production, the increase of the capacity to train craftsmen or managers, the policy of contractors in setting up new regional offices in the UK or abroad.

Short-term forecasts of an earlier stage in the construction process, for example new orders and housing starts, must be based partly on very few relevant indicators and partly on an interpretation of the longer-term demand in the short term.

In order to translate forecasts of demand into forecasts of output it must be considered whether or not the industry will be able to meet demand. Normally it has been able to do so. Exceptions are discussed elsewhere, notably in Chapters 4 and 10.

SHORT-TERM FORECASTS FOR UNDER THREE YEARS

In the short run contractors' output is dependent on orders received. There are, however, difficulties in forecasting output from new orders because the rate at which orders are transferred into output depends on the size of orders and the intensity of work over time. The intended completion date may not be the actual completion date. The intensity varies in any case over a project's life according to a fairly regular pattern, but this pattern may be varied because of extraneous factors, such as supply difficulties, or at the will of the contractor because of his work-load and problems within the firm. In addition, there may be variation orders that upset the original intentions and possibly increase the value of the order without this appearing in any order statistics. All these are real problems and are compounded by problems arising from sampling and price changes. A full discussion of these matters is contained in a paper by Sugden and Wells.[1]

A stage further back in the process is that of design and cost advice. For building there are statistics of new commissions and work entering the production drawings stage by the RIBA[2] and the RICS work-load inquiry.[3] However, the difficulties become even greater. At least new orders and output data for contractors are collected by the same organisation, using the same definitions and since 1980–1 have both been based on projects.[4] In contrast, RIBA survey of work in architects' offices is sent out to a sample of offices and does not tie in well with output by contractors or even with their new orders. One reason is that of the collection of data – well covered by Fleming.[5] Another reason is that the rate at which work goes from new commissions to production drawing stage and then on to a new order for a contractor is extremely variable. Furthermore, work at the design stage may be cancelled and never reach the construction stage. In any case the work is only that covered by private architects' offices and, although it gives breakdowns by very broad type of work, insufficient is known of the overlap of work between private and public architects. It would be expected that the proportions of work done in-house by the public sector would fluctuate over time and therefore that private architects' work for the public sector would be an inadequate guide to public-sector construction. The RIBA figures are best used as a general indicator only rather than a quantitative input to a model.

Similar considerations apply to the RICS inquiry of work-load, especially since this inquiry is less detailed than that of the RIBA.

Indeed many organisations connected with the industry undertake a state of trade inquiry[6] and these all have value as indicators to be used as a general guide on trends. However, they often tend to reflect the current position rather than the future.

For some individual types of building or works more detailed information is available on plans and work in the pipeline. For public-sector work generally there are the government expenditure plans for construction which after much lobbying by the industry, largely through the Group of Eight, are now published for one year ahead only with the annual White Paper[7] giving plans for future overall public expenditure. Statements are available from government departments about policy affecting various types of construction. Unfortunately undue reliance in the past on the trends in the White Papers would have yielded very poor forecasts and within any one sector very substantial changes have taken place in their plans for any one year. For example, in December 1973 the planned expenditure on education for the year 1977–8 was about £450 million at 1970 prices,[8] but the planned expenditure for that year decreased year by year so that by January 1978 the provisional outturn was nearer £150 million at 1970 prices.[9] A similar picture emerges for roads, with smaller falls over the years for water and sewerage and health expenditure.

Within the public sector other sources are most helpful in housing[10] but there is very little specific data for other types of work. Within the private sector, again housing is well documented[11] but there are also a number of indicators for other private work.[12]

Repair and maintenance presents great problems for forecasters because there are no new order figures for repair and maintenance and the only indicators are policy statements on improvement grants, etc. as well as the most important assessments of the general level of economic activity.

There are many very competent forecasts of the economy,[13] and the fact that the resources that are necessary to produce such forecasts are substantial, means that they should first be considered before embarking on any individual forecast. The problem is that they differ quite substantially in their predictions. Any forecast of construction should state explicitly the assumptions on the conomy.

There are two major short-term group forecasts prepared for the construction industry. The first is by the Joint Forecasting Committee of the Building and Civil Engineering EDC.[14] This is prepared every six months with the help of sub-groups, including in their membership many persons from the industry who are concerned with forecasts in their own organisations. It presents a comprehensive review of the outlook about two and a half years ahead. The other is that undertaken by a panel in the National Council of Building Material Producers[15] three times a year and covering similar ground. The two forecasts do not always agree. However, since the reasons for their forecasts are discussed, they provide a foundation on which to make a judgement and to update according to changed circumstances.

In addition, a number of stockbrokers and other firms produce forecasts of construction activity and many of the larger companies make construction output predictions as part of their company planning although in many cases these are based on the NEDO and BMP forecasts.

LONG-TERM FORECASTS FOR THREE YEARS AND OVER

In the longer term almost all the indicators considered, including orders and state of trade inquiries, are of no value because they do not give a useful indication so far ahead, and, in practice, statements of government policies and plans are of slight benefit. Reliance must be placed where possible on an understanding of need and then of the factors that enable or prevent that need being met.

The requirement for buildings and works may be divided into categories all of which have to be considered for forecasts usually distinguishing between the situations in various parts of the country:

(a) The population of users of the building or works and changes in the population. This population may be households for dwellings, children of various age groups for schools, the number of vehicles for roads, the number of dwellings having piped water supply, the number of persons travelling by air, and so on.

(b) The rate of usage per user and changes in this rate. For example, more miles per vehicle will affect the need for roads. Technological factors can play a major part in this category, for example, industry may consume more or less electricity for production processes and there may well be a change towards less space requirements for industry.

(c) Standards and changes in standards. These may, for example take the form of increased space requirements, improved standards of construction and fitments for buildings. Increased standards for sewerage systems are currently being called for.

(d) Replacement of stock because of deterioration due to age or technical factors. Here the age of the stock of buildings and works is a vital factor as well as standards of construction in past periods. This is clearly seen in the present housing situation where the stock built only thirty years ago is deteriorating to the point where demolition is sometimes necessary.

(e) Increase or replacement of stock because of technological change or changes in standards. Changes in harbours and docks were necessary to make them suitable for containerised traffic and change in gas installations because of the change to natural gas.

The difference between the total requirement for building and works and the existing provision represents need for construction.

The separate factors will have very varying importance according to the type of demand being considered, and although broadly the state of the economy is the main factor determining the rate at which need is translated into economic demand, the aspects of the economy that are important vary from one type of work to another.

In determining requirements for dwellings demographic factors play a prime part, in particular the rate of new household formation and the number of households that do not have a separate dwelling.[16] The demand for second dwellings has to be included since it may prevent dwellings being used for other households. There are, however, very few compared with the total.[17] The extent of mobility of the population and potential mobility affects the number of vacant dwellings required as does the market turnover and local surpluses.

Then there is the whole matter of standards and suitability. The English House Condition Survey[18] referred to in Chapter 2 separates dwellings unfit, having not all of five basic amenities and those needing substantial repair, and there are numerical data on all these factors. These as well as data on the age of the stock of dwellings,[19] constitute a basis to assess need for replacement or refurbishment. In addition many dwellings are in the wrong location or are of the wrong size for present needs. For housing there is a considerable amount of data both on the requirement and also on the stock and changes in the stock through losses due to urban redevelopment, road improvement schemes, changes to other use, as well as redevelopment and conversion.[20] It is thus possible to make a reasonable assessment of need.

It is much more difficult to estimate the rate at which this will be met by the creation of economic demand. In the private sector this is determined by many of the factors mentioned for short-term forecasts, such as finance, as well as the economic environment, particularly incomes and expectations and the price of housing relative to other goods. In the public sector government policy is a dominant factor, as well as local authority priorities. Once the main determinants of demand are established, it is possible to construct a model to assist in forecasting and several models of the housing market have been tried – for example those by Whitehead[21] and Holmans.[22]

Industrial building is very substantially determined by the economic environment and 'need' has very little meaning except in this context. Various attempts have been made to relate industrial building to known or predicted economic parameters and thus to make a forecast. One such attempt was undertaken in the long-term forecasts by NEDO.[23] These used a number of variables representing the growth in the economy and related them by equations to some measure of investment by industry.

The problem with this attempt and with the mathematical approach in general is that since each calculation gives different results, judgement still has to be used to choose the most likely answer. However, the preliminary analysis clarifies the thought processes and helps to define limits within which the correct forecast is expected to lie.

For public-sector work other than housing, need is more relevant, especially in sectors such as education, where demographic factors mean that the population of schools, at least to age 16, is fairly certain, or in water treatment where consumption is relatively predictable. The difficulties are greater where there is no defined standard of provision or definite means of assessing potential use – such as in day centres for old people or even the standard of roads.

In the public sector there is always difficulty in determining for how much of the need satisfaction is regarded as vital, and for how much a long-term objective is acceptable. This was a problem when the political parties were generally agreed on objectives. It is even more of a problem now that objectives are not common. In these circumstances a judgement must be made of the social and economic factors and of the politicians' attitude to them. The range of possibilities is wide and hence longer-term forecasts in this area are likely to be particularly subject to error.

Two major long-term forecasts of construction demand have been published. The first was that by the EDCs for Building and Civil Engineering in 1971, looking ten years ahead from the last date for which statistics were available, that is, 1969–79.[24] The second was a regional forecast looking five years ahead on the same basis which was to some extent a sequel to the first.[25] The latter established a methodology for making forecasts at a disaggregated level. In addition, the assessment of the possible ranges and mix of future demand in *Construction in the Early 1980s* and the corresponding Scottish report[26] adopted the methodology of long-term forecasts. Political and economic factors meant that the forecasts were to a large extent out of date before they were published. There is little reason to suppose that one undertaken in the early 1980s would fare substantially better. Yet forecasts are required for decision-making and major companies and other organisations have to make some forecast beyond three years. It is vital that assumptions are stated, that alternative scenarios are discussed and that the forecasts are updated at regular intervals. The most likely outcome must be highlighted in the short tun with a range for the longer term.

7 Structure of Contracting Industry

There are two main types of organisation concerned to produce construction output on site: the private contractors and the direct labour organisations of public authorities. The former account for nearly 90 per cent of the work (Chapter 4). They will be considered first.

PRIVATE CONTRACTORS

There were about 115 000 contracting firms on the DoE register in October 1981 in Great Britain[1] and there were, in addition, a number of firms - mostly small - not on the statistical register. Although the term 'firm' is used throughout, strictly these are 'reporting units' and may consist of a regional office of a contracting company or an associated company, or the whole group may report as one unit. The same problem arises with data from the Census of Production which also reports undertakings 'which are uncertain in scope'. However, since the 1980 census the data published there[2] have been less useful because of the reporting of only the new Standard Industrial Classification Groups,[3] because there is no geographical split of the UK and because there is less detailed information even on the new groups, notably on the split between private and public undertakings. With this limitation, the census of production will be little used and frequent reference will be made to the 1979 and earlier years for which fuller data are available.[4]

It is difficult even using DoE data to make any satisfactory statement about the change over time of the number of firms in the industry because of discontinuities in the series - particularly in 1973 and to a lesser extent in 1978 - and also because of the undercounting of small firms, already referred to, which will almost certainly not be a consistent percentage of the total. However, Figure 7.1 shows the close relationship

113

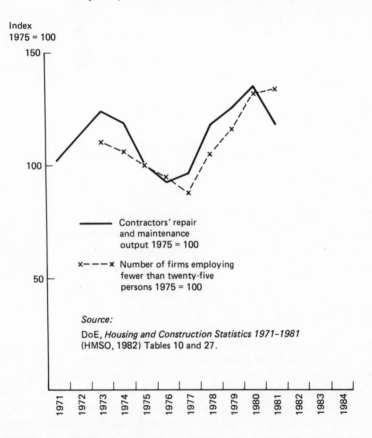

FIGURE 7.1 *Private contractors: repair and maintenance output and number of firms employing less than twenty-five persons from 1971 (indices 1975 = 100)*

since 1973 between the number of small firms and the value at constant prices of contractors' output on repair and maintenance. Figure 7.2 shows a similar relationship between the number of firms employing 115 persons and over and the value at constant prices of contractors' new work. Also on this graph is the estimate of the number of large contracts in 1971, 1976 and 1981 (from Table 4.6) which corresponds with the general trends of output and firms.

These broad size groups conceal greater changes in more specific groups. The greatest percentage fall in 1973-81 has been in the firms employing 1200 and over from eighty to thirty-nine firms.[5] The size

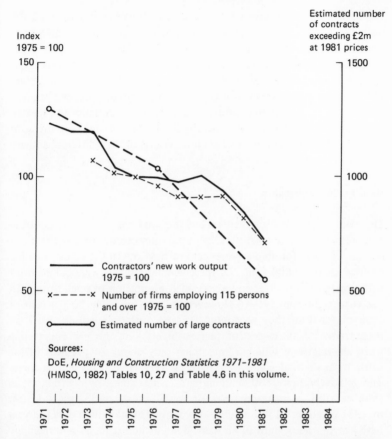

FIGURE 7.2 *Private contractors: new work output and number of firms employing 115 persons and over and estimated number of large contracts from 1971 (indices 1975 = 100)*

group employing 80–114 has also fallen sharply from 697 firms in 1973 to 416 in 1981.[6] These changes of firms in size groups can occur in many different ways, notably a disappearance of firms by mergers, a disappearance of firms by company liquidations or bankruptcies, a change in workforce and in work done or simply in the proportion of directly employed labour, with no change in work done, so that the firm moves into a different size category. Mergers and insolvencies are discussed under separate headings later in this chapter and the change in proportions of directly employed and subcontracted labour force is discussed further in this chapter and in Chapters 11 and 12.

The firms may be divided into the main trades contractors and the specialist trades. These categories do not by any means exactly correspond with main contractors and subcontractors, but for the larger categories of size of firm they are related to it; and since this latter division is related to the process where, under the traditional system and in many other arrangements, the main contractor has the primary role on site, it is useful to consider separately the main trades and specialist trades and also the private housebuilders who are, however, included in the DoE statistics of main trades but because of their different activity are worth considering separately.

Main Trades Contractors

The main trades consist of general builders, building and civil engineering contractors and civil engineers. In total they accounted in the third quarter of 1981 for about 44 per cent of the firms in the industry with a total of about 51 000 firms. Of these general builders were the majority with nearly 46 000 firms and a very high proportion of small firms with less than eight employees.[7] However, in spite of being 90 per cent of main trades firms they accounted for only just over half the work by these trades.[8] Main trades contractors undertaking only civil engineering work are relatively unimportant, doing only about 14 per cent of the work by main trades and they have no very large firms among them. The relatively few 2880 building and civil engineering contractors, in October 1981, were responsible for a gross output in the third quarter of 1981 of about £1500 million of work or £6000 million on a full-year basis – well over a third of all work done including repair and maintenance. Out of the twenty-three large firms in main trades employing 1200 persons or more, eighteen were building and civil engineering and these large firms accounted for 47 per cent of work by all building contractors and civil engineering contractors.[9]

This ties in with the work done by these various trades. General builders in the third quarter of 1981 had 35 per cent of their work in repair and maintenance, for civil engineers the figure was 23 per cent and for building and civil engineering contractors, 13 per cent.[10]

The large number of small general builders is not surprising in view of the nature of the work-load of the industry. There is a very high proportion of small contracts in the industry especially when repair and maintenance is included. The geographical location for much of this work is determined by the location of the existing building stock, which is very widely spread throughout the country. There are difficulties and high costs associated with managing contracts far away from the controlling office and large contractors with high overheads cannot profitably handle small contracts. Hence small jobs tend to be done by a large number of small contractors geographically spread according to the location of the work. There are no data on the geographical distribution of main trades contractors but for all firms the percentage of total small firms in each region bears a close relationship to the percentage of total work in the region.[11] It is also relevant that firms employing fewer than twenty-five persons do over 50 per cent of the repair and maintenance work and over 50 per cent of their work is in repair and maintenance.[12]

Table 7.1 shows the number of all main trades firms of various size groups according to number employed, the gross value of the work for which they were responsible, the work they did themselves, and the derived percentage of the gross output subcontracted. Some explanation of the size groups must be given. The number employed refers to direct employees by the firms concerned, including working proprietors, but does not include the labour force of subcontractors employed on their sites or of labour-only subcontractors. Since some firms run their sites with almost all subcontracting, some relatively small firms may be responsible for a very substantial turnover as a main contractor. However, from Table 7.1 it is possible to say that twenty-three large firms were responsible for nearly 21 per cent of the work and subcontracted all but about 56 per cent of this. Their average turnover in Great Britain – for all these figures refer only to work in this country – was of the order of £260 million a year.

More is known about the operation of the very largest contractors from other sources. Taking information on public companies derived from stockbrokers Savory Milln,[13] the six companies with the largest turnover in contracting in 1980 appear to be George Wimpey, the largest; John Laing; Trafalgar House, which owns Cementation, Trollope & Colls, Ideal Homes and Willett; Tarmac, which owns Holland, Hannen & Cubitts, Kinnear Moodie and McLean Homes; Taylor Woodrow and Costain Group. The next six in size were probably John Mowlem & Co.: Marchwiel Holdings, which owns Sir Alfred McAlpine; Newarthill, which owns Sir Robert McAlpine; French Kier Holdings; Fairclough Construction Group, which owns John Howard and Parkinson; and Higgs and Hill. The merger in 1982 of Fairclough Construction Group with William Press to form AMEC raises them to the top six in second or third place. It is interesting that going back to 1968/69[14] the same six as in 1980 were at the top of the list, although at that time Cementation would

TABLE 7.1 *Gross output, work done and work subcontracted by main trades contractors by size of firm, 1981, Great Britain (Oct. 1981 or third quarter of 1981)*

Size of firm	Number of firms		Gross output		Value of work done		Work subcontracted	
No. of employees	*No.*	*% of total*	*£m*	*% of total*	*£m*	*% of total*	*£m*[a]	*%*[b]
1–7	40 953	80.5	477	11.6	377	13.8	100	21.0
8–24	7 020	13.8	469	11.4	360	13.2	109	23.2
25–114	2 337	4.6	747	18.1	525	19.3	222	29.7
115–1 199	557	1.1	1 565	38.0	982	36.0	583	37.3
1 200 +	23	neg.	863	20.9	481	17.6	382	44.3
Total	50 890	100	4 121	100	2 726	100	1 395	33.9

Notes:

[a] Gross output is value of work done (or output) plus work subcontracted.
[b] Work subcontracted as a percentage of gross output.

Source:

Based on: DoE, *Housing and Construction Statistics 1971–1981* (HMSO, 1982) Tables 31, 40 and 41.

have been there in its own right and not as part of Trafalgar House. Similarly W. C. French and Kier were separate, but together (and perhaps even separately), they would have been in the top twelve or fifteen companies. Going back even further to about 1958 before figures of turnover were published, the list of the top companies was very similar. At that time among the top dozen companies over half were run by or had board members of the founder's family. Now the proportion has fallen but still a quarter or so are in that category. The output of these companies includes in many cases a considerable amount of work abroad – as much as half in the case of Costains. This is described more fully in Chapter 5.

Although for contractors in general, the geographical distribution of firms is similar to the work-load, this does not apply to the large contractors, most of which have head offices in the Greater London area and all in the South East. However, most of them also have regional offices.

Contractors are subject to great uncertainties in their work-load. First, this is due to fluctuations in national work-load and particularly in types of work. Then, since most contractors operate in a specific locality or region, there is often greater fluctuation there. Secondly, the fact that each contract has normally to be won in competition with other contractors means that there is great uncertainty as to whether the work-load of the firm can be evenly maintained. Even when a contract is won its duration, cost and the final price are often uncertain, for reasons discussed in Chapter 3.

The increase in the amount of rehabilitation and improvement work and the decrease in new work has an effect on the organisation of contractors and the largest contractors as well as the medium and small ones are engaged in this type of work. It has implications for the type of management required and for the skills and training.

Subcontracting and Specialist Trade Firms

The demand of an individual contractor for certain types of manpower input would almost certainly fluctuate, even if his overall work-load were stable, because the requirement for various trades over the life of a contract is bunched and different types of contract require different inputs (see Chapter 10). Thus the practice of subcontracting has grown up. This helps the main contractor in a number of ways: first, it enables him to choose the specialist trade inputs when he wants them from a range of specialist firms, who will often have far more skill and know-how of their specialism than he could command; second, he can obtain the advantage of low prices by competitive tenders; third, it enables him to keep his own workforce small and thus minimise the costs of having underemployed operatives on his payroll; fourth, it allows him to keep his working capital requirements down, not only because he doesn't have to pay operatives weekly, but also for other costs of the trade such as tools and materials; and lastly, it gives greater freedom in choosing what contracts he will bid for. Over all it gives greater flexibility in the type of work to be undertaken and in its execution. Additional to the employment of specialist supply-and-fix trade firms, the contractor has increasingly during the last twenty years employed labour-only sub-contractors, sometimes known as the 'lump' or the 'grip' in Scotland, in trades that formerly he would have employed himself (see Chapter 11). The reasons for this are partly the flexibility and also that, if they are employed on a piecework system, it provides a built-in incentive scheme. However, a site with much subcontracting requires supervision and management of a different type to that on a site with directly employed operatives.

There are also disadvantages to contractors. Although it may be easy to negotiate a piece-rate for fairly straightforward work, it is difficult to do so for much of repair and maintenance or rehabilitation and also for the more complicated bits of new work. This has sometimes led to extremes of specialisation such as a bricklayer going from site to site on a motorbike building the corners in walls while others do the straight work. One way in which the problem of standards is overcome is that many contractors employ the same labour-only subcontractors more or less continuously and therefore come to know and trust the quality of their work. The cost of self-employed labour may be higher in terms of payment per day and will be very high in a period of boom. In a recession contractors probably find it cheaper than direct employment. In a boom it may not be possible to obtain the required labour any other way.

With the supply-and-fix subcontracting system and the labour-only system there are great variations. Some supply-and-fix subcontractors employ labour-only subcontractors. The labour-only subcontractors range from large organisations acting as agencies for the provision of labour and organisations providing labour-only gangs to a number of sites, to individual operatives offering their labour to contractors or to householders. The labour-only operative is always self-employed but he may be paid on a piecework basis or on an hourly rate.

One difficulty in interpreting statistics on the structure of the industry is that very little is known about labour-only subcontracting and the self-employed. It should be included in the percentage subcontracted in Table 7.1 but it is possible that not all firms clearly differentiate in their returns between work done by and persons employed on a labour-only basis and a direct-employment basis. It is a potential source of error. Moreover, doubts on the figures are increased by suggestions (see Chapter 11) that the total number of self-employed in construction is considerably greater than those counted by the DoE statistics. While it is likely that many of these work direct to private householders, those working with various types of subcontactors distort the figures of sub-contracting by the large main contractors. It is important in using the figures to compare like with like and the DoE figures of men employed, work done and number of firms are internally fairly consistent.

Bearing in mind the above reservations, the statistics show that the amount of work subcontracted by main trades firms is a total of 34 per cent, but much higher at 41 per cent by building and civil engineering contractors, 32 per cent for general builders and only 17 per cent for civil engineers. In general the amount of work subcontracted rises with the size of firm from an average of about 21 per cent for small firms to 44 per cent for large ones.[15] Apart from labour-only subcontracting, most subcontracting would be to specialist firms, but some would be to other main trades firms, which means that not all work done by main trades contractors is necessarily as a main contractor.

The changes in the amount of subcontracting over the three years 1979-81 throws some light on the reasons for the very rapid fall in the number of contractors employing more than 1200 persons. Whereas the rise in the overall percentage of subcontracting by main trades contrac-tors has been about 2 per cent of their gross output from 31.7 per cent in the third quarter of 1979 to 33.9 per cent in the third quarter of 1981, the comparable figures for contractors employing 1200 and over is 37.5 per cent in 1979 and 44.2 per cent in 1981.[16] This would indicate that some may have fallen into a lower size category because of a change in subcontracting policy. There are in any case regional variations. Of industrial building projects studied in the EDC study on construction times,[17] of those in the south over three-quarters were wholly or mainly subcontracted, compared to only about one-third in the rest of the country.

There were in October 1981 over 64 000 specialist trade firms account-ing for about 56 per cent of all firms counted by the DoE.[18] The statistics distinguish eighteen types of specialist firms, and then there is still a miscellaneous category (see Table 7.2). Generally the size of firm is small but sixteen employ more than 1200 and 285 have between 115 and 1199 employees.[19] Thus the proportion of large firms is less than for main

TABLE 7.2 Gross output, work done and work subcontracted by specialist trades contractors by trade of firm, 1981, Great Britain (third quarter of 1981)

Trade of firm	Firms No. th	Gross output £m	Value work done £m	Work subcontracted[a] %	Gross output per firm[b] £th
Plumbers	9.9	126.8	116.5	8.1	12.9
Carpenters and joiners	7.0	94.7	81.0	14.5	13.5
Painters	12.7	189.7	168.5	11.2	14.9
Roofers	3.5	131.6	119.1	9.5	37.8
Plasterers	3.0	55.9	48.9	12.5	18.8
Glaziers	2.2	63.3	57.5	9.2	29.3
Demolition contractors	0.5	13.6	12.5	8.1	29.7
Scaffolding specialists	0.5	62.7	60.3	3.8	122.5
Reinforced concrete specialists	0.4	25.4	22.3	12.2	69.2
Heating and ventilating engineers	5.6	346.9	283.4	18.3	61.6
Electrical contractors	9.2	273.3	254.9	6.7	29.7
Asphalt and tar-sprayers	0.6	94.4	87.8	7.0	149.8
Plant hirers	3.5	167.1	159.7	4.4	47.6
Flooring contractors	0.9	31.4	29.2	7.0	34.0
Constructional engineers	1.1	81.7	67.8	17.0	74.8
Insulating specialists	0.8	66.2	61.4	7.3	78.2
Suspended ceiling specialists	0.5	22.9	19.3	15.7	45.6

Floor and wall tiling

specialists	0.7	18.2	16.4	9.9	25.7
Miscellaneous	1.7	101.2	88.2	12.8	58.2
All specialists	64.3	1 967.1	1 754.7	10.8	30.6

Notes:

aGross output is value of work done (or output) plus work subcontracted.
bGross output per firm based on numbers of firms before rounding.

Source:

From or based on DoE, *Housing and Construction Statistics 1971–1981* (HMSO, 1982) Tables 31, 40 and 41.

trades contractors. The trades having the greatest number of larger firms are the heating and ventilating contractors and electrical contractors and these are in any case the trades with the largest overall volume of work. Table 7.2 shows some of the differences between trades. The gross output per firm gives a good indication of size. The highest is in asphalt and tar-sprayers at £150 000 per quarter equivalent to about £600 000 a year, followed by scaffolding specialists with £490 000 a year. Although there are large firms among electrical contractors and heating and ventilating contractors, the number of small firms brings the average gross output down to about £250 000 a year for heating and ventilating and £120 000 a year for electrical contractors, the latter being the same as the average for all specialist trades. The average is brought down by the large numbers of firms of painters, plumbers, carpenters and joiners which have a low gross output. The amount of work subcontracted varies from very small for plant hirers and scaffolding specialists – both less than 5 per cent – to over 15 per cent for suspended ceiling specialists, constructional engineers and heating and ventilating contractors. Some of the work subcontracted may be subsubcontracted but for certain types of project, especially in repair and maintenance and renovation, the specialist trade may be the main contractor and will need to subcontract the specialisms that he does not have in his own organisation to specialist trade firms, to general builders normally regarded as main trades, or to labour-only subcontractors. The overall percentage of work subcontracted by specialist firms is about 11 per cent of the gross output compared with 34 per cent for main trades contractors.

There are three main problem areas that arise with the increasing amount of subcontracting of various forms and of self-employment. The first is the situation of the 'traditional' type of subcontractor in the industry. With the increase in management contracting and with the desire of main contractors to keep maximum flexibility with least capital lock-up, the practice of subcontracting has grown so that it is often well over 50 per cent of work on site and rises to 100 per cent on some sites. The place of the subcontractors in the industry has therefore grown to one where on many projects they do all the actual site work, except for the overall management. However the place of the subcontractor organisations in the industry and the conditions of contract under which they operate have not changed in tune with their increased role. Because they are near the end of the line in the contract process, in a recession they can be squeezed by the main contractor and, because they are still mainly small firms, they are not in a good position to bargain with builders merchants and producers from whom they buy their supplies (see Chapter 3). They are unable substantially to reduce their working capital requirements because they have to pay their labour. They, however, are the people who do the work and they must be maintained in a fit state for the benefit of the whole industry. A thorough investigation of their role and operations is required with the objective to ensure treatment which in the long run is going to maintain an effective industry.

The second problem is the growth of the self-employed used by contractors coupled with labour-only subcontracting, although as stated earlier this is often associated with supply-and-fix subcontractors. This issue is causing serious dissension in the industry. The problem must be tackled, so that it does not sour relations between employer and unions. It is very likely that whatever happens now, labour-only subcontracting will still be with us in fifteen years' time as it was fifteen years ago. It has many advantages, especially in productivity. However, the problems created by it are many. Self-employed operatives do virtually no training. Although some main contractors insist that subcontractors on their sites should take trainees and pay them to do so, this is the exception rather than the rule and it is doubtful whether the training received in this way is always satisfactory. This means that the burden of training in the industry falls on contractors employing directly employed labour and on the direct labour departments of public authorities (see also Chapter 11).

Another major disadvantage of self-employment is that it creates two quite separate cohorts of operatives, one of which is being remunerated on a different basis and at a very different level to the other (see Chapter 11). These two sets of operatives may be working side by side on the same site. This is particularly undesirable when the labour-only, self-employed operative is being paid at an hourly rate and this may well be more than double the directly employed, especially in the London area. The reasons that this happens are that output per man is higher; the self-employed person pays very little or no tax; the employer does not pay national insurance contributions for him (and many operatives do not in fact pay self-employed contributions) or holiday stamps and, as mentioned earlier, avoids some of the overheads associated with direct employment.

Various attempts have been made to prevent tax and insurance evasion and in the great majority of cases they have probably been successful. A 714 certificate and strictly a 715 certificate are needed by an operative for the employer not to deduct tax. However, the system is sometimes abused; 714 certificates are now easily obtained legally and can still in some areas be purchased illegally and, by dint of changing addresses frequently, the Inland Revenue does not actually find the man to levy tax. In any case there are many allowable expenses for self-employment which are intended for the small business that takes risks and has *bona fide* expenses but are claimed by the self-employed working on an hourly rate. Another method devised to collect tax is that the employer has to collect, from the operative who does not have a 714 certificate, 30 per cent of his earnings which is to be passed to the Inland Revenue. There is no means for the Inland Revenue to know that this has been collected and it may not always be passed on to them.

The trade unions are extremely concerned at the increase in self-employment for several reasons. They dislike the two sets of operatives and regard the self-employed system as seriously undermining the wages and conditions of employment of their members. The unions have over a long period negotiated improvements in conditions on site from which the self-employed largely benefit but with no allegiance to the unions that created them. They are concerned at the effect on their membership because, although some self-employed – notably drivers of ready-mixed concrete lorries – are members of the union, generally the self-employed are not union members. Moreover they are worried about the effects of self-employment on the industry, especially on training and safety standards.

In any case use of many types of self-employed subcontractors is contrary to all the Working Rule Agreements which, with varying degrees of strength, attempt to ban employment other than direct employment on sites. These clauses in the Working Rules are clearly not being observed in their rigid interpretation by a large number of contractors and have not been for a long time.

Another possible but unproven disadvantage of labour-only self-employment is that of standards. Some consider that standards of construction are reduced by subcontracting and self-employment. Many, however, say that it is the best workers who operate as self-employed and that the quality of work carried out is equal to that of directly employed operatives. The crux of the matter probably lies in the degree of supervision and management.

The same applies to safety on site. A well-managed site will not permit laxity in safety standards by subcontractors or anyone else. There is no statistical evidence that the self-employed are more at risk than the directly employed (see Chapter 11).

The solutions to these problems need urgent consideration. It is suggested that progress might be made in several ways: first a review by government of the rules for the circumstances in which persons may be taxed as self-employed; second, an attempt by unions to find a place within their organisation for self-employed with a valid 714 certificate working as a subcontractor, but excluding certain categories damaging to the general interest and to offer them assistance with the terms and conditions under which they operate and with group schemes for them to obtain some insurance and financial arrangements peculiar to their needs; third, the development of some scheme to involve the self-employed in training, practically and financially with consideration of the present arrangements of some contractors in this respect; fourth, a renegotiation of the relevant Working Rule agreements in a form in which they can be accepted by employers and unions. The contractors must concede that there are types of self-employment that are in the long run damaging to the industry and the unions that it is acceptable with appropriate safeguards.

The third related matter is concerned with labour-only self-employed who work directly for clients – often, but not always, householders. Here the problem is a different one and they are more akin to large numbers of small contractors than to the operatives employed on sites. The major difficulty is one of standards, and the various warranty schemes that are being proposed or actually operating should help in this respect. Beyond that, what seems to be needed more than anything else is that the householder knows the sort of person he is employing. Certification of skills (see Chapter 11) will help if the householder is informed of what it means. Some other 'passport' is, however, required and this could perhaps be provided by some form of record card similar to that of the scaffolders and tunnellers which would at least give an idea of what jobs the person had done. Some checks on validity would be needed. If the householder then employs someone without a certificate or record card, then he should realise the risks involved and the need for supervision.

Private Housebuilders

Table 7.3 shows the distribution of members of the National House-Building Council according to the number of registered starts for each firm or group in 1982 and the percentage of the total number of dwellings registered by each size group. Over 60 per cent of the members started no dwellings at all in 1982 and this percentage has not fallen below 50 per cent in the last few years.[20] They are builders who *might* wish to obtain certification of dwellings at some future data and consider membership worth while. Most active members start very few

TABLE 7.3   *Number of housebuilders in size categories by number of
dwellings started and market share, 1982, Great Britain*

Size of housebuilder No. of starts made	No. of firms	% of total starts
0	12 971	0
1–10	6 907	14
11–30	833	10
31–100	320	12
101–500	122	18
501 +	30	46
Total	21 183	100
	(active in year 8 212)	(total starts in year 138 300)

Source:

National House-Building Council, *Private House-Building Statistics 1982 4th quarter*
(NHBC, 1983) Tables 8 and 9.

dwellings each year. 84 per cent of active members on average build
less than three houses. Thirty firms built more than 500 in 1982 at an
average of 2000 each, with total share of the market of 46 per cent. In
1976 thirty-three builders constructed more than 500 in the year and
accounted for 34 per cent of a larger market (NHBC). Thus, although
the market share of the top firms has increased at the expense of the
medium builders, the total numbers built by them has not increased.

The largest builders may be divided into three categories: part of a
contracting group, for example Wimpey; part of a group that also owns
other very substantial firms, for example, Ideal Homes is part of Trafalgar
House; an organisation devoted mainly to private speculative housing
development such as Barratt. The top forty firms or so have a preponderance of the last category and only Wimpey is really very large operating
under its own name, although most of the large contractors do also have
a housing division.

The Level of Competition Among Contracting Firms

The extent of competition tends to be greater, the greater the number of
firms, the easier entry to the market, the more homogeneous the product
and the greater the degree of knowledge of the market and of what other
persons are doing in the market. How much competition there is in construction depends first of all on establishing the concept of the market.

Sufficient has been said about the diversity of firms and products to show that the industry is not one market. There is no direct competition between, at the extreme, the small builder undertaking repair and maintenance in a small town and the large national building and civil engineering contractor. They are in separate markets. The industry as a whole consists of a series of different, overlapping markets which may be defined in terms of an identifiable service, the size and complexity of contracts and the geographical location of work. Within each market there will be different degrees of competition and, moreover, it has been argued[21] that the extent of competition changes over the various stages of one project. It is desirable here to try to assess how widespread is the exercise of a significant degree of monopoly power and whether this means that the costs to the economy of construction are higher than they should be, or the contrary indicated by efficiency, the level of cost or the level of profits.

There are markets where a very few firms have a large market share and these will include the markets for large, complex projects, where few British contractors are capable of undertaking the work. Within these markets, when one or two contractors have experience of it and the others do not, the experienced one tends to obtain the competitive advantage, both in convincing the client of his suitability and in submitting lower prices in tendering, and it is possible that, because of his expertise, he is able to make greater profits than normal. This is not damaging to the economy. The arguments over specialisation in large road contracts are interesting. In 1966 The Lofthouse Report[22] studied the problem and, after pointing out that previous policies had resulted in contracts being so spread that contractors could not make use of specialised plant holdings nor keep experienced management teams in being, recommended that the execution of major road construction contracts should be concentrated in the hands of fewer teams. This was to some extent achieved and according to the 1977 Labour Party policy document on construction in the early 1970s four contractors had nearly 70 per cent of the motorway programme.[23] This situation could certainly be regarded as one of oligopoly but it was created by the client in his perceived interests of efficiency.

There have been, from time to time, cases of collusion by firms to arrange tendering so that prices did not fall too low. The best known scheme is that of the London Builders Conference in the post-war years and investigated by the Monopolies Commission in 1954.[24] Another case was that of electrical and mechanical services contractors grouping together to determine which firm should obtain the contract with a system of compensation for others. This was dealt with under the restrictive practices legislation.[25]

In addition, there are probably a number of instances where there are small groupings that never become public. Moreover, in order for prices and profits to be higher than under competitive conditions there need be no overt collusion. In a small market town, for example, it is quite possible for there to be a generally accepted level of prices among, say, three or four contractors and it is not in the interest of any, or even necessarily the wish of any, to increase turnover by tendering below this level. It is not possible to measure in how many cases or to what degree overt or tacit collusion exists. However, in a situation of recession where contractors generally are continually seeking to increase their work, the number of contractors in any given market is probably not sufficiently stable to allow it to happen on any large scale. In a period when contractors are satisfied with their work-load in their existing markets, such instances could well develop in quite substantial numbers.

It is also common practice for contractors not wishing to obtain a contract, but being unwilling to tell the client so to put in a cover price, that is, they ask another contractor who is tendering to tell them a price to submit that is higher than his price. The problem is that if a large number of contractors do this the client may not be obtaining real tenders at all but one price that must win the job and can therefore be higher than the competitive price and have an element of monopoly profit. On the other hand, it is argued in Chapter 9 that the tendering process in a period of recession is likely to push prices so low that efficiency is jeopardised.

Data on profits is scanty except for the published accounts of large companies. The analysis of these is undertaken in Chapter 16 and there is no evidence there that large firms in the construction industry are making exceptional profits.

Over all it is likely that there is sufficient competition in construction to produce efficient working at prices that do not contain a profit above that required to keep firms in business. There are, however, periods when demand is high, when there is likely to be such restricted competition so that efficiency is reduced and profits rise. In general, reasons for inefficiencies in the industry are to be found in areas other than the degree of competition.

Mergers and Acquisitions

One way in which the structure of the industry changes is by takeovers and mergers. A study by Ball and Cullen[26] analysed the reported mergers

in the British construction industry in 1960-79. They were few compared with other industrial sectors and they were characterised by the
overriding reasons of extension of the companies' activities into a
different market. The majority were mergers within the industry. The
situation of Trafalgar House owning companies in construction, property,
hotels, newspapers and shipping and of Bovis being owned by P&O are
exceptions to this rule and, because they are among the top companies,
give an impression of diversification not borne out in the rest of the
industry. There were two periods of mergers that by construction standards were intense. The first was in 1967-9 when the industry, especially
public-sector housebuilding, was going through a period of depression.
Firms moved into new markets in order to maintain the momentum of
orders and profits. The second period for mergers was, on the contrary,
in the boom conditions of the 1970-73 upswing when firms did not
have resources to undertake all the orders they could obtain and the
stronger firms acquired others to have the benefit of their management
teams and established places in other markets. Then there was a period
at the beginning of the recession when uncertainity, coupled with the
unusual balance sheet situations of companies that went from extremes
of strength to weakness, slowed merger activity and those that took
place were either for diversification or because of an opportunity to
acquire cheaply. The third surge in mergers of this period took place
in 1977-9, again for reasons of diversification.

Table 7.4 shows the analysis by Ball & Cullen of the dominant reason
and other reasons for mergers for companies between 1970 and 1979.

Product expansion was the dominant reason in 148 out of 484 cases.
It is interesting in this connection that work by Jones and Harris[27] on
acquisitions by construction companies in 1972-7 found that they were
not very successful in achieving growth. Indeed the main conclusion
from their work was that acquisition policy was more often than not
opposed to the interest of the four groups concerned with the companies,
especially shareholders and the economy, and less clearly managers and
employees.

Liquidations and Bankruptcies[28]

The large entry of firms to the construction industry means that many
persons become part of the industry without having all the character-
istices required to ensure success. It would be expected therefore that
there would be a large number of business failures, that is, free entry
also implies free exit. This characteristic is compounded by the high level

TABLE 7.4 *Dominant and total quoted reasons for takeover involving construction firms, 1970–9*

Reason	Number of times reason quoted	
	as dominant	as important[a]
Sectoral diversification into or within construction	50	52
Product diversification within construction	42	61
Product expansion by speculative housebuilders	53	57
Product expansion by specialist contractors	34	37
Product expansion by other contractors	61	81
Land bank	23	68
Potential or current profits	2	35
Ability to win contracts	4	17
Available investment cash	1	2
Complementary activities	7	21
Cheap acquisition	22	43
Rental income	2	4
Product expansion or diversification outside construction	90	103
Geographic diversification national	9	57
Geographic diversification international	16	38
Plant hire: expansion of or diversification into	62	69
Not known	6	6
Total	484[b]	751

Notes:

[a] Includes dominant reason.
[b] Equals also total acquisitions investigated.

Source:

Ball, M. and Cullen, A., *Merger and Accumulation in the British Construction Industry, 1960–79* Birkbeck
____, Discussion Paper no. 73 (Birkbeck College, 1980) Tables 1 and 2.

of risk and uncertainty in the industry. The method of tendering as a pricing method, the necessity to price the product before it is produced, the risks due to uncertainties of weather and ground and so on, all contribute to high risk. In addition, each project may be a high proportion of the firm's turnover and the reserves of capital are usually small. These problems become particularly severe in periods of rapid change in the industry, sometimes due to inadequate work-load but also in an upswing to trading beyond the firm's capacity.

Table 7.5 shows that in the middle and late seventies the chance of a company in the construction industry becoming insolvent was nearly twice as high as in other industries but in the early 1980s was about the same. Table 7.6 shows a similar calculation with similar results for self-employed persons becoming bankrupt. However these last figures are not very reliable because of dependence on the 1971 census data for numbers of self-employed over the whole range of industry whereas the numbers of self-employed in construction has in fact fluctuated considerably in 1971-81. If the number of self-employed including working proprietors is taken for each year, as estimated by the DoE,[29] then the percentages are rather lower as in shown in Table 7.7, especially in the last few years. If even higher estimates of self-employed in construction are taken,[30] then the percentage of bankruptcies falls even lower. A better picture may be produced when the 1981 census results are available.

Figure 7.3 plots the percentage for construction and all industry of total liquidations as a percentage of assessments in 1977. It is clearly seen that the fall in relative risk of insolvency in construction is due to a rise in other industries, not to a fall in construction. Also in Figure 7.3 is plotted the index of all new work by contractors and there is a link between this index and the percentage of insolvencies, the fall in insolvencies in 1979 corresponds with a small increase in output in 1978. In 1975 there may have been an increase in insolvencies still partly as a result of the too rapid expansion of firms in 1972-3. The time lag between output changes and insolvencies seems to be a year or more.

Figure 7.4 plots the data for receiving orders as a percentage of 1971 self-employed and also the index of the repair and maintenance work-load and the fall in receiving orders seems to be closely related to the rise in repair and maintenance. The time lag is apparently much shorter than for liquidations, as would be expected.

Unfortunately the way the statistics are usually presented in official statistics or in reports in the press usually shows the percentage of construction industry liquidations and receiving orders as a percentage of the total in the period. Even the DoE in *Housing and Construction*

TABLE 7.5   *Company liquidations[a] and number of Inland Revenue company assessments in construction and other industries from 1974*

Year	Farming	Manufacturing	Construction	Distribution	Other	Total
Number of liquidations – England and Wales:						
1974	17	1 012	801	684	1 361	3 875
1975	52	1 361	995	1 034	2 160	5 602
1976	25	1 319	977	1 169	2 449	5 939
1977	25	1 179	1 004	1 264	2 359	5 831
1978	29	1 076	929	1 102	1 950	5 086
1979	30	1 039	789	827	1 852	4 537
1980	34	2 095	949	1 192	2 620	6 890
1981	56	2 676	990	1 526	3 348	8 596
1982	55	4 058	1 422	2 313	4 219	12 067
1983						
1984						
Number of assessments – UK (th):						
1977	9.3	97.2	49.1	71.4	186.9	413.9
Liquidations as percentage of assessments:						
1974	0.2	1.0	1.6	1.0	0.7	0.9
1975	0.6	1.4	2.0	1.4	1.2	1.4
1976	0.3	1.4	2.0	1.6	1.3	1.4

1977	0.3	1.2	2.0	1.8	1.3	1.4
1978	0.3	1.1	1.9	1.5	1.0	1.2
1979	0.3	1.1	1.6	1.2	1.0	1.1
1980	0.4	2.2	1.9	1.7	1.4	1.7
1981	0.6	2.8	2.0	2.1	1.8	2.1
1982	0.6	4.2	2.9	3.2	2.3	2.9
1983						
1984						

Notes:

[a] Compulsory liquidations and creditors' voluntary liquidations.

The number of assessments is used as a basis for broad comparison. The fact that it refers to the UK and the insolvencies refer to England and Wales should not materially affect the relative percentages.

Sources:

Department of Trade, 'Insolvencies in England and Wales', *Trade and Industry*, quarterly articles 1975–9; Department of Industry and Trade, 'Insolvencies in England and Wales', *British Business*, quarterly articles 1981–3; Board of Inland Revenue, *Inland Revenue Statistics 1981* (HMSO, 1982) Table 3.3.

TABLE 7.6 Receiving orders administered (bankruptcies)[a] and numbers of self-employed from 1974, England and Wales

Year	Farming	Manufacturing	Construction	Distribution	Others	Total
			Receiving orders:			
1974	90	152	1 056	1 018	1 216	3 532
1975	167	199	1 543	1 220	1 660	4 789
1976	133	183	1 554	1 254	3 576	6 700
1977	67	128	972	921	2 007	4 095
1978	54	144	890	697	1 755	3 540
1979	55	137	832	678	1 512	3 214
1980	50	143	783	683	2 045	3 704
1981	70	192	922	960	2 676	4 820
1982	78	208	988	1 072	3 019	5 365
1983						
1984						
			Self-employed – Great Britain:			
1971	278.4	201.5	312.4	437.7	613.1	1843.1
		Receiving orders as percentage of self-employed:				
1974	0.03	0.08	0.34	0.23	0.20	0.19
1975	0.06	0.10	0.49	0.28	0.27	0.26
1976	0.05	0.09	0.50	0.29	0.58	0.36
1977	0.02	0.06	0.31	0.21	0.33	0.22
1978	0.02	0.07	0.28	0.16	0.29	0.19
1979	0.02	0.07	0.27	0.15	0.25	0.17

1980						
1981						
1982	0.02	0.07	0.25	0.16	0.33	0.20
1983	0.03	0.10	0.30	0.22	0.44	0.26
1984	0.03	0.10	0.32	0.24	0.49	0.29

Notes:

[a]Includes a small number of deeds of arrangements.

The number of self-employed is used as a basis for broad comparisons. The fact that they refer to Great Britain and that receiving orders refer to England and Wales should not materially affect the relative percentages.

Sources:

'Insolvencies in England and Wales', *Trade and Industry*, quarterly articles 1975–9; Department of Industry and Trade, 'Insolvencies in England and Wales', *British Business*, quarterly articles 1981–3, Office of Population Censuses and Surveys (OPCS), *Census of Population, Economic Activity Tables Part II* (HMSO, 1975).

TABLE 7.7 *Receiving orders administered (bankruptcies) compared with number of self-employed in construction from 1974*

Year	% based on 1971 census of self-employed	% based on annual DoE figures of self-employed[a]
1974	0.34	0.25
1975	0.49	0.41
1976	0.50	0.46
1977	0.31	0.30
1978	0.28	0.24
1979	0.27	0.21
1980	0.25	0.21
1981	0.30	0.29

Note:

[a] Including working proprietors.

Sources:

Based on DoE, *Housing and Construction Statistics 1971–1981* (HMSO, 1982) Table 15; Table 7.6 in this volume.

Statistics[31] shows construction liquidations and receiving orders as a percentage of the total and the percentages are far in excess of the share of GDP of construction. Of course construction has a high percentage because the number of firms and the number employed are high. Sometimes the statistics are given in rank order of absolute numbers for each industry separated in the official statistics. Construction is not subdivided but manufacturing industry and distribution are further subdivided so that in absolute numbers it is inevitable that construction will be the highest, leading to captions in the press such as 'construction heads the league of insolvencies'.

A similar difficulty arises with the figures of Trade Indemnity Ltd often quoted in the media – again for similar reasons construction is highlighted as the worst industry. In any case the figures of Trade Indemnity Ltd need careful interpretation. The company insures its client companies against failure of their clients. Not every transaction of its clients is reported to the company because it has some blanket provisions in its policies and the coverage of the company is not evenly spread across all industries. Moreover, if the turnover of Trade Indemnity Ltd increases so will the number of failures even if there is no change in economic conditions.

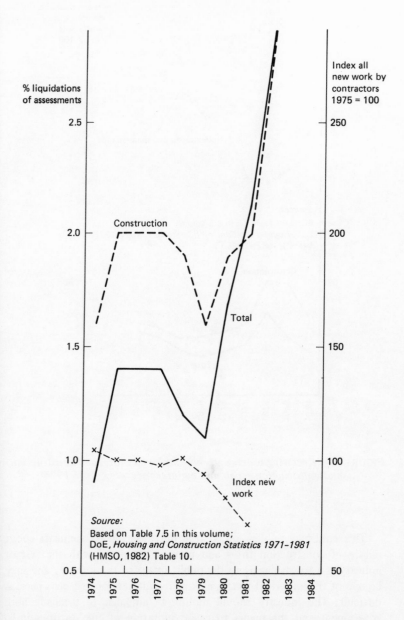

% liquidations
of assessments

Index all
new work by
contractors
1975 = 100

Construction

Total

Index new
work

Source:
Based on Table 7.5 in this volume;
DoE, *Housing and Construction Statistics 1971–1981*
(HMSO, 1982) Table 10.

FIGURE 7.3 *Liquidations and assessments – total and construction –
and construction new work from 1974*

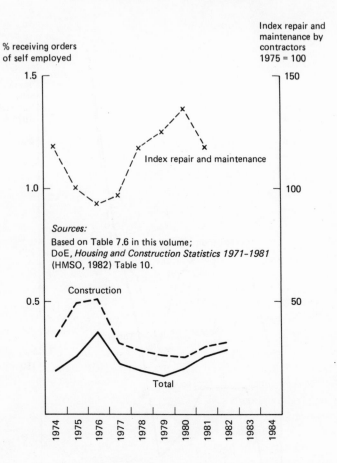

FIGURE 7.4 *Receiving orders and self-employed – total and construction – and construction repair and maintenance work from 1974*

This continual publication of true but misleading statements about failure of construction firms and persons compared with the rest of industry is very damaging to the public image of the industry and may be one of the important factors making recruitment of first-class persons difficult. The industry should mount a campaign to persuade both government and the media to cease quotation of the statistics in so misleading and damaging a way.

Contractors' Organisations

The contractors have joined together in associations, the main ones being as follows:

The National Federation of Building Trades Employers (NFBTE) is the major organisation representing building contractors and most of the large contractors are members. It includes under its umbrella a number of other federations and associations.[32] The total membership is of the order of 11 000 firms and includes many medium and small firms. It was estimated that in 1978 the membership accounted directly or indirectly for some 60-75 per cent of the industry's annual work-load.[33] This would of course not be the value of work done but rather the gross output for which its members were responsible. It has ten regions and a number of local associations in each region. Funds are raised by a subscription levied on members according to their payrolls. The staff exceeds 300 persons. There are a number of specialised groups within the Federation, notably the National Contractors' Group, the System Builders and Smaller Builders' Sections, Federation of Building Subcontractors. The Building Advisory Service (BAS) is virtually part of the NFBTE. The reorganisation of the NFBTE has been under discussion for some time.

The NFBTE is a party of all the major relevant construction industry organisations, such as the National Joint Council for the Building Industry (NJCBI) which deals with wages and apprenticeship, the Construction Industry Training Board (CITB) on training, the Joint Contracts Tribunal (JCT) on contracts, the EDC for Building. It represents contractors' interests on matters such as building regulations, standards and research. The president is a member of the Group of Eight which represents the industry's views to government, mainly on demand. Services to members, apart from representation of their interests on industry matters, includes advice on safety, security on sites, contracts and other legal matters, insurance and taxation; a state of trade inquiry; publication of information to members through its journals and other publications; arrangement of courses and conferences.

The Federation of Master Builders (FMB) generally represents the smaller firms in the industry although some are quite substantial. Subscriptions are a flat rate assessed annually. It provides a forum for members and advises on industry matters through publications and through an information service. It will represent members in dispute and since 1980 has negotiated with the Transport and General Workers' Union on wages and conditions of employment through the Building and Allied

Trades Joint Industrial Council (BATJIC). The level of services to members is less than the NFBTE but the subscription is small and within the reach of the very small contractor.

The Federation of Civil Engineering Contractors (FCEC) is the contractors' association for civil engineers in the industry. It has some 500 members representing most of the large firms in the industry. It is represented on the organisations involved in civil engineering such as the Construction Industry Research and Information Association (CIRIA), the CITB, EDC for Civil Engineering, Civil Engineering Construction Conciliation Board (CECCB) and the Building and Civil Engineering Joint Board for Wages, and the president is a member of the Group of Eight. It is also widely represented on national organisations such as the Confederation of British Industry and the British Standards Institution. It advises members and negotiates on their behalf on wages and industrial relations, legal matters, safety health and welfare and training. It keeps members informed by its publications. It monitors and tries to influence where necessary legislation and government policies on the industry.

The Committee of Associations of Specialist Engineering Contractors (CASEC) was formed in 1961 as a group of more technically orientated specialist trades contractors who felt they needed separate joint representation from FASS (see below). There has, however, since 1978 been a liaison committee between the two subcontracting federations. There are eight constituent associations.[34] As with the other associations CASEC is represented on a number of industry bodies including the JCT, the NJCC, EDCs for Building and for Civil Engineering. CASEC has a less unified structure than the NFBTE and hence direct services to members are provided usually by the constituent associations.

The Federation of Associations of Specialists and Subcontractors (FASS) has since CASEC broke away from FASS in 1961 represented the less technical subcontractors. There were fourteen separate associations in membership at January 1983.[35] It is represented on similar bodies to CASEC. There have been disagreements within FASS as to the level of services that should be provided and paid for and this will almost certainly lead to some realignments of subcontractors' organisations.

The Export Group for the Constructional Industries (EGCI) is a forum and source of advice and of negotiation with government on exports by contractors, suppliers and services mainly in building and civil engineering, but also in the electrical and mechanical fields. There are twenty-eight members of the general contractors' group.

PUBLIC AUTHORITIES' DIRECT LABOUR ORGANISATIONS

The work of public authority Direct Labour Organisations (DLOs) is split between local authorities and new towns on the one hand and other public authorities on the other. The local authorities and new towns probably account for nearly three-quarters of the total output of DLOs,[36] the remainder being other public authorities. The information is separate and that on local authorities is more comprehensive. Local authorities are dealt with here first.

Local Authorities and New Towns

All except 17 of the 548 local authorities in Great Britain in October 1981 directly employed some operative construction labour. Of the seventeen that did not, twelve were new towns (out of a total of twenty-seven new towns), four were Scottish District Councils and one a Metropolitan County. The 531 DLOs are divided as shown in Table 7.8 between the various types of authority. The GLC is probably the largest authority and at a total operative employment of over 2500 it ranks in employment among the largest contractors. However, in output terms at an annual output of about £35 million, it would be lower down in the list of contractors, the difference being due to the fact that repair and maintenance work, which it mostly does, is labour intensive.

However, Table 7.9 shows the numbers, work done and employment by size of DLOs of local authorities and new towns and, whereas some are small, the size distribution is very different from that of contractors. Those employing seventy operatives or less do only 4 per cent of the work, while those employing 500 or more do nearly 60 per cent of the work. For contractors 3 per cent of the work is done by one-man firms while those employing up to seventy operatives do well over a third of the work. At the other extreme contractors employing 500 or more probably do only a little over a quarter of the work.

None of the small DLOs do any new work and over 80 per cent of new housing work and over 75 per cent of other new work is done by DLOs employing 500 operatives and over. Small DLOs are most important in housing repair and maintenance but even for that over 50 per cent is done by those of 500 and over. For other new work over 65 per cent is done by the large authorities. Table 7.10 illustrates this as well as the importance of the various work types to authorities of various sizes.

The advantages and disadvantages of direct labour departments of

TABLE 7.8   *Direct labour organisations of local authorities and new towns by type of authority, 1981, Great Britain (third quarter of 1981)*

Type of authority	Number	Value of work done £m	Employment of operatives th
England and Wales:			
GLC	1	8.6	2.3
Metropolitan Counties	5	13.5	2.7
Non-Metropolitan Counties	47	93.2	23.5
London Boroughs	33	61.2	16.1
Metropolitan Districts	36	109.0	35.4
Non-Metropolitan Districts	334	136.9	43.6
New towns	10	1.3	0.5
All England and Wales	466	423.7	124.1
Scotland:			
Regional Councils	9	36.4	10.4
Island Area Councils	3	3.1	0.7
District Councils	49	27.9	11.8
New towns	4	1.2	0.5
All Scotland	65	68.6	23.4
Great Britain	531	492.3	147.4

Source:

DoE, *Housing and Construction Statistics 1971-1981* (HMSO, 1982) Table 46.

public authorities, particularly local authorities, and their deeds and misdeeds have been the subject of comment, much of it biased and ill-informed in the last twenty or thirty years. Unfortunately the split of opinion has been along broadly party political lines, with the NFBTE, backed by the Conservatives, conducting a campaign against direct labour and many of the local authorities themselves, and the trade unions, supported by the Labour Party, being for direct labour departments with of course minor dissenting voices on both sides. It is a pity that an issue which ought to be considered calmly and impartially on the basis of establishing the efficiency, in its broadest sense, of the two organisational types of direct labour departments and private contracting should have become a political football, because there are few aspects of the construction industry where there is so much doubt as to the overall relative advantages and disadvantages. Many instances have been cited of inef-

TABLE 7.9 *Direct labour organisations of local authorities and new towns – number, work done and operatives, 1981, Great Britain*

Size of organisation (no. of operatives)	Number Oct 81	Value of work done third quarter 1981		Operatives Oct 81	
		£m	%	Number (th)	%
1–70	153	17.8	3.6	5.9	4.0
71–99	67	18.1	3.7	5.7	3.9
100–249	158	82.1	16.7	25.8	17.5
250–499	66	86.3	17.5	23.1	15.7
500–999	67	161.3	32.8	46.8	31.8
1 000–4 999	20	126.7	25.7	40.1	27.2
5 000 +	–	–	–	–	–
Total	531	492.3	100	147.4	100

Source:

DoE, *Housing and Construction Statistics 1971–1981* (HMSO, 1982) Table 46.

146

TABLE 7.10 Types of work done by direct labour organisations of various sizes, 1981, Great Britain (third quarter of 1981)

Size of organisation (no. of operatives)	New work				Repair and maintenance				All work	
	Housing		Other		Housing		Other			
	% size group	% total	% size group	% total	% size group	% total	% size group	% total	% size group	% total
1–99	–	–	0.6	0.5	75.5	13.1	23.7	3.7	100	7.3
100–499	2.1	19.7	4.9	22.7	47.3	38.6	45.7	33.3	100	34.2
500–4 999	5.0	80.3	9.7	76.5	34.6	48.3	50.7	63.1	100	58.5
		100		100		100		100		100

Source:
Based on DoE, *Housing and Construction Statistics 1971–1981* (HMSO, 1982) Table 46.

ficiency, malpractice of direct labour organisations but similar instances can be cited for contractors. What is needed is an independent investigation of the value for money of the two organisational types, and the social costs and benefits of their operations. Those that have been undertaken have been by those with vested interests. Such an investigation could probably have been undertaken impartially twenty years ago but in the last ten years or more the strength of the political feeling involved and the jealous guarding of entrenched positions would probably have made it very difficult to obtain the necessary data.

The situation has been considerably affected by Part III of the Local Government Planning and Land Act 1980[37] which came into force on 1 April 1981. This Act specifies that local authorities must adopt separate accounting for the main categories of work and that tenders must be obtained for works above certain levels. Strict accounting procedures must be observed along the lines of the CIPFA Code of Practice 1981[38] and no transfer of funds is permitted between the four accounts. A return on capital employed must be obtained, at present designated as 5 per cent.[39]

It is yet too soon to say whether the Act will be broadly accepted by both sides as a workable basis for regulating procedure. However, it does not place the two types of organisation on an equal footing and it is doubtful whether there is a completely satisfactory way of doing so, given the different objectives and styles of the two types. It is agreed, for example, that in not allowing DLOs to average their returns between the four categories, the Act is penalising the DLOs because contractors have only to make a profit over all.[40] Moreover the DLOs have much less independence of the client than the contractor and the contractor is able to compete for any work, whereas the DLO may compete only on public-sector work.[41] The Act has been criticised as being biased against the DLOs[42] but it is conceivable that by placing the DLOs on a sound accounting basis and introducing competition so that the efficiency of their operations are clearer, the efficient organisation could turn the Act into a charter for expansion. Only time will tell.

The argument continues, but it may in future be confined more to whether local authorities are meeting the provisions of the Act and on the other hand, on the social costs and benefits of the two sorts of operations. An investigation is still needed because policy-makers should understand why well over 10 per cent of construction resources are being used in directly employed labour departments of public authorities so that they can sensibly decide whether it should be more or less.

Once it becomes possible with a run of years to consider the money costs of work done by the direct labour, compared with the price charged by contractors, the main emphasis will switch to broader measures of efficiency in the use of national resources. Output per person employed is clearly a major component in this, although with a high level of unemployment the case for the method producing the highest output per person may be questioned. A discussion of the available data on output per man and of other measures of efficiency in the use of manpower is included in Chapter 12. It is clear from the analysis there that, although output per man is apparently lower in direct labour organisations than in private contractors for broad types of work, the difference is not as great as has often been suggested, especially when comparison is made between identical work types. There are, moreover, other costs and benefits to be considered. Without further research no overall conclusion is possible.

Other Public Authorities

Apart from local authorities and new towns, public authorities that have DLOs are the public entities of railway; canal, dock and harbour boards; tramways; trolley-bus, omnibus, etc.; Coal Board and British Airports Authority and two government departments, namely Department of the Environment/Property Services Agency (PSA) and United Kingdom Atomic Energy Authority. They in total account of 25-30 per cent of the total DLO work.[43] Of this the great majority of the work is done by PSA, railways and canal boards who all employ a large number of direct labour personnel.[44] Some indication of their work is given in Chapter 4.

DISCUSSIONS ON PUBLIC OWNERSHIP

Discussions of a greater public-sector participation in construction work have been going on, not only in relation to the direct labour departments of public authorities, but also in relation to other parts of the construction industry. The Labour Party's policy background paper, *Building Britain's Future*, produced in 1977 suggested the formation of a National Construction Corporation, based initially on the acquisition of one or more major contractors, in consultation with the trade unions in the industry. The aim would be to establish a public enterprise base in each of the major specialised sub-sectors of large-scale construction work, and in each regional construction market. An extension of the work of DLOs and the formation at local level of workers' co-operatives were also proposed.

This document produced a response by the contracting industry of the organisation of a Campaign Against Building Industry Nationalisation (CABIN) which commissioned the Economist Intelligence Unit to produce a report entitled *Public Ownership in the Construction Industries*.[45]

Many of the arguments for and against are similar to those discussed for the direct labour organisations with emphasis on overcoming job insecurity and improving working conditions as well as reducing the power of a few contractors in the market for large projects. On the other hand, there are arguments about the dangers of inefficiency of large public organisations and the increased costs that would be imposed. It is difficult to discuss the matter except in the wider context of the instability of work-load and the advantages and disadvantages of greater national planning of construction. That the industry has problems few would doubt, and the debate on how to solve them will continue.

8 Structure of the Professions

A profession may be defined as an occupation possessing a skilled intellectual technique, a voluntary association and a code of conduct.[1]

All the major construction industry professions establish and enforce a code of conduct and uphold the standards of knowledge of the profession - the latter by setting entry standards and by promoting the advancement of knowledge. Beyond that their roles vary from one professional organisation to another.

ROLE OF PROFESSIONAL ORGANISATIONS

The architects have the umbrella organisation of the Architects Registration Council of the United Kingdom (ARCUK) which recognises qualifications for registration as an 'architect', which is a protected description, and lays down rules of conduct for registered architects. Anyone wishing to practise as an architect must be registered with ARCUK.

Nearly 80 per cent of architects are members of the Royal Institute of British Architects (RIBA)[2] which has its own code of conduct, is a learned society that cultivates improved standards in architecture and represents the collective interests of its members. In the 1960s the RIBA was active in promoting efficiency in architectural firms (see Chapter 13). Since then this part of its activity has declined, although there are moves being made through, for example, the Practices Membership Scheme to do something to revive it.

There are other smaller professional organisations for architects: the Faculty of Architects and Surveyors (FAS), the Incorporated Association of Architects and Surveyors (IAAS) and the Royal Incorporation of Architects in Scotland (RIAS).

151

The code of conduct for architects has undergone dramatic changes in the last few years. Formerly the code prohibited advertising in any form and did not allow architects to become directors of limited liability companies connected with construction, property or development. Thus while they could become an employee of, for example, a building company or a developer, they could not become a member of the board. After much debate this was changed and in January 1981 architects were permitted to form companies to undertake development, etc., but not to mix this activity with their professional practice. Indeed they have to register their intention of forming their own company or becoming directors of companies in areas previously forbidden.

The members of the Royal Town Planning Institute (RTPI) are usually involved in broader fields of interest in the built environment and planning the overall use of land. They are therefore mostly involved in the stage before the construction process commences.

Quantity surveyors in private practice are for the most part members of the Quantity Surveyors' Division of the Royal Institution of Chartered Surveyors (RICS) which undertakes similar activities to those of the RIBA. The code of conduct for the quantity surveyors is not the same as for other divisions of the RICS. Quantity surveyors were not permitted to work for a limited liability company in the construction field and hence quantity surveyor members of the RICS were precluded from taking any part in, for example, contractors' estimating. This restriction was removed in 1967 and quantity surveyors and architects are now more or less on an equal footing so far as this matter is concerned. Partly because of the restrictions on quantity surveyor members of the RICS, many quantity surveyors joined the Institute of Quantity Surveyors (IQS) which permitted its members to work for contractors and the employment of the members of the two professional bodies reflected this past situation. With the change in the RICS rules, the major impediment to merging had gone and the two organisations merged in March 1983.

The other members of the RICS tend to be associated with the creation and demand before it is put to the industry and with land purchase and with estate management after initial construction.

The Chartered Institute of Building is the last major professional institution on the building side of construction. Its role is described later in this section.

The engineering professions are set up differently. The main engineering professions concerned with construction are the civil engineers, the structural engineers and the building services engineers with the institutions, all of which are chartered. The lead is taken by the Institution of

Civil Engineers (ICE). The last of the three to receive its charter was the present Chartered Institute of Building Services in 1976, when it took the opportunity to change its name from the Institute of Heating and Ventilating Engineers and to broaden its scope. Its growth and development are indicative of the increased sophistication of the heating and ventilating, air conditioning, acoustics, fire and security systems, etc. in building in the last two decades. Electrical and municipal engineers also have a role in the construction industry but it is not so central.

The chartered engineering institutions joined together in 1965 to set up the Council of Engineering Institutions (CEI) which is the umbrella professional organisation setting standards and providing a forum for discussion of matters of interest to all engineering professions, most of which are unrelated to construction. The Finniston Report[3] recommended the establishment of an Engineering Authority appointed by government. In the form of the Engineering Council, it was set up in 1982 and is liaising with the Council of Engineering Institutions about arrangements for the transfer of some executive functions. It is not yet known whether both organisations will exist side by side.

The engineering institutions also act as learned societies and have their own rules for membership. These professional bodies are not, however, involved with professional firms as are the RICS and the RIBA. Another organisation, the Association of Consulting Engineers (ACE), is concerned with the professional firms of electrical, mechanical, civil and structural engineers. It lays down rules of conduct for its members, including that they shall not operate as a limited liability company and shall not compete on fees. As a result a few substantial consulting engineers are not members of the Association, partly so that they can have limited liability including some tax advantages.

However, ACE is concerned only with professional firms. One of the features of the engineering professions is that members of the Institution can either become consultants or work in any capacity in the contracting industry. Although individuals tend to have preference for one or the other at a fairly early stage, many have some experience of both worlds and, in any case, they speak the same language, whether on the design side or on the contracting side. This has undoubtedly done much to facilitate good relations and a smooth process of construction in civil engineering as compared with building, where architects and quantity surveyors often do not really understand the mentality of the contractors with whom they are dealing – or indeed each other.

The lack of a profession on the building contracting side had important repercussions for the way the industry worked. The builder had a poor public image and, in general, until shortly after the Second World War, most directors of building companies had worked their way up from the crafts. The only obvious source of well-educated persons for building contracting – the architects and quantity surveyors – were not permitted to participate in commercial activities and, very often, after building increased in complexity and size in the post-war period, the man in charge of a building firm or the building part of a large contracting firm was a civil engineer by training.

The effects of this on the way the process works have been far-reaching. Because the architect could not be concerned with contracting, he tended to have little knowledge of construction and the separation of design and construction was reinforced. His education emphasised artistic creativity and the management element was for a long time virtually ignored. The education was broadened in the 1960s and 1970s and the changes in the rules for conduct in 1981 enable him to do all the things that he might have done earlier to narrow the gap. If the change had taken place at the end of the Second World War, during a period of rapid growth and change in the industry, the pattern of relationships in the industry might now have been different, but they tend to have developed to leave the architect almost entirely to his design role and even the traditional role of leader of the construction team is being eroded. It is likely that it will need a new generation of architects before they play any significant role in the production process as a contractor, as the civil engineer became a civil engineering contractor.

The vacuum was filled by a resuscitation of the Institute of Builders, originally formed in 1834 as the Builders' Society, but which, in the early 1950s, was virtually moribund. In 1955 it had just over 2000 members; the standards set in the examination were low and general; the public image was poor. It was revived with increasing standards, increasing emphasis on management and increasing potential for specialisation. It now has about 27000 members and in 1980 received recognition by being granted a Royal Charter and is now the Chartered Institute of Building. Increasingly it is supplying the needs of contractors and other organisations connected with the industry for qualified expertise on construction. It is different from most of the other professional organisations in construction in that its members do not, with a few exceptions, engage in private consultancy practice. Construction management could well, however, be undertaken by building consultancy practices.

All the major construction professions are represented on industry organisations appropriate to their interests including the NJCC (architects and quantity surveyors) (see Chapter 3), the Economic Development Committees for Building and Civil Engineering, the JCT for building and the civil engineering contracts body. The Presidents of the RIBA, RICS and ICE are members of the Group of Eight.

The construction professions meet together in the Presidents' Committee for the Urban Environment (PCUE) comprising the presidents and chief executives of seven institutions, namely ICE, CIBS, CIOB, I.Struct.E., RIBA, RICS and RTPI. It is an informal but helpful committee, meeting once a quarter to discuss matters of common concern. There is, however, no overall umbrella organisation for the building professions, as for example the CEI for engineering. In view of the large number of building professions some more organised meeting of them might be valuable, although the danger of another tier of organisations must be borne in mind.

EMPLOYMENT OF PROFESSIONALS

Some of the differences in the roles of the professions are reflected in the statistics of where the members of professional organisations are employed. Table 8.1 shows membership and employment information.

Firms in private practice in the professions are fairly small. Data are available for the RIBA for 1980 and are shown in Table 8.2. The importance of small practices is very clear from this table; 47 per cent of all principals and employees in architectural practices are in firms employing ten or fewer architectural staff and, at the other extreme, the thirty-five large firms employing fifty-one or more architectural staff account for only 12 per cent of the value of work entering the production drawing stage. Some 21 per cent of the value of new commissions went to practices employing between one and five architectural staff.[4]

Over time the trend is towards an increase in the number of very small practices and their employment. From 1968 to 1980 the actual number of practices with one or two architectural staff more than doubled, partly reflecting 'the growth in the size of the profession and also deteriorating job prospects for salaried architects in established private practices and public authorities, encouraging more of them to become self-employed by starting their own small businesses'.[5] The work done by these small firms as a percentage of the total has also increased.

The latest available data for the RICS quantity surveyors are for 1973 and the results are not comparable to the RIBA data, even for that time because the size groups are based on all staff, not just architectural staff.[6]

TABLE 8.1 *Main building and civil engineering professions: membership and type of employment*

	ARCUK[a]	RICS[b]	IQS[c]	CIOB[d]	CIBS[e]	I. Struct. E.[f]	ICE[g]
Membership (th)	28.4	13.4	6.7	27.3	5.9	10.8	41.1
% in employment in:							
Private practice – principals	30.8	27.9	27.4	8.1	24.7	34	19.4
Private practice – employees	23.2	34.3	47.4	67.1	37.1	37	19.7
Other private employment	6.8	11.1		4.5		9	13.5
Central government and nationalised boards	11.0	9.8	4.5	7.4	28.7	15	39.5
Local authorities	25.3	14.9	16.8	12.5	4.5	4	4.2
Education	2.9	1.9	2.0				3.5
Miscellaneous	–	–	1.9	neg.	5.0	2	

(RICS and IQS membership combined: 18.1[h])

Notes and sources:

a Membership in the UK and overseas, Jan 1983; employment from RIBA Statistics Section, *Architects' Employment and Earnings 1982: A Report of the RIBA Survey* (RIBA, 1982) Table 2.

b Membership in UK and overseas, 22 June 1981; employment table of 22 June 1981 from RICS excluding those retired and not employed.

c Membership; employment based on sample of IQS survey undertaken by Reward Regional Surveys Ltd, *Salary Survey of Members of the Institute of Quantity Surveyors* (IQS, 1980).

d Membership UK and overseas, 31 Dec 1982; employment from Institute of Building, *Survey of Home Members 1975* (IOB, 1976) Tables 2–7.

e Membership UK and overseas, Jan 1983; employment from Journal of CIBS, *Readership Survey* (Building Service Publications Ltd, 1981) section 2.

f Membership UK and overseas, Jan 1983; employment from Institute of Structural Engineers, 'Survey of Professional Engineers Summer 1981', *The Structural Engineer*, vol. 60A, Mar 1982, Tables 4 and 5. Many of the self-employed are probably as firms of consultants. Local authorities includes teachers.

g Membership in UK and overseas, Jan 1983; employment from Institution of Civil Engineers, 'ICE Salary Survey', *New Civil Engineer*, 6 Mar 1980.

h After merger because of previous overlapping membership.

TABLE 8.2 *Full-time mainly architectural practices and numbers employed by size of practice, 1980, UK*

Practice size (no. of architectural staff)	Practices	Principals		Employees				Total	
				Architects		Other staff			
	Number	No.	Av. per practice	No.	Av. per practice	No.	Av. per practice	No.	% of total
1–2	2 216	2 604	1.2	181	0.1	438	0.2	3 223	11.5
3–5	1 189	2 106	1.8	818	0.7	1 976	1.7	4 900	17.5
6–10	629	1 529	2.4	1 099	1.7	2 429	3.9	5 057	18.0
11–30	434	1 992	4.6	2 353	5.4	3 948	9.1	8 293	29.6
31–50	72	574	8.0	1 097	15.2	1 490	20.7	3 161	11.3
51 and over	35	553	15.8	1 293	36.9	1 538	43.9	3 384	12.1
Total	4 575	9 358	2.0	6 841	1.5	11 819	2.6	28 018	100

Source:

RIBA Statistics Section, *Census of Private Architectural Practices 1980* (RIBA, 1981) Tables 1 and 7.

Bearing this in mind the quantity surveyors' private practice structure was not very different from that of architects. The RICS is undertaking a study of quantity surveying practice and client demand for quantity surveyors' services, which will be available at the end of 1983.

No data are available for other professions but the impression is that some of the largest mostly civil engineering practices are at least as large as the largest group of architectural or quantity surveying practices.

In many cases the type of work done by the smaller firms is quite different from that of the large ones. Clearly the larger firms design larger projects, but sometimes there is a difference in kind as well as in scale. For example, many of the smaller firms of structural engineers are concerned to a large extent with advice on building regulations consents rather than structural design.

One of the matters on which all professional bodies have some views is that of the method of fixing fees for design work. Some, notably the Association of Consulting Engineers, lay down that the competition for appointment shall be on qualification for the job and not on fees. Once the appropriate consultant has been chosen then, and only then, may fees be discussed. If they are unsatisfactory then negotiations can be terminated and commenced with another firm. Until recently architects and quantity surveyors in the RICS could not compete with fellow members of their professions, and the RIBA had a mandatory fee scale, mainly as a percentage of the cost of buildings but in some cases on a time basis. Other professional architectural organisations tended to follow the RIBA scales. They were upheld by ARCUK because they required an architect to be remunerated on a recognised fee scale and the only recognised scales were those laid down by the professional bodies. This practice was challenged as long ago as 1967 in a report by the Prices and Incomes Board on Architects Fees.[7] Then in 1973 the Department of Trade and Industry referred the supply or architects' services by practices to the Monopolies Commission, and in its report[8] the latter found that the practices were in many respects against the public interest and recommended that they be discontinued and that architects should be permitted to compete on fees. Published fee scales were to be allowed under certain conditions but would not be mandatory. After further discussion and argument – indeed a battle royal – the RIBA finally gave in and 'voluntarily' agreed to make the necessary changes in the code of conduct. As from 1 July 1982 there are no mandatory fee scales for architects.

The RICS fees for quantity surveyors were also referred to the Monopolies and Mergers Committee.[9] Their fee scales were more complex than those of RIBA and, although they could be negotiated with individual clients, competition in fees were prohibited. The RICS had, however, to conform to the Monopolies Commission ruling on competition and, after an alteration in the by-law, quantity surveyors can now compete (since the end of March 1983).

The basis of the fee structure for all professions remains broadly that of a percentage of the value of the contract. This is based on the idea that the amount of work involved is proportional, subject to various adjustments, to the value of the project. This is not necessarily the case and professional practices make losses on some jobs and profits on others so that on average they may be or may not be appropriately renumerated. It also means that some clients are effectively subsidising others. A difficulty is that this system gives no direct financial incentive to the architect, quantity surveyor or other professional to design a building with value for money. It seems wrong that the financial interests of professionals should often be in direct contradiction to their professional duty, and thus some alternative fee structure for the design should be devised and more regularly used. In international work this is increasingly so.

Data on the number of professionals employed in local authorities and new towns are difficult to interpret because of differences in definition. The DoE statistics,[10] discontinued after 1980, are for those qualified and engaged in their profession. They are not necessarily members of a professional institution except in the case of architects, presumably because of the protected designation. For quantity surveyors and engineers the figures do not bear a close resemblance.[11] However, the figures are of some interest for trends. The year 1973 was a boom one for employment of all three categories. Since then architects have suffered a reduction in their numbers from 6200 to 4800, engineers from 15 500 to 14 300 but surveyors have stayed the same at 5000.

Greater problems exist for employment of professionals by contractors because the DoE has not published this information for separate professions since 1974.[12] There is no information other than that already referred to the Table 8.1 and in Chapter 4.

PRESENT AND FUTURE ROLES OF THE PROFESSIONS

In Chapter 3 on the construction process several patterns of organisation were indicated, each one having different roles for the professional members of the construction team. For civil engineering projects the situation, so far as the role of the professional is concerned, is fairly clear for, since more or less all civil engineers are members of the Institution of Civil Engineers a member of that organisation is likely to be the leader of the design team and another the leader of the contracting team, no matter whether employed by a private practice, a public-sector design office or a contractor. The client is also likely to be a civil engineer. A civil engineer would also probably be the project manager if there is one. This clear-cut situation is assisted by the relative simplicity of the process (although not the technical know-how), and the civil engineer will normally himself undertake the role of designer and quantity surveyor and indeed is responsible for so doing.

In the case of building, however, the roles of the various professions are in a state of fluidity, partly because of the very substantial increase in size and complexity of buildings. In particular, there is the question of who takes the lead in the whole construction process. The building team is constantly seeking to determine who is its leader or captain, whereas one of the problems is that a captain chosen from one of the players may not be sufficient. It is perhaps not leadership but management that is required and it is stated in Chapter 13 that this is in short supply. It might come from an existing team member or, in the case of project management and construction management, from outside the traditional team, from a person having no role in the process other than management. The original training of the person in this role can be from any of the construction professions.

The RICS quantity surveyors in 1971 considered the future of the quantity surveyor.[13] By this time the role of the quantity surveyor had already extended beyond the 'distinctive competence [of] skill in measurement and valuation in the field of construction' and they defined the role of the quantity surveyor as 'to ensure that the resources of the construction industry are utilised to the best advantage of Society by providing *inter alia* the financial management for projects and a cost consultancy service to client and designer during the whole construction process'. The report identified ways in which the role could be extended into mechanical and electrical services and civil engineering, higher management roles in contracting and in economic management of the project – although not necessarily as total project manager – and greater involvement in environmental economics. They were concerned that there should more often be appointment of the quantity surveyor direct to the client. Since then the quantity surveyors have made more strenuous attempts to act as project controllers[14] and to extend their functions.

There are several reasons for the extension of the quantity surveyors' role, apart from the obvious one that there is a need for better financial and cost management of the project. One is that the work with bills of quantities, while providing most of the 'bread and butter' of quantity surveyors' practices, is a narrow meticulous process which is however not very intellectually stimulating. The quantity surveyors with initiative and imagination wish to do more constructive things. At the same time, it is expected that computers will take much of the drudgery out of this traditional function leaving some qualified quantity surveyors with spare capacity. Moreover, the method of recruitment of quantity surveyors has changed with a majority of graduates who will, it is hoped, have a broader view of their role. If the quantity surveyor is to become increasingly broad in his work, then so must his education and training. The RICS itself recognises this and it is interesting that it was the first of the institutions to set up a mandatory scheme of continuing professional development (CPD) for the new entrants to the profession (see Chapter 13).

The architects also have problems with their role. Traditionally they are the leaders of the team in that they are appointed first by the client and advise on the appointment of other team members. They are responsible to the client for the organisation of the process of the project. But partly because of their long divorce from the business of contracting, referred to earlier, and the selection of the education process, they are basically designers, often with an artistic inclination; only a few have any management bent. Moreover the period of training for architects, in spite of its length, is very demanding, and they must learn not only about design but increasingly about technology also. It is difficult to make room in this programme to do more than brush the fringe of management and most students regard the subject as outside their sphere. Thus the architect is not selected or trained to manage; therefore if he is good at it, it is an unexpected and welcome bonus.

Yet management of the whole process is becoming increasingly important and complex. Unless architects can come to terms with the need to improve their management ability, through, for example, improved management training generally or for a cohort to specialise in management of design and the process, they are unlikely to be able to retain their traditional role as leaders of the building team and will continue to lose it to other parties to the process.

CONTINUING PROFESSIONAL DEVELOPMENT

The CPD in Construction Group was formed in September 1980 with eight member institutions: ARCUK, The Building Centre Trust, CIBS,

CIOB, I. Struct. E., RIBA, RICS and RTPI. The group acts as a focal point for CPD and brings together the efforts of a number of individual institutions in this field.[15]

ARCUK has done much to support CPD among architects. It has made grants to the Institute of Advanced Architectural Education at York and partly financed the York Centre for CPD. The Building Centre Trust has helped to finance the CPD in Construction Group and is concerned in a project for the production of audio-visual material for use in programmed CPD among small groups.

Of the institutions with professional membership within the Group only RICS has yet made any compulsory requirement for CPD among new members, but the CIOB and RIBA are considering whether they should take action in this way. Most institutions do in fact have some CPD activity through publications, meetings, etc. Progress is however slow, with the exception of RICS where there is considerable activity including well-attended short courses.[16]

9 Costs and Prices

The cost of construction work to the main contractor may be split into the several parts of materials, labour, management, plant, work sub-contracted and overheads. His price will include profit - positive or negative - that is, he may in certain circumstances price his work in such a way that the price not only excludes any profit element, but does not make a full contribution to overheads.

In its turn the cost to the main contractor of work subcontracted will be the price charged by the subcontractor; this consists of similar components to those of the main contractor.

The price of work carried out by the contractor, plus professional fees, is the price paid by the client and becomes to him a cost of acquiring the building or other works that he requires. However, it is important to point out that the actual capital cost of the building is a relatively small part of the cost of a building over its life.

COSTS OF CONSTRUCTION

Material costs indices are available from the DoE[1] for new housing, other new work, repair and maintenance and a combined index for all work. Movements in these indices have not differed greatly and the overall index is shown in Table 9.1. The changes in the prices of individual materials are dealt with in Chapter 14.

The cost of labour is difficult to assess and, although there is an index of basic weekly wages for construction industry manual workers, this takes no account of overtime, bonuses, etc. Nor does it consider the movement of productivity, all of which would affect the cost of labour per unit of work. There is also an index of average earnings based on the overall salaries and wages of all employees in construction firms and this

163

TABLE 9.1 Selected cost and price indices from 1970 (1975 = 100)

Year	Cost indices				Tender price indices						Output price indices
	DoE[a] Average earnings	DoE[a] Material costs all work	BCIS[b] Cost of building	DB & E[c] Cost of building	DQSS[a] Firm price contracts	DQSS[a] Variation of price contracts	DQSS[a] Total index	DoE[a] Variation of price contracts roads	BCIS[b] All tenders	DB & E[c] Fluctuating price contracts	DoE[a] All new construction
1970	44	50	n.a.	49	n.a.	n.a.	44	n.a.	n.a.	n.a.	40
1971	47	55	n.a.	53	n.a.	n.a.	50	n.a.	n.a.	n.a.	44
1972	53	58	n.a.	58	n.a.	n.a.	61	n.a.	n.a.	n.a.	51
1973	69	66	n.a.	68	n.a.	n.a.	86	n.a.	n.a.	82	66
1974	80	84	81	81	n.a.	n.a.	100	n.a.	95	98	85
1975	100	100	100	100	101	99	100	100	100	100	100
1976	112	122	117	117	106	106	106	93	107	100	109
1977	125	146	136	134	122	115	119	112	122	107	118
1978	140	158	150	145	139	132	136	138	143	122	131
1979	161	182	173	167	181	168	176	173	182	153	161
1980	191	217	207	199	217	190	206	225	211	189	203
1981	216	235[p]	229	223	209	176	192	206	199	193	216
1982	237	254[p]			205	186	195				211
1983											
1984											

Sources:

[a] DoE, *Housing and Construction Statistics 1970–1980* (HMSO, 1981) Table 2; DoE, *Housing and Construction Statistics 1971–1981* (HMSO, 1982) Table 2; DoE, *Housing and Construction Statistics 4th quarter 1982*, no. 12 (HMSO, 1983) Table 2.1.
[b] Building Cost Information Service, *Quarterly Review of Building Prices*, issue no. 9, (Feb, 1983) Table 2.
[c] Davis, Belfield and Everest, 'Cost Forecast', *Architects' Journal*, vol. 177, no. 12, 23 Mar 1983.

does take account of overtime bonuses, etc. – but not of course productivity. Productivity is extremely difficult to measure for reasons discussed in Chapter 12. The index of average earnings is shown in Table 9.1.

The cost indices in Table 9.1 do not take account of the varying effective discounts for large customers nor of the changes in the amount of credit available for material purchases, both of which depend on the state of the market. Nor do they take into consideration the relative efficiency of the process in different environments such as adverse weather, delay in obtaining material, inefficiencies in management of materials and labour due to overload, all of which affect the real cost of materials and labour.

There is no overall composite cost index produced by the DoE since all the other indices they produce, with the exception of repair and maintenance index, are based on tender prices as well as costs and therefore reflect the state of the market as well as the cost of the inputs in construction. However, the Property Services Agency of the DoE publishes construction indices monthly for use with the NEDO price adjustment formulae.[2]

The Building Cost Information Service (BCIS) of the RICS produces indices of cost based on a cost model of an average building.

The model was derived from the analysis of 80 Bills of Quantities. These Bills were broken down into the work categories defined in the National Economic Development Office's formula method of calculating fluctuations under a building contract.

The inputs to the index are the work category indices prepared by the Property Services Agency (DoE) for use with the NEDO Formula. The indices allow for changes in cost of nationally agreed labour rates, material prices and plant costs.[3]

A further cost index is prepared by Davis, Belfield and Everest and is published quarterly in the *Architects' Journal*.[4] It is based on the labour costs from contractors' wage sheets and the material cost index of the Department of Industry applied to the elements of a building. The cost indices shown in Table 9.1 move in approximately the same way.

PRICES OF CONSTRUCTION

The tender price for a project will include estimates of direct costs and a mark-up to cover overheads and profits. This mark-up will vary with the circumstances of the individual firm and the market situation. If a firm wants a job, it puts in a price as high as possible compatible with getting that job. If the market is oversupplied with work, it will consider that its competitors are likely to put in a high price. If it does not especially want the work because it itself has full order books it may still put in a price so high that it does not expect to get the work, but that if it does, it will be very profitable. In a period of recession the reverse is the case and each firm will expect the market price to be low and, if it wants the job, will put in a low price to obtain the work. Since there is in a recession nearly always one firm on a tender list who wants the work very badly and may be prepared to go in to the tender at a mark-up making no contribution to overheads, tender prices fall very low to the detriment of the long-term financial situation of all firms in the industry, since in the long run overheads must be covered.[5]

The tender price of a project is not always the final price for a number of reasons:

(a) adjustment according to the contract for increases in costs of materials and manpower
(b) claims by the contractor due to developments in the course of the work for costs for which the client is contractually responsible – such as some of the consequences of 'unusually' bad weather or inadequate or wrong technical data or drawings provided late by the professional team
(c) adjustment to the project as a result of the client's variation.

Contractors will often anticipate the likelihood of this cost variation and price their initial tender accordingly, hoping to make the profit on the variations by, for example, assessing the type of work in which these are likely to occur and pricing these higher than other items in the bill of quantities. Thus for any single contract the likely increase in final price over tender price is variable. However, generally the movements in tender prices and final prices are likely to be similar.

The DoE publishes several indices of tender prices based on the prices in bills of quantities weighted according to the type of work under consideration.[6] The output price indices, used to deflate the value of output from current to constant prices, are based on the tender price indices, after making adjustment for the time at which the current output was let and the effect of variation of price clauses.

Since 1975 some of these tender price indices have been available for variation of price contracts and firm price contracts (see Chapter 3). Clearly, since the movement of prices of materials and labour over the life of a contract over one year (since 1974) is taken care of by the variation of price contracts, contractors pricing these contracts would be able to price tenders lower than those without these clauses, although the final price would not necessarily be different. Each new contract tendered for would of course start with the base of current prices. However, as would be expected, the firm price contract index has risen more than the variation of price contract index, and the firm price contract index gives a better indication of what will be the final price to the client than does the index of variation of price contracts. Selected indices of these tender prices are shown in Table 9.1.

The BCIS tender price index is based on the examination and analysis of priced bills of quantities and comparison of the same bill priced at a base schedule of rates.[7]

The Davis, Belfield and Everest index of tender prices is based on fluctuating tenders on a method similar to that adopted by the BCIS.

COSTS AND PRICE COMPARISON

It is very difficult to compare indices of costs, output prices and tenders. The output price index is a combination of what is currently happening to costs (as measured) weighted for past tender prices; the cost indices reflect what is happening to costs as measured, and the tender index reflects what contractors think is going to happen in the future to costs not covered by the fluctuations clauses for materials and labour, as well as what they think they can add in mark-up and still obtain the work.

Davis, Belfield and Everest regularly calculate what they call a 'market factor' obtained by deflating their tender index by their cost index using 1976 as the base year because that was regarded as a fairly 'normal' year and in fact both indices coincided in 1970 and again in 1976. Thus the exceptional boom of 1973 is isolated. The resultant graph is shown in Figure 9.1. At the height of the 1972–4 boom the tender price index was about 50 per cent higher than the cost index. This could have been caused by real costs of materials and labour being understated by the cost index, expectations of contractors that costs not covered by the fluctuating clauses would be higher than in fact they were, as well as higher margins for overheads and profits.

FORECASTS

Contractors are continually making cost and price forecasts in their tendering and some of them make them explicitly.

The published forecasts are those by the BCIS[8] and Davis, Belfield

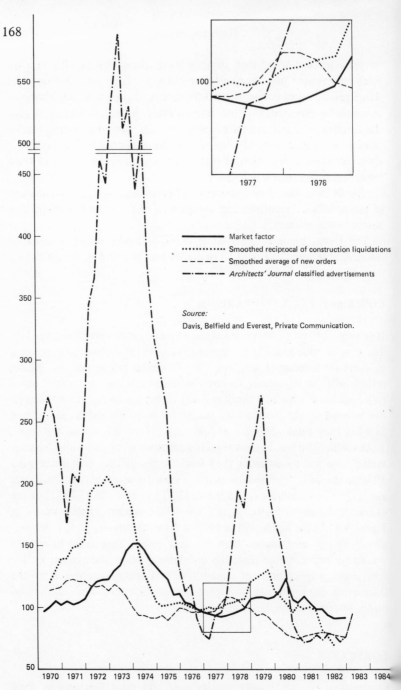

FIGURE 9.1   *Construction indicators (indices 1976 = 100)*

and Everest.[9] Both are based on a number of assumptions about the state of the economy, construction output and labour and material costs and these are more explicit in the BCIS forecast than in the published forecast by Davis, Belfield and Everest. The latter use several indicators to assist in forecasting their 'market factor' and these are shown in Figure 9.1. They are contractors' new orders and the level of insolvencies (shown on the graph reversed, i.e. a high graph represents low insolvencies) which precede the market factor by about a year and the number of classified job advertisements in the *Architects' Journal* - a very sensitive indicator - which precedes the 'market factor' by about six months. Having made a forecast of costs these indicators are of considerable assistance in forecasting tender prices.

PRICE OF CONSTRUCTION COMPARED WITH OTHER COSTS AND PRICES

Table 9.2 shows that the cost of new construction, as measured by the DoE output price index for all new construction, has risen faster (over five times, 1970-81) than other categories of goods listed and much faster than durable consumer goods, which rose only about three times and also faster than capital goods as a whole. Stone[10] suggests that this is a general experience partly due to the fact that technological change in construction is slow compared with other industries. He shows that in seven EEC countries in 1960-74 construction prices rose by 8-91 per cent faster than consumer goods. In the UK the figure was 21 per cent. This is made up of a period from 1958 to 1968 when they rose less fast than retail prices and 1969 to 1980 when, as has been seen above, the rise was considerably greater. The implications of this faster rise have already been discussed in Chapter 2.

TABLE 9.2 Indices of costs of construction compared with other costs and prices from 1970 (1975 = 100)

Year	All new construction[a] (output price index)	Repair and maintenance[b] cost index	Land for private housing[c] (price per plot or hectare)	Retail prices[d]			Capital goods prices[e]		
				Total	Durable household goods	Transport and vehicles	Housing	Total	Plant and machinery
1970	40	46	49	54	61	52	56	49	57
1971	44	50	56	59	65	58	61	53	63
1972	51	54	94	64	68	62	68	59	63
1973	66	65	146	69	72	66	75	67	72
1974	85	80	145	80	82	77	84	82	81
1975	100	100	100	100	100	100	100	100	100
1976	109	117	100	117	110	115	114	114	120
1977	118	131	106	135	127	132	129	128	137
1978	131	139	129	135	139	144	138	143	150
1979	161	163	183	166	154	169	165	164	162
1980	203	199	241	196	172	201	215	193	177
1981	216	220	250	219	181	224	254	210	186
1982	211	239	281	238	186	239	285		
1983									
1984									

Notes and sources:

[a] DoE, *Housing and Construction Statistics 1970–1980* (HMSO, 1981) Table 2; DoE, *Housing and Construction Statistics 1971–1981* (HMSO, 1982) Table 2; DoE, *Housing and Construction Statistics 4th quarter 1982*, no. 12 (HMSO, 1983) Table 2.1.

[b] DoE unpublished information. Average of repair and maintenance deflators based on costs of materials and labour. The series is being revised by the DoE.

[c] DoE, *Housing and Construction Statistics 1970–1980* (HMSO, 1981) Table 3; DoE, *Housing and Construction Statistics 1971–1981* (HMSO, 1982) Table 3; DoE, *Housing and Construction Statistics 4th quarter 1982*, no. 12 (HMSO, 1983) Table 2.2.

[d] CSO, *Annual Abstract of Statistics 1982* (HMSO, 1982) Table 8.1; Department of Employment, *Employment Gazette*, vol. 9, no. 3, Mar. 1983 (HMSO, 1983) Table 6.4.

[e] CSO, *National Income and Expenditure, 1981 Edition* (HMSO, 1981) Tables 10.4 and 10.5; CSO, *National Income and Expenditure, 1982 Edition* (HMSO, 1982) Tables 10.4 and 10.5.

10 The Links between Resources and Output and Capacity

Analysis of the construction industry involves its dissection to understand the nature and functioning of each separate part. An understanding of each part separately is however insufficient for the understanding of the industry. The interrelationship of the parts must also be studied. Some of these relationships have been described in Chapter 3. This chapter concentrates on those between resource inputs and output on the one hand and between demand and output on the other. There are several ways in which these relationships can be viewed of which the main ones covered here are:

(a) the resource inputs required to produce a given level and mix of output
(b) the capacity of the industry to produce outputs of various types
(c) the effects of demand exceeding capacity, of capacity exceeding demand and of fluctuations.

INPUTS IN RELATION TO OUTPUT

Very little was known of the requirements of various types of inputs to produce different types of construction output until the Building Research Station undertook a substantial research programme to obtain data on the average inputs of site manpower and materials for various types of construction output, measured in square metres of floor space and in thousand pounds worth of output. The first part of the research for new work was based on some 550 projects around 1968. The least variable relationship was of requirements of inputs per £1000 of work. For building contracts in the public sector the margin of error is generally less than 5 per cent. For private-sector contracts it was less easy to obtain data and the margin of error is higher. The commercial building coefficients, that is, man-days per £1000 of output, were obtained from a few contractors who were probably above average efficiency. The industrial building is mainly based on publicly owned sites and may not therefore be representative of industrial work as a whole.[1] Table 10.1 shows some of the results of the first stage of this research. The figures are expressed in £1000 contract value updated to 1975 prices. It must be stressed that these figures are averages and there is often a wide range about the mean.

The outstanding difference between sectors is between building and civil engineering. The latter uses about half the labour of the building sectors and very little craft labour but a high proportion of general labourers and plant operators. There are also some quite large differences within building, for example housing uses a substantial number of bricklayers and is high on the finishing trades. Hospitals use a large proportion of services.

Since the data for Table 10.1 were collected there have been changes that will affect the number of operatives required. First there have been changes in output per man. These are discussed in Chapter 12 and a series is shown in Table 12.1. Productivity to 1981 probably fell. This would be expected by reason of the composition of work, notably the increase in repair and maintenance, and may not be the case for new work as a whole. There is too little evidence to draw any satisfactory conclusion. There have, however, been technological changes in construction which may have affected the manpower coefficients. In particular the weighting of various types of construction within the broad work categories has changed, for example, multi-storey flat construction has declined and timber-frame housing has increased (see Chapter 4). Any user of the statistics must consider these changes and the impact they are likely to have had on the coefficients, along the lines undertaken in the study *Construction into the Early 1980s*.[2]

More recently work has been undertaken by BRE on repair and maintenance by private contractors and direct labour departments of public authorities. These data are summarised in Table 10.2. It will be seen that the trades have not been specified because of the greater flexibility of tradesmen employed by small contractors on repair and maintenance. However the major work types of each contract give an indication of the trade. The total number of man-days for contractors work was thirty-four man-days. For general contractors the labour requirements were 35 ∓ 3 man-days per £1000 with 95 per cent confidence limits and for specialist contractors the figure was 32 ∓ 6 man-days per £1000. There was no analysis by work types but the work of firms included 56 per cent of repair and maintenance on housing, 12 per cent other public, and 32 per cent other private.

The man-days on repair and maintenance over all by contractors were over 60 per cent higher than on new building by all agencies (see Table 10.1). It is difficult to obtain from these figures any overall information on the man-days required for broad types of repair and maintenance to compare with those for new work in Table 10.1. However in order to be of practical value data are required for the work categories usually specified in DoE figures. Table 10.3 represents an attempt to provide these. The estimates for new work are based on Table 10.1. Those for repair and maintenance are based on Table 10.2 and on other supporting data. The overall average for repair and maintenance is rather over 60 per cent greater than for new work which corresponds with the result from the contractors' repair and maintenance data in Table 10.2. This means that correspondingly less within the £1000 expenditure is left for other inputs.

Similar work undertaken by BRE on materials usage is shown in Table 10.4 and 10.5 based on work from the mid sixties to the late seventies. The data given are grouped by customer sector and they are weighted by the frequency of building type investigated in each sector. As with manpower, consideration must be given before use of the data to the extent of technological and other changes and checks made accordingly.

Lastly it would be desirable to have similar data on plant but unfortunately no similar survey data are available. An indication of the usage of large plant may be obtained from the number of plant operators employed on various types of work in Table 10.1. There it will be seen that the highest number per £100 of work is in road, water and sewerage work followed by harbours. In building, perhaps surprisingly, the largest number per £1000 work is in private housing and 'other public work'. This number of operatives is probably not well related to the value of plant because the size of plant is likely to vary greatly from one type of work to another and some of the civil engineering plant is very large and so too are tower cranes used on large building works but normally only one or two to a large site. This matter is further discussed in Chapter 15.

A rough estimate of the inputs for various types of work is given in Table 10.6 which should be regarded as a basis from which to work for greater accuracy and improvement. Meanwhile it brings together in approximate quantitative terms the data so far available.

TABLE 10.1 *Employment of site operatives in man-days per £1000 of work at 1975 prices for various market sectors of new work*

Trade groups	Housing		General building					Civil engineering			
Trades	Private	Public	Education	Hospitals	Other public	Industrial	Commercial	Roads	Harbours	Water	Sewerage
			Site man-days[a] per £1000 contract value at 1975 prices								
Structure:											
Bricklayer	3.7	3.5	2.2	2.0	2.1	2.0	1.3	0.1	0.1	0.3	0.3
Roofer	0.5	0.4	0.4	0.3	0.3	1.3	0.2	–	–	–	–
Steel erector	–	0.1	0.2	0.1	0.2	0.6	–	–	–	–	–
Erector	0.1	0.1	–	0.3	0.1	0.3	0.2	–	–	–	–
Glazier	0.1	0.1	0.2	0.1	0.1	0.3	0.1	–	–	–	–
Others	0.1	–	0.2	0.1	0.3	–	0.3	0.2	0.1	0.3	0.3
Total	4.3	4.1	3.2	2.8	3.1	4.6	2.1	0.5	1.3	1.3	1.4
Carpenter	3.4	3.1	4.6	3.6	3.8	2.5	2.5	0.5	1.3	1.3	1.4
Services:											
Plumber	1.1	1.0	0.7	0.7	0.6	0.5	0.4	–	–	–	–
Heating	0.1	0.3	1.6	2.6	1.3	1.2	1.1	–	0.1	–	–
Electrician	0.7	1.0	1.4	1.8	1.4	1.2	1.2	–	–	–	–
Others	0.1	0.2	0.4	0.3	0.2	–	0.3	0.1	0.1	–	–
Total	2.0	2.4	4.1	5.5	3.5	2.9	3.0	–	–	–	–
Finishes:											
Plasterer	1.7	1.4	0.7	1.1	0.7	0.2	0.5	–	–	–	0.1
Painter	1.8	1.8	1.2	1.0	1.0	1.4	0.4	–	–	–	–

Other:

General labourer	5.9	6.6	6.4	5.2	6.7	6.2	3.8	5.4	3.2	3.3	5.9
Plant operator	0.8	0.4	0.4	0.3	0.8	0.2	0.3	2.5	1.5	2.5	2.5
Scaffolder	0.3	0.1	0.2	0.1	0.3	0.1	0.4	0.1	–	–	–
Steelfixer ⎱ Welder ⎰	–	0.1	0.1	0.3	0.3	0.1	0.3	0.2	1.3	0.3	0.3
Pipelayer ⎱ Drainlayer ⎰	0.1	0.3	0.1	0.1	0.1	–	–	0.3	0.2	0.9	0.8
Tarmac/asphalt	0.1	0.1	0.3	0.1	0.1	0.1	0.2	0.6	2.1	1.1	–
Others	0.3	0.2	0.3	0.1	0.3	0.2	5.0	0.9	8.2	8.1	0.3 9.8
Total	7.6	7.8	7.7	6.2	8.6	6.9		9.8			9.8
General foreman:	1.4	1.2	1.3	0.9	1.4	1.1	0.9	0.7	0.1	0.2	0.1
All trades	22.8	22.1	23.9	21.7	22.4	20.1	15.0	11.3	9.8	9.9	11.7

Notes:

— nil or negligible.

[a] 8½ hours per day (5½ days per week) for building; 9 hours per day (6 days per week) for civil engineering.

Sources:

Based on EDCs for Building and Civil Engineering, *How Flexible Is Construction?* NEDO (HMSO, 1978) Table 6.2 updated to 1975 prices; using relevant output price indices in DoE, *Housing and Construction Statistics 1970–1980* (HMSO, 1981) Table 2.

TABLE 10.2 *Man-days per £1000 of turnover/expenditure on various work types in repair and maintenance, 1975 prices*

	Man-days per £1000
Contractors' work:	
Various building types:	
Glazing	32
Roofing	44
Brickwork	41
Carpentry	32
Plumbing	35
Electrical	63[a]
Painting	50
Mixed	32
All above	37[b]
All average including above	34[b]
PSA work for government including some new work:	32
Direct labour work:	
Housing in local authorities	47
Hospital in Health Service	53
Roads in county council	23

Notes and sources:

[a] Based on one contract only.
[b] Not all contracts for which total work was available could be split into types; 34 is the overall figure, 37 is the average of those contracts on which detail was available. Based on preliminary data collected by Building Research Establishment.

The requirements for the various input types over the life of a contract are important in understanding some of the problems of the industry. First the build up of labour requirements is slow at the beginning and tails off at the end so that it is not unusual for three-quarters of the work to be done in the middle 60 per cent of the time. Then there are differences in the requirements for skills. The finishes and services are usually bunched towards the second half of the contract and the structural work at the beginning. Figure 10.1 shows the distribution of labour over the contract period for various types of hospital work but the same type of pattern emerges from other types of work.[3] This bunching of requirements for skills is one of the factors encouraging the employment of subcontractors (see Chapter 7).

30 Treatment units-traditional construction

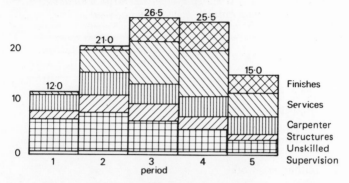

30 Service and residential units-traditional construction

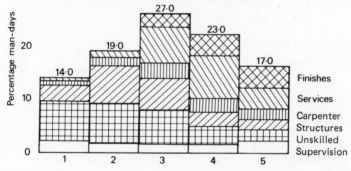

Work including alterations and additions

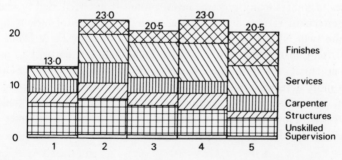

Source:

Lemessany, J., and Clapp, M. A., *Resource Inputs to New Construction −
The Labour Requirements of Hospital Building* CP 85/75 (BRE, 1955) Figure 4.

FIGURE 10.1 *Distribution of labour over the contract period −
hospital building*

TABLE 10.3 *Estimated average operative man-days per £1 000 of work by broad types of work, 1981 (1975 prices)*

Type of work	Estimated operatives man-days per £1000 work
New work:[a]	
Housing:	
Public	22
Private	23
Other new work:	
Public	18
Private industrial	20 ⎱ 17
Private commercial	15 ⎰
Repair and maintenance:[b]	
Housing	37
Other public	29
Other private	27

Notes and sources:

[a] Based on Table 10.1 weighted by 1981 work proportions.
[b] Estimated, based broadly on Table 10.2 and other preliminary data collected by Building Research Establishment.

The availability of data on resources required for various output types facilitates many types of investigation. It has been used to analyse the effects of various demand patterns on the demand for various inputs in the twin NEDO publications *Construction into the Early 1980s* and *Scottish Construction into the Early 1980s*.[4] It can be used to assess the potential capacity of the industry along lines suggested below. Lastly, at a more detailed level it can assist in the planning of training programmes, in manufacturers' decision on plant requirements for building materials or on the effect of the pressure of demand on resources of a change in the demand for any one type of work.

CAPACITY

The definition of capacity adopted here is the maximum output attainable by the industry in the time under consideration within the limits of

TABLE 10.4 *Estimated mean inputs of major building materials per £1000 of work at 1975 prices*

Sector or sub-sector	Aggregates (tonnes)	Cement (tonnes)	Brick/block wall (m² of single skin)	Softwood[b] (m³)
Housing	6.0	1.1	36.0	0.6
Private industrial	8.0	1.4	11.6	0.3
Private commercial	5.7	1.0	6.2	0.3
Roads	73.8	1.8	–	0.3
Water and sewerage	12.2	2.1	–	0.3
Education incl. universities	5.7	1.0	11.1	0.3
Health	3.7	0.7	9.8	0.4
Other public[a]	5.9	1.1	9.6	0.3
Repair and maintenance	11.1	0.6	2.3	0.4

Notes:

[a] 'Other public' covers public corporations, harbours and docks, personal social services, miscellaneous public services, coal, road passenger transport, road haulage and storage and forestry.
[b] Including shuttering and scaffolding.

Sources:

Estimates primarily based on BRE information from EDCs for Building and Civil Engineering, *Construction into the Early 1980s*, NEDO (HMSO, 1976) Table 4.8 converted to 1975 prices using relevant output price indices of the DoE, *Housing and Construction Statistics 1970–1980* (HMSO, 1981) Table 2 and unpublished data from the DoE on repair and maintenance deflators.

acceptable strain. What is acceptable will vary according to the economic and political objectives of the government of the time and the social climate. If the objective is, for example, rapidly to increase the stock of some military installations, then the necessity to import materials or components which, given time, could be produced in this country would not be regarded as a limiting factor and nor perhaps would higher prices to be paid for the output. If, on the other hand, there was a period of balance of payments crisis and an urgent government demand was not under consideration, then it would not be acceptable to define capacity so high that it could be achieved only with large imports or at the expense of price rises.

Capacity varies over time and responds to demand over time. It should therefore be considered in a dynamic sense. Table 10.7 shows a schematic basis for the discussion of capacity. It is concerned with the industry as a whole rather than the individual firm and deals with the situation

TABLE 10.5 Mean[a] input of some selected building materials per £1000 of project value (at 1975 prices)

Material	Unit	Education	Health	Housing (public)	Government	Industry	Commercial[b]
Bulk excavation	m^3	11.2	5.9	8.0	9.3	12.8	6.8
Hardcore	m^3	3.17	1.46	2.06	2.04	6.75	2.47
Concrete in situ	m^3	1.57	1.44	1.98	3.00	3.90	2.66[b]
Precast concrete	m^3	0.34	0.28	0.41	0.53	0.23	0.44[b]
Rod reinforcement for in situ concrete	kg	17[c,d]	52[c]	21[c]	208	39[c]	171[b]
Mesh reinforcement for in situ concrete	m^2	3.8	2.0	1.8	5.4	14.3	3.8[b]
Formwork	m^2	1.4	3.8	2.1	7.9	3.5	8.1
Brickwork (half brick wall equivalent)	m^2	8.1	7.1	16.9	5.2	6.5	5.8
Blockwork	m^2	1.67	2.40	8.39	1.06	2.07	2.98
Structural and joinery timber	m^3	0.164	0.077	0.306	0.051	0.039	0.030
Total timber	m^3	0.34	0.18	0.50	0.16	0.08	0.10
Steel frame	kg	76	44	neg.[d]	90	401	61[c,d,b]
Unframed steel	kg	6.8[d]	2.0[d]	3.0[c,d]	4.6[d]	0.8[c,d]	4.0[c,d,b]
Glazing	m^2	1.32	0.70	1.39	0.99	0.96	1.26[c]
Timber doors	no.	0.356	0.357	1.587	0.190	0.129	0.154
Boarding (Hardbd. and blockboard, etc.)	m^2	5.2	1.6	3.1	1.7	1.4[c]	1.1[c]
Roof decking (mainly woodwool)	m^2	1.35	0.92	1.10[c,d]	1.29[c]	0.23[c,d]	0.45[c,d]
Drainpipes	m	3.37	1.34	3.38	2.18	2.33	0.93
Service pipework	m	1.61	1.31	5.95	0.76	0.89	1.43
Roof pipework	m	0.43	0.29	1.44	0.36	0.51	0.33

Sectors

Sanitary fittings	no.	0.335	0.218	0.512	0.058	0.096	0.093
Electrical prime cost	£(1975)	53	91	39	47	39	55
Heating and ventilating cost	£(1975)	90	203	45	136	56	107
Lifts prime cost	£(1975)	0.6[c,d]	18.6[c,d]	4.0[c,d]	34.5[c,d]	1.5[c,d]	25.5
Painting (one coat)	m²	53	45	95	37	26	12
Rendering, screeds (beds and backing)	m²	4.8	4.7	5.6	3.8	1.7	4.6
Plastering 2 coat + 1.5 × 3 coat	m²	4.0	6.7	17.5	4.5	1.1	4.8
Plasterboard	m²	0.84	1.07	6.00	0.67[c]	6.67	0.18[c,d]

Notes:

[a] Mean inputs were calculated as the mean of per unit inputs to each project in the relevant sample. This weights large and small projects equally.

[b] Shops and places of entertainment were not adequately represented. This may have led to a slight underestimate of structural steel and overestimate of concrete and reinforcement.

[c] The range of usage from one project to another is such that the standard error of the mean exceeds 25 per cent.

[d] The material occurred in less than 50 per cent of projects surveyed.

[e] Including structural timber, joinery timber, doors, boarding, woodwool slabs, fittings and furniture units, formwork, shelving, floorboarding and woodblock flooring.

Source:

Preliminary analysis of data from Building Research Establishment.

TABLE 10.6   *Estimated percentages[a] of value of various work types accounted for by main inputs*

Work type	Operative Manpower[b] %	Materials[c] %	Plant[d] %	Other[e] %
New housing	30	43	2	25
New other building	28	42	4	26
New civil engineering	15	35	22	28
Repair and maintenance	46	30	2	22
All work[f]	35	37	5	24

Notes and sources:

[a] Percentages are not accurate to one digit.

[b] Based mainly on BRE work especially that in Tables 10.1 and 10.2, and on BCIS work for new building.

[c] Based on BRE work especially for repair and maintenance, on BCIS work for new building and on discussions with the industry.

[d] Based on data in Chapter 15, on the usage of plant operators by type of work in Table 10.1, adjusted for estimates of value of plant per operative, on type of work done by plant-hire firms in 1978 (DoE, *Private Contractors' Construction Census 1978* (HMSO, 1979) Table 28); and on EDCs for Building and Civil Engineering, *How Flexible Is Construction?* NEDO (HMSO, 1978) pp. 65–6.

[e] Based on a broad assumption that, on average, management return on capital and other overheads represents about a quarter of turnover. This is then adjusted for expected differences in management component based on data in Chapter 13.

[f] A weighted average using 1981 output data from DoE, *Housing and Construction Statistics 1971-1981* (HMSO, 1982) Table 9, but corroborated as far as plant is concerned by output of plant hire and scaffolders as percentage of total value of work done (ibid, Table 43) and by *How Flexible Is Construction?*, p. 65.

where expansion of output is being considered in relation to the capacity of the industry. Three time periods are studied: short term for which a rough indication is up to three months, medium term up to say one year and the long term which may reach to five years or more. The time categories overlap and some actions of the medium term may be started in the short term and extend to the long term and similarly for other time periods. The short and medium term are different in kind from the long term in that the resources available in the short and medium term exist and have usually been utilised in a past period, whereas the long-term resources have to be created.

EXPANSION OF OUTPUT TO MEET DEMAND

In the short term output can be expanded by using up stocks of materials held by manufacturers and merchants and by imports. In the short term, however, imports will be possible only from established sources of supply – it may take longer to seek out new suppliers. The unemployed operatives – skilled and unskilled – can be re-employed and the utilisation of the existing labour force extended by overtime. For managers, designers and other non-operative workers, since firms tend to hang on to these in a period of slack output more than they keep on operatives, there will probably be some underemployment as well as the pool of unemployed. Plant and equipment can be expanded by making better use of underutilised plant in the hands of plant hirers and contractors and by buying stocks in the hands of plant manufacturers. Finance may be a problem dealt with in the construction industry in the short term by an extension of bank overdrafts and, if possible, longer credit from builders merchants. Lastly there is the organisational structure of firms which is not a resource in the ordinary sense but is a factor that could restrict expansion of output and is closely linked to management. The slack in the short run can usually be taken up within the existing structure.

How much expansion is possible in the short run depends on the levels of the factors mentioned, for example, stocks, unemployed and under-utilisation of men, plant and organisations, only some of which are measurable. It will also depend on the mix of these available resources compared with the demands to be put upon the industry. It is clear from Tables 10.1–10.6 that the amounts of resources required for different types of output vary greatly and therefore that the capacity of the industry to do work measured in £ sterling will be different according to the matching of resources of different types with requirements for output of different types. It may be possible to undertake much civil engineering work, for example water and sewerage which needs much plant, cement and aggregates and relatively little labour, in a situation where labour is scarce. However, if there is massive unemployed craft labour and a general surplus of materials but a shortage of plant, then more work could be undertaken by concentrating on repair and maintenance, improvement, rehabilitation and housing.

In the medium term there will be sufficient time to expand production in underutilised plant and to bring back into use plant that had been mothballed, assuming that there is sufficient raw material supply and appropriate labour to man and organise it. Moreover there would be time

TABLE 10.7 *Time/supply relationships for sources of resources for expansion of output of industry*

Resource	*Time for expansion*		
	Short term (say 0–3 months) *(existing resources)*	*Medium term (say 3–12 months)* *(existing resources)*	*Long term (say 1–5 years)* *(new resources)*
Materials	Stocks held by suppliers Imports from established sources Substitution for scarce materials	Under-utilised and mothballed plant Imports Substitution for scarce materials	New factories Imports
Operatives	Unemployed Overtime	Workers in other industries abroad and retired Increased productivity Delayed retirement	Increased level of recruiting and training Increased productivity
Managers, designers and other personnel	Underemployed Unemployed	Ex-construction managers in other industries, abroad and retired Increased responsibility to existing managers Delayed retirement	Increased level of recruiting and training
Plant and equipment	Under-utilisation of existing plant Stocks at manufacturers	Increased production Imports	New factories Imports
Finance	Increased credit from suppliers Bank overdrafts	Loans from wider range of investors	Raising new capital

Technology	Substitution of existing technologies	Substitution of existing technologies	Developing new technologies
Organisations of contracting and professional firms	Slack in existing structure	Expansion within existing organisational structure	Reorganisation for larger output Formation of new firms

Source:

Based partly on Hillebrandt, P. M., 'The Capacity of the Industry', in Turin, D. A. (ed.), *Aspects of the Economics of Construction* (George Godwin, 1975).

to organise new sources of supply of imports. Once the unemployed are re-employed it might be possible to attract back into the industry from other industries or from abroad some who had previous experience in it, and in Chapter 11 it is found that the potential may be considerable. However, this will be possible only if construction is attractive to this labour by the conditions and pay it offers relative to the present employment of these persons, so that this may involve some rise in costs. Men may similarly be attracted back from retirement. Ways of increasing productivity may also be found by methods of payment, provision of better tools or the scope for better deployment of manpower with a larger workforce. Managers may similarly be enticed back, although, because of the peculiar specific characteristics of construction, there may not be many in other industries. Existing managers can be stretched with larger projects and more responsibility and retirement delayed. In this period of time imports of plant and equipment can be arranged as well as increased production from existing factories. Better arrangements can be made for the finance of expansion and some adjustments and extensions can be made to the existing structure of firms to enlarge the organisational capacity. It may be that expatriate firms will be brought in if the domestic professional firms or contractors do not appear to have the right approach to the organisation of the process or do not have the capacity to produce.

Expansion beyond these medium-term measures utilising basically existing capacity will take place only if the industry foresees a continuing demand for larger output, because only in these circumstances will it be economic to invest resources in capital equipment that can produce over many years or in training that will potentially provide a working life of usefulness. Neither investment in new factories nor in training can bring any substantial increase in output for at least a year and it is usually many more. If, however, the prospect of a continuing larger output is envisaged then, not only will investment in factories and housing be expanded, but also new technologies will be developed often leading to higher productivity. For this expansion new capital for construction firms must be raised and the firms themselves often reorganised to take account of the increased work-load and the change in production techniques. At this stage too new firms will be formed.

The rate at which expansion can take place is determined by a number of external factors many of which are discussed elsewhere, including planning and building regulation procedures (Chapter 3), taxation allowances on investment of plant (Chapter 15), training support (Chapter 11), and research and development (Chapter 17). It will only happen at all, however, if there is confidence produced by the state of the economy and the industry. This was discussed in Chapter 2 in relation to demand, but it affects not only demand but the willingness and ability of the industry to supply.

The scope of expansion therefore in the short and medium term depends on the extent of underutilised resources but in the longer term much more on expectations of the future demands on the industry.

Suppose that capacity is not adequate to meet demand, what are the effects of the industry? There will be shortages of manpower of all types, including managers and professional staff, shortages of materials, increases in prices of labour and materials and inefficiency in production from the design stage to the completion of the project. Tender prices will rise because of increases in costs, actual or anticipated and because of the possibility of increasing profits. Construction times will lengthen. The effects do not stop at the construction industry, for the increase in prices cause inflation in the economy and the failure of buildings to be delivered on time at the agreed price creates inefficiences in the rest of the economy.

There was a feeling in 1964 that the industry was very strained and that it was in danger of working at over-full capacity. Output in 1964 was over 11 per cent higher than in 1963 when the industry was already busy and new orders were nearly 15 per cent up. The mood of the time may be summed up by a report to the National Economic Development Council as follows:

> The broad conclusion of Section I was that there is uncertainty whether the construction industry will be able to meet the demands which are likely to be placed upon it. The industry may be overloaded and there is a possibility that costs and prices may rise with harmful effects, not only in construction, but in other parts of the economy as well. It is therefore important for the well-being of the economy as a whole that the load on the industry should be in approximate balance with its capacity. The question arises whether steps should be taken to reduce demand. In considering the question of any reduction, it has to be borne in mind that the high level of demand is helping to create conditions under which all sections of the industry are accepting change more readily than ever before.[5]

In fact prices rose but not by more than in previous years[6] and not by an amount that would be regarded as politically unacceptable, partly because the rate of increase in output in 1965 and subsequent years slowed down. There was, however, still expansion to 1973 apart from a small fall in 1969. But in 1973 the industry did seem to be overloaded and working for a very short time beyond the acceptable levels of strain. The highest level of output of the industry in any quarter was in the 1st quarter of 1973 and during 1973 there were severe shortages of many materials with stocks of materials at their lowest for most materials sometime between the end of 1972 to the end of 1973[7] (see Chapter 14). Prices rose steeply; the DQSD tender price index rose more than 50 per cent from the 4th quarter of 1972 to the 4th quarter of 1973 and while the index of the cost of new construction rose just over 20 per cent, the retail price index rose just 10 per cent.[8] Part of this was due to the wage settlement after the 1972 national building strike but the degree of overload was also important.

There was time and cost overrun on a disproportionate number of projects. There was difficulty in obtaining sufficient tenderers for much work, especially in the public sector, and some projects had to be postponed. It was often difficult to have repair and maintenance done and although there is no repair and maintenance index equivalent to that for tender prices of new work the price was almost certainly rising very fast. Indeed it seems likely that whenever there is a high demand for new work, repair and maintenance is the sector that is squeezed most.

CONTRACTION IN OUTPUT DUE TO A FALL IN DEMAND

In a period of contraction of output, to some extent the short-term and medium-term changes shown in Table 10.5 will be reversed. If a decline in output continues for any length of time the industry will seek to minimise the cost of operating at low levels. For materials stocks will be decreased at the expense of current production so that more plant is underutilised. If enough plant is underutilised the less economic plants will be mothballed. However, to keep a plant in being without production is itself expensive and unless there are prospects for an upturn in output some facilities will be scrapped and be lost completely. Similarly with men, the unemployed may emigrate permanently or obtain skills in other industries, the long-term unemployed and retired will lose their willingness and ability to work. There will be in the short run no apparent requirement to train and the training apparatus may be run down and in some cases disbanded. Morale will be low and the initiative and enthusiasm to innovate will be lost. Not all the effects are easily reversible, however, and the shrinking process will be painful with likely top-heavy organisations and financial structures. Moreover, because of the tendering situation, work for contractors is likely to be relatively unprofitable and profits will fall and with them the money to pay a return on past capital borrowings. Some firms and parts of the industry may be able to maintain themselves by obtaining work abroad or by export of goods but this may be less profitable and more risky than the well-tried home market and some firms will eventually go out of business.

The longer the capacity of the industry is underutilised the more it will shrink and hence the slower the rate at which output can be expanded again and the higher the costs of doing so.

Since 1973 the output of the industry has declined with minor recoveries to well into the 1980s. The process has followed the lines outlined above and has been painful. By the end of 1982 the amount of surplus capacity was probably diminishing fairly rapidly as firms were unable to remain in business (see Chapter 7) or to maintain the past level of their resources. A return to the levels of the 1970s would not be possible except over a considerable time period and with very favourable conditions, although it could be speeded up at the expense of a high level of imports and earnings levels.

Thus it is not possible to reverse the expansion or contraction process without considerable loss of investment in plant, expertise and the organisational framework. The costs to the economy of expansion, and particularly of contraction, are very high. The level of demand itself is not as important as the process of going from one level to another and that can be a very painful process indeed. It is time the prevailing view that the industry is flexible be tempered by an understanding of some of the costs of that flexibility.

FLUCTUATIONS IN OUTPUT AROUND THE TREND

Large fluctuations in demand and hence in output over a long period of time lead to the type of investment in plant and machinery to achieve flexibility rather than efficiency at a particular output; to an industry structure and employment structure to achieve flexibility even at a cost; to a low level of investment in training in research and development and in plant and to poor career prospects and transitory management and production teams. These are damaging and with each up and down in output the same sort of processes will take place on a smaller scale as those outlined above.

Minor fluctuations in demand along an upward trend such as occurred in the 1960s are less damaging although some of the disadvantages mentioned above will be apparent. However, a quick stimulus to improvement followed by a period of consolidation may also have some advantages. Indeed the 1960s was a period of long-term expansion when the underlying feeling was one of optimism and challenge. In spite of stop-go (see Chapter 4), it was a period of innovation and experimentation. There was development in new building material technology; a substitution of capital for manpower in civil engineering, especially earth moving, and in the industrialisation of housing, schools and other buildings (see Chapter 4); a reorganisation of firms and a period of mergers (see Chapter 7); a boost for training, not only of operatives but of managers in construction and in design and indeed a whole examination of the industry by itself leading to innovative ideas, many of which fell by the wayside but some of which bear fruit today.

11 Manpower

TOTAL MANPOWER OF THE INDUSTRY

Excluding the professionals in private practice but including those professionals employed by public authorities and contractors, the total manpower in the construction industry in 1981 (shown in Table 11.1) was estimated at between 1.5 and 1.8 million persons and, including unemployed construction workers, at between 1.8 and 2.1 million. This is remarkably little different from the 1973 levels of 2.0 to 2.2 million in the peak employment and output year of 1973 (see Table 11.2). The reason for the upper and lower figures is the uncertainty about the number of self-employed. The lower figures are based on DoE estimates and the higher ones on Inland Revenue statistics of assessments of individuals in construction.[1] It will be seen that the number of self-employed may now be nearly equal to the number of operatives directly employed by contractors, although some of the self-employed on the Inland Revenue basis may be Administrative Professional Technical and Clerical (APTC) - for example self-employed draughtsmen working in contractors design offices, but these according to the CITB, would be only 1300.[2] The OPCS survey on mobility[3] gives some further clues about the numbers of self-employed. They were concerned with manual workers employed in the construction industry and in their sample they found 20 per cent of the hireable workforce were men working as self-employed manual operatives in construction. This would give a total of about 300 000 self-employed manual workers. One problem is that it is not clear where the working proprietors would fit in - would they be classed as self-employed manual workers or not? If not, then 300 000 plus the 126 000 working proprietors bring the total midway between the Inland Revenue assessment figure and the DoE figure.

There is some evidence for 1974 from the survey undertaken by the

194

TABLE 11.1 *Manpower of the construction industry, 1981, Great Britain (annual averages)*

	No. of persons th
Employees in employment:	
Contractors	
Operatives	659
APTCs[a]	226
Public authorities	
Operatives	207
APTCs[a]	105
Total	1 198
Self-employed:	
Estimate 1[b]	
Working proprietors 126	
Others 188	314
(Estimate 2)[c]	(570)
Total manpower in industry:	
Estimate 1	1 512
(Estimate 2)[c]	(1 768)
Unemployed:	352
Total labour force:	
Estimate 1	1 864
(Estimate 2)[c]	(2 120)

Notes:

[a] Administrative, Professional, Technical and Clerical.
[b] Figures for working proprietors are for the self-employed in firms on the DoE statistical register. Figures for other self-employed are estimates of those not so covered.
[c] Based on Inland Revenue data (see text).

Sources:

DoE, *Housing and Construction Statistics 1971–1981* (HMSO, 1982) Table 15; CSO, *Monthly Digest of Statistics*, no. 441, Sept 1982 (HMSO, 1983) Table 3.12; Leopold, E., 'Where Have All the Workers Gone?', *Building*, vol. 243, 22 Oct 1982, pp. 29–30.

TABLE 11.2   *Operatives, self-employed and APTCs in the construction industry from 1970, Great Britain*

Year	Operatives	Self-employed[b]		APTCs[a]	Unemployed
		Est.1	Est. 2[c]		
	th	th	th	th	th
1970	1 170	300	494	333	106
1971	1 106	328	550	330	128
1972	1 110	367	644	324	133
1973	1 148	428	667	338	89
1974	1 104	427	573	347	104
1975	1 055	375	470	353	162
1976	1 023	341	424	350	207
1977	983	325	435	340	208
1978	974	365	475	341	186
1979	990	395	547	349	164
1980	975	375	555[E]	346	217
1981	866	314	570[E]	331	352
1982	776		600[E]	310	n.a.
1983					
1984					

Notes:

[a] [b] and [c] See corresponding notes in Table 11.1. The regular collection of unemployment statistics for the construction industry ceased during 1982.

Sources:

DoE, *Housing and Construction Statistics 1970–1980* (HMSO, 1981) Tables 15 and 20; DoE, *Housing and Construction Statistics 1971–1981* (HMSO, 1982) Tables 15 and 19; DoE, *Housing and Construction Statistics 4th quarter 1982*, no. 12 (HMSO, 1983) Table 2.9; Leopold, E., 'Where Have All the Workers Gone?' *Building*, vol. 243, 22 Oct 1982, pp. 29–30.

CITB and the NFBTE in the London Region and Midland Region of the NFBTE, which showed 22 per cent labour-only subcontracting as a percentage of total operatives in London and 24 per cent in the Midlands.[4]

The Construction Industry Training Board (CITB) now collects figures of self-employed labour-only working for contractors and these were 55 000 in April 1981.[5] These would represent, according to the OPCS survey,[6] say 120 out of a sample of self-employed of 313 or 35 per cent which, applied to the CITB figure, brings the total self-employed manual workers to only about 150 000 compared with 300 000, applying the 20 per cent to the total available operative labour force. It seems that either the CITB is missing a lot of self-employed or the Inland

Revenue data include a high number who are not really in construction in the accepted sense or a combination of the two. The uncertainties over the number and type of self-employed bedevil the understanding of the current manpower position in construction, as will be seen not only in this chapter but also in Chapter 12.

The breakdown of the self-employed, according to the OPCS survey,[7] shows that about 42 per cent work for contractors usually supplying neither labour nor plant, about 26 per cent work direct to the client usually supplying materials or plant and 33 per cent work for both, but over half of these supply material or plant. The OPCS study unfortunately did not ask how the self-employed were paid – piece-rate or hourly rate. Both are used and particularly in London hourly payment seems to be prevalent. There is therefore a variety of different ways in which they arrange their work.

The change from 1973–82 in total employment has been only 5–7 per cent whichever figures are taken, and this is in spite of a fall in output of 27 per cent. In part this is due to the change in the type of work undertaken, with the shift from new work to repair and maintenance which is far more labour intensive. This is borne out by calculations based on the figures in Tables 10.1 and 10.2, discussed in Chapter 12. Employment of APTCS has kept remarkably stable in spite of changes in the work-load.

OPERATIVES

Operatives include the traditional crafts, such as carpenters and joiners, and newer skills such as mechanical equipment operators as well as labourers. The data on crafts are now collected by the CITB so far as its jurisdiction goes, that is, excluding the direct labour of public authorities and certain other parts of construction. In their present form statistics are available only since 1974. Table 11.3 shows the percentage of various tradesmen among operatives employed by contractors and by public authorities and of self-employed working for contractors. It also shows estimates for self-employed working direct to the public. Similar estimates from the same survey are available for those who work either direct to the public or for contractors. This last category falls in between the other two in trade distribution.[8]

It is striking that the very high proportion – over 50 per cent of self-employed labour on contractors' sites – is accounted for by the trades of carpenters and joiners, bricklayers and masons and plasterers. Indeed,

TABLE 11.3 *Percentage of total operatives employed by contractors, local authorities and new towns and self-employed by main crafts, 1980 or 1981, Great Britain*

Craft	Operatives employed by contractors April 1981[a]	Self-employed working for contractors April 1981[a]	Self-employed working direct to public[b]	Operatives employed by LAs and new towns 1980[c]
Carpenters and joiners	15.5	21.9	10	13.9
Bricklayers and masons	7.2	23.0	5	6.4
Plasterers	1.8	6.1	0	2.0
Painters	8.4	1.8	20	14.3
Plumbers and gasfitters	4.0	3.4	10	7.6
Heating and ventilating workers	2.7	1.3	nss	0.6
Paviours	0.3	0.7	nss	2.4
Electricians	7.5	1.6	1	4.2
Mechanical plant operatives	7.7	1.1	0	3.7
All others	44.9	39.1	54	44.9
Total	100	100	100	100

Notes and sources:

[a] Construction Industry Training Board, *Annual Report 1981/82* (CITB, 1983) Table 1.
[b] Marsh, A., Heady, P., and Matheson, J., *Labour Mobility in the Construction Industry*, OPCS (HMSO, 1981) Table 7.3 (estimate based on survey).
[c] DoE, *Housing and Construction Statistics 1970–1980* (HMSO, 1981) Table 47 (not published in 1982 edition).

according to the CITB figures self-employed bricklayers and masons and plasterers on contractors' sites accounted for 22–24 per cent of all labour in these crafts on these sites but only 11 per cent for carpenters and joiners. Not surprisingly, for work direct to the public, it is the housing repair trades of painters, plumbers and carpenters who were most important. Local authority direct labour departments have a high proportion of directly employed painters and a relatively high proportion of plumbers and paviours.

These figures are consistent with what is known of the work-load of these groups (Chapter 4, Tables 4.1 and 4.2) and the intensities of skills required for various types of work (Chapter 10, Tables 10.1 and 10.2).

Training

Training in the construction industry is in a state of flux, partly because there have been many changes in the system over the last few years and partly because of the government's initiative in training, notably the Manpower Services Commission (MSC) Youth Training Scheme (YTS) which started in September 1983.

The basic scheme was that a would-be craftsmen enters into a training service agreement with the industry of three years for most building crafts, four years for plumbers and either three or four years for electricians. The organisations concerned are, for the CITB crafts, the National Joint Council for the Building Industry (NJCBI) usually through the NFBTE Regional Organisation, and the national joint boards for plumbers and for electricians. There are in addition special arrangements for glaziers, mastic asphalters and wood-cutting machinists.

The preferred CITB scheme was known as the Standard Scheme under which the trainee had the first six months as off-the-job training to achieve a sufficient range of skills for him to be useful on site. In any case his work experience should be linked to practical training in an employer's workshop, at a training centre or college. This might be a block release or day release scheme. The trainee would be required to study for the craft certificate of the City and Guilds of London Institute. There is difficulty at the moment in finding places for trainees. This scheme is now in abeyance with the introduction of the new YTS scheme.

A problem of the whole training programme is that it is nowhere stated exactly what work experience should be and how it should be organised. The quality and range varies considerably from one firm to another.

The new scheme introduced from September 1983 for school leavers under the Manpower Services Commission Youth Training Scheme (YTS) provides, it is currently intended, a year additional to the existing training arrangements although there will need to be some alterations in these as a result of the introduction of YTS.

Some 20 000 training places will be offered to school leavers in construction, that is, five places for every two previously entering the industry. The CITB will be the primary managing agent for most of the industry in this scheme.[9] There will be courses intended for potential craftsmen, general operatives, clerical workers and technicians. The precise arrangements are still subject to alteration. However, the intention is that the training will consist of a four-week induction course, followed by vocational training off-the-job and planned work experience. The training may be specialised or can be general to enable trainees to determine what skill they would like to learn after the first year. The costs of the training in the training centres or colleges, the allowance of £25 a week for the trainees and other incidental expenses, such as protective clothing, will be met by the MSC or CITB. The contractor does not have to employ the trainee and will have the opportunity to choose those he wishes to employ as a full trainee after the YTS year. However the advantages of this are partly being nullified by the contractors themselves determining in advance who will be retained.

The electricians, the plumbers and some other parts of the industry will have schemes that diverge somewhat from the general scheme. In particular the JIB for the Electrical Contracting Industry is introducing a radically changed system of training to replace apprenticeship, in which the first year meets the requirements of the MSC YTS. Progress depends on achievement both technical and practical and not upon any age or service criteria. It includes a considerable proportion of off-the-job training.[10] In the case of the civil engineers the YTS year will form the first of three years of a proposed three years Civil Engineering Operative Training Scheme (CEOTS) which would qualify operatives in a wide range of civil engineering skills. It is due to start as a pilot scheme at the CITB training centre at Bircham Newton in September 1983.

From the construction contractors' point of view, the scheme could be beneficial, in providing, at little cost to him, a first year of training so that when the trainee is employed, he has some idea of what happens on site and is more likely to be immediately useful. There are, however, many problems: the first is whether the CITB will be able to place all the required members for work experience. However they face a penalty if they do not and are in fact confident of doing so. Secondly, there is the question of whether the training colleges and centres will be able to mount training courses for the YTS intake, without reducing the standards of other teaching and training within the same institutions. There is some evidence that staff are being drawn for the YTS provision to the potential detriment of, for example, technician training. It will not however be known for some time what practical effect the scheme will have on overall standards.

Lastly, what will happen to those not employed by contractors at the end of the year? It seems unlikely that all can be given employment in view of the very high intake. The industry is apprehensive lest they become part of the industry self-employed particularly in the household sector.

Other types of skills such as plant operators, scaffolders, steel fixers, kerb layers or concreters may be obtained from off-site training programmes arranged by the CITB and the Cement and Concrete Association combined with work experience on site with supervision. This training takes about six months.

Many skilled persons, and also some not so skilled but claiming to be skilled in a craft or other trade, have learnt on the job and have not followed any formal training programme. The OPCS survey[11] analysed the level of skills claimed by the men and these are shown in Table 11.4. Some of those stating that they had no 'formal' training may have had quite rigorous training by an employer on the job but the proportion of some of the trades with no formal training looks alarming, especially where safety is involved (e.g. scaffolders or mechanical equipment operators). Government training scheme could mean a variety of schemes from the six months' training for ex-service men to the TOPS schemes. Apprenticeship was of course the standard arrangement now replaced in nomenclature by the Training Agreement.

The statistics of numbers being trained are not very reliable because very little is known of the drop-out ratio or of exactly when training agreements are registered. However, Table 11.5 shows the percentage of operatives employed by contractors and by the direct labour departments of local authorities and new towns who are trainees. It will be seen that the proportion of contractors' labour force who are trainees is higher than those of direct labour although if the self-employed on contractors' sites are included their performance goes down. The self-employed in Table 11.5 are simply those on contractors' sites counted by the CITB and these, as has been shown earlier, may be low. There are, in addition, those working direct to the client and those only sometimes working for contractors, and these also do virtually no training. One of the great disadvantages of self-employment, and labour-only subcontracting which is but a part of it, is that the burden of training for the whole industry is put on the contractors and the direct labour departments of public authorities. The direct labour departments are not 'in scope' to the CITB, that is, they do not pay levies or obtain grants. They may, however, send people on CITB courses on payment of the appropriate fee. It would seem appropriate that the direct labour departments should be included in the CITB scheme.

The boundaries of skills have changed little and from time to time suggestions have been made for a division of skills more in keeping with modern requirements. As long ago as 1966 a study by the Building Research Station[12] pointed towards the need for change in trades and their training, including a requirement for broadly based trades able to undertake a wide range of building work, possibly, for example, wet trowel trades and dry trades. The different requirements of repair and maintenance and new work were also shown. Very little has happened as a result of this, although the City and Guilds Institute does have a syllabus covering all the trowel trades except plastering. Nevertheless the study by Hatchett[13] of the Inner London Education Authority (ILEA) craft students found that changing from one craft course to another simply does not take place. Flexibility is very limited.

Within trades there have been changes in requirements. The increasing proportion of repair, maintenance and rehabilitation in the workload requires different types of skills. The existing training is geared towards skills for new work and not for repair or rehabilitation. Furthermore, the tendency for skills to be split up on site and hence in trainees' experience into sub-skills (e.g. shuttering carpenter, first and second fix carpenter and joiner) means that the generally skilled carpenter is getting scarce but he is just the type of person required for rehabilitation work. The Civil Trust is concerned that the necessary skills should be available for the construction and renovation of high-class buildings and old buildings and has proposed a registration scheme.[14] At the other extreme the increase in sophisticated components means that different skills are required for their installation.

Certification of Skills

Certification of skill under which the skill of an operative is tested and a certificate of competence given has been under discussion for some years. It is now accepted as an objective and a pilot scheme operating in 1983 will pave the way for its general introduction in 1985. The general plan was described to a Construction Industry Training Officers' Conference by Fulcher of the CITB.[15] Surveys are being undertaken to establish the

TABLE 11.4 *Skill and*

	Carpenters and joiners	Bricklayers	Electricians	Plumbers	Painters
	%	%	%	%	%
Skill:					
Skilled	97	98	92	97	92
Semi-skilled	2	2	5	2	6
Unskilled	1	0	3	1	2
	100	100	100	100	100
Training: [a]					
Apprenticeship	83	74	77	76	65
Government training scheme	6	9	4	7	4
Other formal training	12	5	8	11	3
No formal training	14	16	16	14	31
Base – no. in sample	159	124	98	114	144

Note:

[a] Some men underwent more than one form of training so totals will exceed 100%.

Source:

Marsh, A., Heady, P., and Matheson, J., *Labour Mobility in the Construction Industry*, OPCS (HMSO, 1981) Table 2.4.

training by craft group

Mechanical equipment operators	Plasterers and tilers	Scaffolders and steel-fixers	Other construction skills	Labourers and mates	Drivers and miscellaneous occupations
%	%	%	%	%	%
49	81	59	38	8	36
44	17	39	43	37	34
7	2	2	19	55	30
100	100	100	100	100	100
15	46	20	21	9	14
4	7	6	4	4	6
4	6	24	6	2	2
81	46	55	70	86	81
90	55	51	221	231	127

TABLE 11.5 *Percentage of operatives (including trainees) who are trainees in contractors and local auhorities and new towns – selected trades and total operatives, 1980, Great Britian*

Trade	Contractor trainees as % direct employees (Oct 1980)	Contractor trainees as % direct employees and LOSC contractor sites (Oct 1980)	Local authorities and new town trainees as % employees (Oct 1980)
Carpenters and joiners	17.3	13.2	11.1
Bricklayers and masons	19.8	13.1	9.2
Plasterers	13.6	9.2	8.4
Painters	14.1	11.2	8.3
Plumbers and gas fitters	27.0	19.9	14.0
Heating and ventilating workers	22.1	17.6	12.7
Electricians	36.2	26.2	15.4
Total operatives	11.2	9.3	6.2

Notes and sources:

DoE, *Housing and Construction Statistics 1970–1980* (HMSO, 1981) Table 49 (not published in later edition); DoE, *Housing and Construction Statistics 1971–1981* (HMSO, 1981) Tables 16 and 17; information provided by CITB.

tasks commonly used by most craftsmen to act as a base on which tests can be developed. Practical tests are being developed for carpentry and joinery, brickwork, plastering and painting and decorating and these will be used in pilot schemes in sixteen test centres. The CITB staff will develop the tests of skills to be administered, probably over two days. The marking may be on a local basis but to national standards by a test panel including an employer, a skilled craftsman, a teacher and a CITB staff member. This is similar to continental practice. In addition to the skill test, there will probably be a knowledge test and a minimum period of site experience. The tests should be open to persons of any age and at least · one retake will almost certainly be permitted. The whole final scheme will, before implementation, be agreed by representative committees.

The advantages are that it gives a skilled man a recognition that should enable him to have better job opportunities and therefore is an incentive for persons in the industry to reach the standard or standards set. It will make it more difficult for unskilled persons to pose as skilled and therefore should increase client satisfaction with the industry, particularly in those areas where the private client is small and inexperienced, notably on housing repair and maintenance and rehabilitation. It would facilitate a scheme of registration of employees because it would, for younger workers, provide an outside assessment of who should be registered and in what categories.

It is interesting that opinion among operatives is also now in favour of certification. The OPCS survey found that nearly three-quarters (73 per cent) of employees and 61 per cent of self-employed thought it was a good idea and among the employed there was remarkable agreement among skilled, semi-skilled and unskilled.[16] Skill certification would be beneficial, not only in helping to raise standards generally, but also in dealing with some of the problems of the self-employed.

Entry to the Industry

Reasons for deciding to go into the construction industry were investigated by the OPCS Construction Industry Mobility Study.[17] They found that a small majority of reasons for entering construction are of a positive optimisitc character, having to do with the intrinsic attraction of building being out in the open air and seeking better pay. For unskilled men a majority gave negative reasons such as the only type of work available, or entering or re-entering the industry. About a third of both skilled and semi-skilled men admit to being reluctant recruits to construction. This is part of the result of the low public image in construction aptly described in 1968 by the Central Youth Employment Executive and published as an appendix to the Phelps Brown Committee Report:[18]

> The disadvantages of the construction industry in the eyes of parents can be grouped under two headings:
>
> (1) Conditions of work
> (2) Status and prospects.
>
> So far as the first is concerned some parents discourage their sons from entering the industry because of the degree of casual employment; the likelihood of redundancy or short time during the winter and during economic recessions; and unpleasant conditions, including exposure to bad weather, working at heights, long journeys to work, etc. Parents' own experience of the industry or the experience of relatives can sometimes act as a deterrent.
>
> The second group of objections include a suspicion that many of the crafts have been de-skilled or about to become obsolete; that the industry is technologically backward; that opportunities for promotion are limited; and that there is insufficient differential between the pay of craftsmen and others. Some parents are said to feel that there are undesirable elements in the industry's work force with whom they do not want their sons to mix and that the status accorded to building trade workers is comparatively low. This sort of attitude is more prevalent amongst the parents of able boys. One Youth Employment Officer commented 'The more ambitious the parent, the less likely are they to encourage their sons to enter the industry.'
>
> Although a substantial number of parents have reservations of the industry, it would be wrong to suggest that this attitude is universal. Many raise no objection at all and many are keen for their sons to enter the industry, especially in areas where other opportunities are limited.

There may have been an improvement since 1968 in standards of entry but the public image of the industry is still poor.

However, it is possible that the influence of family is positive. Nearly a third of the OPCS sample had fathers in the building trade but only 7 per cent said they consciously and willingly followed the family tradition.[19] A study undertaken by Hatchett of ILEA craft students in 1978[20] found that 67 per cent of students had some members of the family working in the industry and that 24 per cent of students had members of the family in the same craft.

Some workers come from other industries but 75 per cent had spent all or most of their working lives in the construction industry, 13 per cent had divided their time between construction and other work more or less evenly, and the remaining 12 per cent had worked mostly at other, overwhelmingly manual jobs. Moreover, most of the operatives (89 per cent) were native born. 'Whatever may be the conventional wisdom on the subject, only 6 per cent claim to have been born in Ireland, a further 3 per cent claim Irish fathers.'[21] Thus immigration from outside the industry is not very important in supplying the labour force. Initial entry when young is much more important and this has implications for the importance of training.

Exit from the Industry

Men tend to leave the construction industry earlier than the normal retirement age and this is shown by the age distribution of construction workers compared with those in other industries.

> In other large, long established industries one would expect to find men's age distribution to be divided in half either side of forty. Among the employees in construction 64% are under 40 and only 36% between 40 and 65. This suggests that old men leave the industry in quite large numbers. . . It is certainly noticeable that older men tend to accumulate in public sector employment where 52% are over forty compared to 32% in the private sector. . . It is interesting to note that 43% of currently employed construction workers are thinking about leaving the industry – although possibly only in the vaguest terms, while 54 per cent of the currently unemployed are definitely considering working elsewhere.[22]

Many leave the industry and come back again. The OPCS survey found that 27 per cent of the workforce had worked outside the industry in the last five years at least once and that 5 per cent had done so three or more times. But these had come back again.

Reasons for leaving the construction industry or for thinking about doing so were first for better pay, second, more job security, third, for better working conditions and fourth, health reasons. Then came the lack of work and dismissal.[23] Most of these matters are dealt with below.

One question that should be considered here is where the construction workers who leave the industry go. One possibility is that they seek work abroad and these would be by definition excluded from the OPCS survey. There have been suggestions that the number working in EEC countries was substantial. An article in *Building* in 1981[24] suggested that most of the 10 000 or so 'black market' workers in Holland and West Germany were English or Irish. Government sources are more cautious and say they do not know how many are abroad but it is thought that emigration exceeds immigration. But in any case 10 000 is a very small number.

The National Training Survey of the Manpower Services Commission (MSC)[25] obtained data on carpenters, joiners and bricklayers. Nearly half of those whose first job was in construction were no longer in this occupation in 1975. Some 20 per cent left to go to woodworking occupations in industries other than construction and nearly a quarter were promoted out of the craft occupation, but more than half those leaving construction went to jobs having nothing to do with construction or woodworking, some of the more notable being zookeeper, nautical cook, bookmaker, butcher, jockey, coal-miner, bus-conductor and policeman. It is, however, much more difficult to go into other industries in a period of rising unemployment throughout the economy.

Another possible destination of construction workers is the black economy, that is, where persons are doing jobs without the notice of the tax or national insurance authorities. It is thought that this practice is substantial in the economy generally and construction is an area where it is relatively easy to operate in this way because of the large amount of repair and maintenance by private householders.

Mobility within the Industry

It is not surprising if the client demands new building or civil engineering projects anywhere in Great Britain or abroad, to a specific unique design, and at any time, that employment in the construction industry on new work should fluctuate over all and be casual and erratic for the individual site employee. In fact the repair and maintenance work and rehabilitation and extension work introduces stability and so does the tendency for building to occur in existing centres of population.

The main focus of the OPCS survey[26] was to find out about mobility – voluntary or involuntary – in construction. Although other studies, such as the Phelps Brown Report and the Manpower Services Commission Report, had thrown light on this subject, they were not as single-minded in finding out about mobility specifically in construction. Some of the major findings of the OPCS on the current workforce of the industry are summarised in Table 11.6. From there it will be seen that 40 per cent of the labour force had only one job in the five-year period. Nearly 20 per cent had two but of these only just over a third were made redundant or sacked, the remaining two-thirds presumably being a more or less voluntary change. The likelihood of being made redundant or sacked increases as the number of employments increases. For about 18 per cent of the workforce they had each job only for an average maximum of a year and for a few it was six months and these experienced involuntary changes very often.

TABLE 11.6 Number of employments of current workforce of the industry during the past five years and number of times made redundant or sacked

Number of employments	% of workforce	Number of times made redundant or sacked					
		% by number of employments					
		None	Once	Twice	Three times	Four times +	Total
1	41	97	3	–	–	–	100
2	19	64	31	5	–	–	100
3	13	39	40	18	2	–	100
4	11	27	43	15	11	4	100
5	7	14	21	25	21	18	100
6	5						
7	2						
8–14	4	4	14	20	20	44	100
Total	100	62	20	9	5	4	100

Source:

Marsh, A., Heady, P., and Matheson, J., *Labour Mobility in the Construction Industry*, OPCS (HMSO, 1981 Tables 4.1 and 4.5.

This casual nature of employment is one of the matters that is of concern in the industry and outside it. Its causes are several – first the fluctuations in the level of demands on the industry that mean that the overall demand for labour is not constant; second, the 'allocation' of the work-load among a number of contractors whose own demand for labour fluctuates, especially over geographical areas where it is reasonable for operatives to travel; third, the one-off nature of the project even within individual contractors, so that once a project comes to an end the labour is no longer required; and fourth, within each project the requirement for various trades is not constant but reaches a peak and then declines. Even with perfect organisation, to give constant employment would be difficult and the fluctuations in work-load and the contracting system does not help this situation. One of the main reasons for registration schemes for employees and for employers is that it would facilitate the granting of public-sector contracts only to the registered employers who have accepted the objectives of decasualisation so that vacancies and availability of manpower can be better matched. However, alone it cannot do very much unless there is greater stability of work-load throughout the whole construction industry, planned according to areas and types of work.

Even without a registration scheme, however, the Phelps Brown Committee Report[27] felt that more attention should be given by individual firms to ensure that the vacancies on new jobs are offered to men becoming redundant on others and pointed out the advantages for labour stability of subcontracting and of reducing seasonal fluctuations by better winter building measures.

Conditions of Work

Wages, earnings and hours and insecurity of employment are described in other sections. There are, however, a number of other characteristics of the work of building operatives. The first is the type of work and the general conditions under which it is done. Construction work is generally carried on with very little protection from the weather and involves a large amount of physical effort. Even a skilled worker on a building site is often handling heavy materials or scaffolding and needs to be fit to deal with the work. For repair and maintenance the exposure to the weather may be less for indoor work but most trades involve outdoor work to a large extent. It is, however, a job where the effort can be seen to produce results and may be a highly individual job giving considerable satisfaction.

The weather and nature of the work can be damaging to health and poorer health, which in any case comes with age, decreases the ability of workers to cope with the work conditions. The OPCS survey found that one in six or seven men have some sort of health problem or disability that affects the *kind* of work or *how much* work they can do. Chronic bronchitis, some affliction of the joints or hands like arthritis, or the legacy of some injury and back problems were common complaints. Nearly half of these men thought their complaint could be traced to some accident or contamination of one kind or another. The incidence of disability increases with age and is presumably an important reason for persons leaving the industry before normal retirement age.

Moreover, construction has a very bad record for accidents. In 1981, as shown in Table 11.7, there were 134 fatal accidents and at least 1783

TABLE 11.7   *Accidents in construction compared with other industries, 1981, Great Britain*

I Construction:		
	Employees	*Non employees*
Fatal injuries	105	29
Fatal and all major injuries	1 696	87
All injuries	43 070	n.a.

II Incidence rates in construction and other industries:	
	All injuries per 100 000 employees
Construction	3 970
All manufacturing industries	2 440
mining	13 290
metal manufacture	4 070
All industries	2 000

Source:

Health and Safety Executive, *News Release*, 10 Nov 1982 (HSE, 1982).

fatal and serious accidents. The fatal accidents are more than in all manufacturing industry and compare with 62 in 1981 in mining, a notoriously dangerous industry. The incidence rates for all injuries are higher in construction than in any other industry except metal manufacture.[28]

A high proportion of fatal accidents in construction is caused by falls and roofing workers, painters and scaffolders are particularly at risk. Reasons are that the men work in small groups, the work is repetitive, there is usually an incentive scheme to work quickly, the work is dangerous and attracts men who find this stimulating, and as the men are specialists the main contractor does not like to interfere. Another important point is that most of the accidents that occur could have been prevented.[29] A safety campaign is being mounted in 1983. It is hoped it will help to reduce the accident level.

The high mobility of the construction industry means that certain benefits such as sickness pay and company pensions, which are often available to manual workers in manufacturing industry, have not been available in construction. This is being to some extent overcome. (See pp. 214–15.)

Unemployment

Statistics are no longer regularly collected for unemployment in construction. Using Department of Employment figures, in May 1982 it was about 25 per cent of total employed plus unemployed in construction compared with the national figure of about 11 per cent.[30] Part of the reason for this very high level of construction unemployment is the large decline in the level of construction work. Part is the casual nature of employment which means that construction has long periods when its unemployment level is higher than the national average and in part it is due to the nature of the statistics. In the statistics the unemployed are allocated to industries according to the last job held. Because construction is a casual industry, it is often possible for the unemployed from other industries to find a job – usually unskilled – in construction and from then until they obtain their next job they are allocated to construction unemployed. It is not known how important this factor is but it will not substantially alter the disastrous situation. Not only is the level of unemployment a tragedy for the persons concerned but it is also a waste of national resources.

A cessation of the very considerable pressures on the construction industry to increase output is an opportunity to utilise the spare resources to undertake work which is badly needed but always previously got squeezed out by other apparently more urgent demands or demands with more financial influence. This has not been done in spite of the relatively small cost in public-sector borrowing requirement (see Chapter 1), and the high level of unemployment with its appalling waste of resources and human misery continues.

Trade Unions

The trade union membership is relatively low in construction on account of the casual nature of employment, the large number of small firms and the self-employed. Only 40–50 per cent of directly employed operatives are members of a union but less than 30 per cent of all operatives.

The Union of Construction, Allied Trades and Technicians (UCATT) was formed in 1971 by amalgamation of notably the Amalgamated Society of Woodworkers, the Amalgamated Society of Painters and Decorators, the Association of Building Technicians and the Amalgamated Union of Building Trades Workers representing essentially trowel trades – notably bricklayers and stonemasons. These unions had been working together in the National Federation of Building Trades Operatives (NFBTO) but merger was a different matter. However, all the unions were suffering severe loss of membership and finance due to the growth of labour-only subcontracting and thus saw the necessity to merge. The process was eventually completed at the end of 1971.[31] UCATT represents many skilled craftsmen in the industry including a high proportion in direct labour organisations and its membership at the beginning of 1983 was about 278 000. Financial problems persist in spite of merger.

The Transport and General Workers' Union (TGWU) is the second largest union in construction. The construction section includes not only site operatives but also transport workers in construction and construction materials. Its operative membership in construction at the beginning of 1983 was estimated at about 65 000. These members are mainly in the civil engineering side of the industry and in semi-skilled and unskilled trades, although the plasterers' union merged with the TGWU some years ago. Backed as it is by the resources of the TGWU, its financial position is satisfactory and its membership is said to be increasing. The link with the FMB through BATJIC may help to increase membership.

The General and Municipal and Boilermakers and Allied Trades Union (GMBATU) have generally non-craft members, many of whom work in direct labour organisations of public authorities and in building material producers. The Furniture, Timber and Allied Trades Union (FTAT) membership in construction has mainly woodworking machinists, french polishers, etc. in construction joinery shops including some in the DLOS. The Electrical, Electronic, Telecommunications and Plumbing Union (EETPU) represents the plumbers and the electricians in the construction industry.

These last three unions together probably account in construction for about the same numbers as the TGWU.

Wages and Other Earnings

Wages and conditions of employment are agreed between employers and unions through joint boards for various parts of the industry. They have much in common. All fix minimum wages and extra payment for special respónsibilities or arduous conditions of work. They also fix hours of work including arrangements for shift work, holidays, travel pay, etc. They regulate the conditions of trainees and apprentices. They deal with safety and they all have some form of benefits scheme for death and often for other circumstances too, but with considerable variation from one scheme to another.[32]

The National Joint Council for the Building Industry (NJCBI) is the negotiating body for a large part of the industry. On the union side it is dominated by UCATT with the TGWU, FTAT and GMBATU also being represented. On the employers' side the NFBTE is dominant with the National Federation of Roofing Contractors also represented.

There has for long been a system of holiday stamps and from April 1982 a lump-sum retirement benefit has been paid. The source of funds for this is a £50-million surplus on the holidays with pay and death benefit schemes plus 50p week per person paid by employers. There is now pressure to extend the scheme to annual pension benefits.

The Civil Engineering Construction Conciliation Board (CECCB) negotiates civil engineering wages. There the TGWU is the dominant union with the FCEC on the employers' side. The NJCBI and the CECCB are both concerned also in a joint board for building and civil engineering which regulates matters common to both parts of the industry.

The Building and Allied Trades Joint Industrial Council (BATJIC) negotiates wages and conditions for the FMB operatives with the TGWU on the union side. BATJIC was formed as a result of the FMB being excluded for so long from the NJCBI. When it was offered a place on that body it decided that it was better served by continuing on its own. The TGWU sees it as an opportunity to extend its membership among FMB employees.

The Joint Industry Board for the Electrical Contracting Industry has as the employers' party the Electrical Contractors' Association and the union is the EETPU. It negotiates wages and other conditions. However, it also goes further than the industry boards mentioned above in that it operates a grading system for electricians. Each grade carries its own rates of pay. The JIB is advanced in its benefit scheme for operatives including health and health screening. It is considering establishing an industry based pension scheme on a contributory basis.[33]

The Joint Industry Board for Plumbing Mechanical Engineering Services in England and Wales consists on the employers' side mainly of members of the National Association of Plumbing, Heating and Mechanical Services contractors, but also one from the NFBTE and on the union side, the EETPU. There is a separate board for Scotland and Northern Ireland. The Board is the body responsible for wages and conditions of work of plumbers in the industry. As with the electrical contractors it operates a grading system for plumbers with differential rates of pay for each grade. It too has a benefit scheme. There is a pension scheme for the industry created by the National Association of Plumbing, Heating and Mechanical Services Contractors and the Scottish and Northern Ireland Plumbing Employers' Federation with the EETPU also represented on the board of trustees, This is separate from the Plumbing JIB but in its Industrial Agreement is a requirement that every operative be enrolled in the scheme or a company scheme giving equivalent benefits.

There is concern in the unions that the wages negotiated by these organisations are considerably lower than the rates actually paid and therefore that to some extent an increase in the basic negotiated rates can be offset by less generous bonus payments and attraction money especially in time of recession. In April 1981, for example, carpenters and joiners received an average of £106 gross earnings a week excluding overtime whereas the NJCBI rate at that time for craft operatives including the Guaranteed Minimum Bonus was £80.40 so that at even that time of depression in the industry the actual payments received were over 30 per cent greater than the negotiated rate. For bricklayers the difference was even greater.[34] On the other hand there were still 10 per cent of full-time manual workers in construction whose pay, including overtime, in April 1981 was less than £81 a week.[35] Differentials in the construction industry are not very high. In April 1981 foremen were receiving 24–25 per cent more than craftsmen bricklayers, carpenters and joiners who were in turn receiving 10–11 per cent more than craftsmen mates and building and civil engineering labourers.[36] Recorded average gross weekly earnings in construction are now generally rather lower than in all industries and services but in the boom period of the early seventies they were actually higher.[37]

The above earnings apply to employed persons. There are in addition in construction the self-employed about whom there is virtually no statistical information. However, discussions with contractors suggest that the weekly earnings of self-employed, when they are working, may be two, three or even, exceptionally, four times those of the directly employed persons and the hourly rate may be over double. As discussed in Chapter 7, this causes severe problems in the industry.

Industrial stoppages in the construction industry are few and considerably less in most years, measured in working days lost per 1000 persons in employment, than in industry as a whole. In 1981 there were 78 days lost per 1000 compared with 201 in all industries and services and in 1982 there was even more difference with 43 per 1000 in construction compared with 376 in all industries.[38]

Self-employment and Labour-only Subcontracting

The first major investigation of labour-only subcontracting was undertaken by the Phelps Brown Committee. Most of the advantages and disadvantages found by that committee are still valid and feelings in the industry run high on the pros and cons of labour-only subcontracting. These are dealt with mainly under subcontracting in Chapter 7. However, some matters specific to the manpower are mentioned here.

It is said that labour-only subcontractors, in order to complete their work quickly, do not observe the appropriate safety precautions. Any disregard for acknowledged safety standards puts at risk not only their own lives and safety but also those of others on the site. There are some data on fatal accidents only. In 1978 there were 120 fatal accidents reported under the Factories Act 1961 and there were a further thirty-five that occurred to genuinely self-employed persons mostly on small sites or on works or operations to which the 1961 Act did not apply.[39] This in fact is about the same percentage of self-employed in the total fatalities as self-employed labour in the operative force. But this does not necessarily apply to other accidents. If it is a fact that the safety standards of the self-employed are lower than of other operatives, then this needs to be examined to see how action can be taken to prevent this by education and enforcement of the law. The main contractor must be made to supervise this aspect of his subcontractors' work.

There is the question of training already referred to above. Some contribution of labour-only subcontractors to training is required, and some contribution to the industry's training bill – perhaps by a levy collected through the main contractor. Some large contractors do require labour-only subcontractors to do some training.

In general the operative who chooses to be self-employed does so voluntarily according to the OPCS Survey.[40] Only 14 per cent over all said that they became self-employed because it was the only way of obtaining work. The main reason they gave for becoming self-employed was a desire for independence, especially among those who work always or sometimes direct to the public. Money was also important for those working for contractors. The operative working for himself will be able to pay less tax because he can charge more to expenses. But he has to make provision for periods of unemployment. He has to organise his own work but is able to take time off when he wishes and has a feeling of pride in being his own boss. Many self-employed would regard it as a retrograde step to become directly employed.

However, many construction workers may be working as employed during the day and moonlighting with no tax being paid, or claiming unemployment benefit or social security benefit and in fact also working as a self-employed person for private householders. This is what is meant by the black economy and these catagories are not included in the statistics above.

ADMINISTRATIVE, PROFESSIONAL, TECHNICAL AND CLERICAL

Contractors

The employment of APTC staff has been stable over the last ten years or so. Employment by contractors according to trade of firm is shown in Table 11.8. It is interesting that within the main trades the large differences arise only at larger sizes of firm – above 115 employees. For firms over 1200 employees in building and civil engineering contractors, APTCs account for 35 per cent of the total employment compared with less than 30 per cent for the other two groups. This is partly because these contractors subcontract much of their work, which still has to be managed, so that their employment of operatives is low compared with their gross output and with the APTC employment. It is also because they offer a different type of service including design and build for which they need professional staff. There are similar explanations for some of the differences between specialist trades. The highest proportional employment of APTCs is in the more sophisticated trades, such as heating and ventilating engineers, who undertake a considerable amount of specialist design. It is possible that glaziers are high, partly because of the boom in replacement and secondary glazing. At the other extreme, the low proportion of APTCs in painters, plasterers and carpenters and

TABLE 11.8 *Employment of APTCs by contractors by trade or firm October 1981, Great Britain*

Trade	Number APTCs th	% of total employment %
Main trades:		
General builders	66.1	24.1
Building and civil engineering	55.6	33.0
Civil engineers	14.0	24.1
All main trades:	135.7	27.1
Specialist trades:		
Plumbers	5.0	23.7
Carpenters and joiners	2.8	17.7
Painters	6.2	15.0
Roofers	5.4	26.0
Plasterers	1.7	.15.2
Glaziers	3.2	32.3
Demolition contractors	0.6	19.4
Scaffolding specialists	4.7	28.1
Reinforced concrete specialists	1.2	25.0
Heating and ventilating engineering	16.6	32.9
Electrical contractors	13.0	22.5
Asphalt and tar-sprayers	3.7	24.8
Plant hirers	7.1	25.2
Flooring contractors	1.6	31.4
Constructional engineers	4.0	32.5
Insulating specialists	2.9	24.0
Suspended ceiling specialists	1.0	34.5
Floor and wall tiling specialists	0.8	25.8
Miscellaneous	4.5	28.8
All specialist trades:	86.1	24.8
All trades:	221.8	26.1

Source:

DoE, *Housing and Construction Statistics 1971–1981* (HMSO, 1982) Tables 33 and 36.

joiners is partly due to the nature of the work and partly the large number of small firms who generally employ a lower percentage of APTCs.

Data on the breakdown of APTCs employed by contractors are no longer available. However, in 1976 about 40 per cent[41] were clerical and sales staff, about 30 per cent technical, of whom over half were foremen, and the remainder managerial and professional.

The vital question of training of technical, supervisory and management staff is discussed in Chapter 13.

Direct Labour Organisations of Public Authorities

The basis of the statistics of APTCs employed by public authorities is different from that for contractors because they include all those engaged on the design, management, control, etc. of building and civil engineering work, irrespective of whether the work is to be carried out by the industry's own direct labour force or by a contractor.[42] In 1980 there were 111 000 APTCs employed by public authorities of whom about 87 000 were employed by local authorities and new towns. In all public authorities they accounted for 34 per cent of the total labour force in 1980 and in local authorities and new towns alone 36 per cent of the labour force,[43] but because of the different definition mentioned above, these figures are *not* comparable with those of contractors. Table 11.9 shows the importance of types of APTCs in local authorities and new towns for 1980 - the last year for which this detailed information was collected. It will be seen that the professional staff and the 'other technical staff' are large - presumably mostly engaged on work not connected with the construction operations of direct labour organisations, for example in the design offices of local authorities. By 1981 the total employed APTC staff had fallen to 105 000 in all public authorities and 80 000 in local authorities and new towns.[44]

TABLE 11.9 *Importance of types of APTCs in local authorities and new towns, 1980, Great Britain*

	Number th	% of total APTCs
Technical grades		
Foreman	10.7	12.3
Draughtsmen and tracers	2.3	2.7
Other technical	25.1	28.9
Total technical	38.2	43.9
Managerial	3.9	4.4
Professional staff		
Architects	4.8	5.5
Surveyors	5.0	5.8
Engineers	14.2	16.4
Total professional	24.1	27.8
Clerical and office staff	20.8	23.9
All APTC staff	87.0	100

Source:

DoE, *Housing and Construction Statistics 1970–1980* (HMSO, 1981) Table 50.

12 Productivity and Efficiency of Manpower

DEFINITIONS

Productivity is here defined as some measure of the output per man while efficiency is regarded as the best possible utilisation of resources under given circumstances. Productivity may be difficult to measure and sometimes hard to explain so that the link between productivity and efficiency, which depends in part on the reasons for productivity differences, is weak. No satisfactory means has, however, been found of measuring efficiency. First the question arises as to efficiency for whom to what? An efficient utilisation of resources on a project for a client may mean that which produces the building at the lowest cost in the time required. The contractor will, however, also have to consider the opportunity cost of using, say, his site agent or plant on that site rather than another and it may well have been an inefficient operation so far as his firm is concerned. Moreover, while high output per man may be efficient, yet, if it implies large overtime payments, it may not be the cheapest way to produce. From a national point of view the situation is even more complicated. Although high output per man on the site may be cheapest for the contractor, for the nation as a whole if there is substantial unemployment it could be cheaper in money terms to use more men and pay less unemployment and social security benefits. In social terms, the diminution of unemployment and job satisfaction may be overridingly important. In general, high productivity is desirable, but not at the expense of everything else.

The measurement of output per man is fraught with difficulties and in recent years there have been few attempts to assess it. However, output per man and efficiency in the use of resources are vital data for anyone concerned with understanding or monitoring the industry. Hence an attempt is made here to use the statistics that are available and to comment on them so that at least a start may be made to bring the subject into the light of day.

OVERALL PRODUCTIVITY

There are three main sources of data that may be used to measure output per man in the construction industry. DoE[1] data of the money value of work done by the industry (including value of materials) divided by the corresponding manpower figures; census of industrial production data[2] which give gross value added (i.e. excludes materials) at factor cost per head; and lastly, the national income and expenditure[3] accounts data which give figures of net gross domestic product in construction, that is, wages and salaries, employers' contribution, gross profits of companies and income from self-employment. This is then divided by numbers employed as in the DoE calculation. Thus two methods measure net output, that is, excluding the value of materials, and one measures gross output which includes materials (but avoids double counting of work subcontracted).

The problem with using a gross output measure is that if the value of materials rises but not their quantity and/or the labour to put them in place, then the output per man automatically goes up. If the value of materials rises because more are being used, for example, more bricks of the same type are being laid, then this alone is a good indication of productivity. If, however, the value of materials goes up because gold-plated taps are replacing chromium-plated taps, then efficiency is not rising. Consider two hypothetical office blocks. The first is a four-storey office block with average construction but no lift and no air-conditioning and costs £1 million. The second is identical, except that it has an expensive lift and air-conditioning and costs £1.2 million, that is, the value of the building is higher by 20 per cent. The cost of the lift and the air-conditioning is high but the labour used to install them is relatively low and the amount of labour used on site may increase by 5 per cent. The output per man has increased but has productivity in any meaningful sense? Similarly, if the building uses more factory-made components, the gross output per man in construction rises, because site labour is replaced by factory labour which appears in the statistics of another industry. The major reason for using gross output data is that it is available for a more detailed breakdown than other measures of output.

On the manpower side it is important that the numbers used should correspond with the selected output. This raises problems of how to deal with the self-employed. In fact all self-employed in the DoE statistics are attributed to contractors under 'contractors' output'. The DoE state that 'The value of output tables at both current and constant prices include estimates of the 'unrecorded output' of small firms (including self-employed workers) not on the statistical register.'[4] If direct labour organisations employ the self-employed at all their labour force will be understated and their output per man overstated. Their use of the self-employed is, however, likely to be nil or small since it is against their policy. In the case of the employment figures used with the national income statistics, derived largely from Inland Revenue data, again all the self-employed estimated are included. The 'black economy' manpower and its output would be excluded from both sets of figures. However, the census refers to employees only so that self-employed would not be included with the manpower figures.

The three measures are shown in Table 12.1. It will be seen that in 1970–81 gross output per man fell by 12 per cent. Taking the ten-year period 1971–81, the fall was 16 per cent. The fall in net output was much less. An important reason for the reduction in output per man in recent years is the change in the relative proportions of new work and repair and maintenance.

A calculation based on the man-days required for each £1000 at 1975 prices of output of various types from Table 10.3 shows that 22.7 man-days for the work-load would be required on average for £1000 of work if the mix of work was as in 1971 but 24.5 man-days if the mix of work was as in 1981. This, put another way, means that the change in the mix of work types alone over the ten-year period would reduce average output per man-day from £44.1 to £40.8, or a fall of 7.5 per cent. This represents nearly half the fall in output per man in this period. The reason that net output falls much less than gross output is that new work, which has decreased, has a higher material content, and repair and maintenance, which has increased, has a low material content. Thus if the material content is removed the effect of the change in the mix of output is substantially reduced.

Table 12.1 also shows the index of total output. There seems to be a very definite connection between low productivity and low output. In the 1973 boom, however, gross output per head and net GDP per head turned down before the peak of output was reached and this confirms the generally held view that in 1972 and the beginning of 1973 the industry was operating beyond its proper capacity and that therefore

TABLE 12.1   Output per man from three sources from 1970, 1975 prices

	DoE gross output[a] ÷ DoE manpower £	Census gross[b] value added £	Net GDP[c] ÷ DoE manpower £	Index of[d] total output 1975 = 100
1970	7 299	n.a.	4 231	115.2
1971	7 520	n.a.	4 420	116.2
1972	7 445	n.a.	4 715	117.4
1973	7 048	n.a.	4 261	118.1
1974	6 441	3 795	3 702	106.0
1975	6 407	4 021	3 810	100.0
1976	6 566	4 097	4 046	98.5
1977	6 709	4 132	4 146	98.0
1978	7 105	4 195	4 402	104.5
1979	6 638	3 929	4 137	100.7
1980	6 440	3 594	3 776	95.7
1981	6 342		4 147	83.9
1982				
1983				
1984				

Notes and sources:

[a] Value of work done by all agencies divided by the total number of men in the industry. Great Britain. DoE, *Housing and Construction Statistics 1970–1980* (HMSO, 1981) Tables 9 and 15; DoE, *Housing and Construction Statistics 1971–1981* (HMSO, 1982) Tables 9 and 15.

[b] Gross value added at factor cost per head, that is, gross output minus the cost of purchases (adjusted for stock changes), the cost of work subcontracted out and of other industrial services and of non-industrial services received divided by numbers employed. The figures have been converted to 1975 prices using DoE output price index for all new construction. They refer to the UK. Prior to 1980 the figures were based on the CSO, *Standard Industrial Classification Revised 1968* (HMSO, 1968), but in 1980 they were based on the *Standard Industrial Classification Revised 1980*; Business Statistics Office, *Report of the Census of Production: Construction PA500, 1976–82*, Table 1; DoE, *Housing and Construction Statistics 1971–1981* (HMSO, 1982) Table 2.

[c] Net gross domestic product in construction, that is, wages and salaries, employers' contributions, gross profits of companies and income from self-employment plus self-employed excluding Northern Ireland. (Only operative employment in the UK divided by DoE number employed plus self-employed excluding Northern Ireland. (Only operative employment is available for Northern Ireland as there is not a consistent series till 1976. Since it is change over time that is of most interest, it seemed preferable to use only Great Britain manpower.) The figures have been converted to 1975 prices as above under [b]. CSO, *National Income and Expenditure*, 1981 Edition (HMSO, 1981) Table 3.1; CSO, *National Income and Expenditure*, 1982 Edition (HMSO, 1982) Table 3.1; DoE, *Housing and Construction Statistics 1970–1980* (HMSO, 1981) Tables 2, 9 and 15; DoE, *Housing and Construction Statistics 1971–1981* (HMSO, 1982) Tables 2, 9 and 15.

management was unable to maintain efficiency, including productivity (see also Chapter 10).

Another factor to be considered is that tender prices were very high in 1972 and 1973 and would have contained a higher element for risk, profits and overheads than in the early 1980s. This would increase the differences over time in output per man. Similarly, wages were raised after the 1972 strike.

After the decline in output per man, 1981 shows a small improvement in net output and a fall in the rate of decrease of gross output. It is too soon to judge from one or two years, but it is possible that the industry is beginning to restructure to come to terms with the lower work-load. The industry reports improvements in output per man with the use of more subcontracting but this is not evident in the overall figures.

DIRECT LABOUR ORGANISATIONS AND CONTRACTORS

As has already been mentioned in Chapters 7 and 11, the relative productivity and efficiency of direct labour departments, public authorities and contractors has been a matter of controversy in the last fifteen to twenty years. However, serious attempts have been made to understand and interpret the differences in output per man, notably by Fleming,[5] O'Brien,[6] and Sugden,[7] but the argument is not resolved. Yet since the objective should be to make the best use of resources, it is wrong that so much uncertainty surrounds the efficiency of about 10 per cent of construction resources.

An attempt is made here to re-examine the problem. It must be stressed again that comparisons of productivity are valid only if both output and persons are measured in a comparable way. In construction, because of the diversity of products, the only way to add up production is to use money values. Hence output is expressed in pounds sterling. For contractors this is the value of work done which in turn is the result of past tender prices. For direct labour it is the expenditure.

Until April 1981 local authorities did not make proper allowance for return on capital employed and other elements of profit included in the value of output of contractors. An allowance should therefore be added for this. According to statistics from *Company Finance*,[8] quoted in Table 16.3, the profit on capital employed was about 15 per cent and on turnover about 5 per cent for quoted companies in construction but this includes non-construction activities. Large construction companies had a higher return on capital and a lower one on turnover; 5 per cent is the notional return on capital required from direct labour organisations according to regulations under the Housing and Local Government Act 1980. This seems very low. Probably around 5 per cent or even more should be added to total output of direct labour organisations to take account of the different valuation of their work and contractors' work.

It seems that VAT is now excluded from contractors' output so the two sets of figures would at least since 1977 be comparable in this matter.

There may be some undercounting of men in the public authorities since some of the management may not be attributed to construction activities. On the other hand, construction labour is often used for snow clearance, etc. which is not a construction activity. Thus the number of men may not represent the correct number on construction but there is at the moment no way of making any correction for this - indeed the direction of the correction is not known.

There is overcounting of labour by direct labour departments because there are no figures of APTCs excluding those engaged on professional functions not comparable with contractors generally. Some contractors have architects and others employed on design rather than construction so there is overcounting there too. Because of these complications only operatives are included in most of the numerical analysis.

There is also under-counting of contractors' labour unless all the labour they employ on their output, including labour-only subcontractors, is counted in the total operative force.

The first crude comparison of productivity of the two types of organisations (with local authorities and new towns, which account for about three-quarters of the work done, separately specified) is shown in Table 12.2. For convenience for later comparisons, figures for 1978-81 are given.

Thus in 1981 gross output per man was 77 per cent more for contractors than for direct labour organisations of all public authorities. When the non-comparable APTCs are removed the difference was 43 per cent. The only measure of net output available is that of the census data which before 1980 is split into public and private undertakings. This is not shown in the table because the information is so scant. However, there was a difference of 17 per cent in 1979. This lower figure for net output is due to the exclusion of materials of which very different proportions are used because of the differences in the types of work undertaken.

Account must be taken of the types of work undertaken by the two kinds of organisation. Of the work undertaken by direct labour organisations, 80-90 per cent is repair and maintenance.[9] This is the activity

TABLE 12.2 *Comparison of output per man of contractors and direct labour organisations based only on output and employment statistics from 1978 (current prices)*

	(1) Contractors[a] £	(2) All public[b] authorities £	(3) (1) as % of (2) £	(4) Local[c] authorities and new towns only £	(5) (1) as % of (4) £
Gross output ÷					
Employed[d] and self-employed					
1978	10 610	5 617	189	5 573	190
1979	11 882	6 420	185	6 110	194
1980	14 230	7 794	183	7 532	189
1981	15 464	8 686	178	8 721	177
1982					
1983					
1984					
Gross output ÷					
Employed excl. APTCs[d] +					
Self-employed					
1978	12 808	8 375	153	8 532	150
1979	14 288	9 718	147	9 512	150
1980	17 176	11 812	145	11 688	147

1981	19 055	13 092	146	13 361	143
1982			
1983			
1984			

Notes and sources:

[a] DoE, *Housing and Construction Statistics 1971–1981* (HMSO, 1982) Tables 10 and 15.
[b] DoE, *Housing and Construction Statistics 1971–1981* (HMSO, 1982) Tables 11 and 15.
[c] Annual rate based on one or two quarters. DoE, *Housing and Construction Statistics 1971–1981* (HMSO, 1982) Tables 44, 45 and 47.
[d] Some Administrative, Professional, Technical and Clerical personnel undertake design and other non-contracting activities.

where output per man is relatively low both for contractors and direct labour organisations. There are two possible ways of separating the effects of type of work. The first is to take the estimates of man-days per £1000 of work from Table 10.3 and apply them to the work of direct labour and contractors to see the effect of mix of work assuming the same output per man for each type of organisation. It shows that in 1981 the average man-days required per £1000 of work at 1975 prices for contractors' mix of output would be 23.6 and for direct labour mix of output 30.5. This implies output per man-day of direct labour would be £32.8 and contractors £42.4 on these assumptions, that is, just because of mix of output, contractors' output per man-day would be 129 per cent of that of direct labour departments. This leaves still 17 per cent difference according to a comparison with Table 12.2. Perhaps 5 per cent or so of this is accounted for by the failure to include return on capital employed and some other overheads but still leaving a difference in favour of contractors of over 10 per cent after allowing for mix of work.

The other way of assessing the effect of work mix is possible only up to 1978. Up to and including that year figures were published of operatives employed by contractors by type of work and such data were also available until 1980 for local authorities and new towns. This raises the problem of how to apportion the self-employed by types of work. An indication is that contained in the NFBTE/CITB Study of Manpower 1974[10] but that was based only on the London and Midlands regions and is becoming very out of date. However, there it seemed fairly clear that more labour only was used by firms whose main activity was private housebuilding than by other firms. A more recent indication is that of the payments made to labour-only subcontractors by contractors[11] for new housing, new non-housing and repair and maintenance. In 1978 54 per cent of total payments went on housing, 22 per cent of new non-housing and 24 per cent on repair and maintenance. If these percentages are applied to the total self-employed in 1978 and the split within these totals allocated according to the work of the self-employed, then the data in Table 12.3 may be produced. These total manpower figures and output by types of work are then used to obtain the figures of output per man shown in Table 12.4. It will be noted that the output per man is not always in agreement with the figures of man-days per £1000 of output used in Table 10.3, and especially not for the split within repair and maintenance. In Table 10.3 housing repair and maintenance has a low output per man compared with other but this is reversed in Table 12.4 for the private contractors but not for direct labour organ-

TABLE 12.3 *Labour employed by contractors and allocation of self-employed by broad types of work, 1978, Great Britain*

	Directly employed th	Self-employed th	Total th
New housing:			
Public	105	107[a]	212[a]
Private	88	90[a]	178[a]
Total	193	197	390
Other new work:			
Public	143	35[a]	178[a]
Private	178	45[a]	223[a]
Total	321	80[a]	401
Repair and maintenance:			
Housing	114	42[a]	156[a]
Other public	56	20[a]	76[a]
Other private	68	25[a]	93[a]
Total	237	88	325

Note:

[a] Although the totals are derived from DoE data the split within the totals allocates the self-employed in the same proportion as the employed.

Source:

Based on DoE, *Housing and Construction Statistics 1970–1980* (HMSO, 1981) Tables 14 and 16.

isations. Since the allocation of self-employed within repair and maintenance is arbitrary and since housing is not split into public and private, these results must obviously be treated with great caution. Taking the results of the table it seems that direct labour organisations have as high or higher output per man as contractors on housing but less on other types of work.

Apart from differences in output per man in the broad types of work, within the published types of work the sort of construction may be quite different. The BRE report on resource inputs to construction for house-building[12] throws light on this matter. Whereas the man-days per £1000 or per dwellings of traditional housing for public and private clients (both built by contractors) were about the same, the man-days required for non-traditional housing built largely by local authorites was a little over two-thirds of that for traditional. Similarly there were large differences according to storey heights, etc. No statistics are known of which types of project are let to contractors and which done in-house by direct labour, but there is no reason to suppose that the mix is the same. There will be similar differences in the types of work done in repair and maintenance and improvements by direct labour and contractors. It is known, for example, that public authorities employ about double the percentage of painters in their labour force than that employed by contractors and hence presumably do a lot of painting. But the productivity of painting firms is well below the construction industry average. The position in housebuilding repairs and maintenance is complicated by the very high level of work done on a DIY basis and/or by the 'black economy' which is probably as important or more important than the work by contractors in the repair of housing mostly in the private sector (see Chapter 4). This will leave the contractors to do the larger jobs so that probably, within the housing-repair sector, the types of work done by contractors and direct labour are very different.

The characteristics of the labour force of the two organisational types are different too. Table 12.5 taken from the OPCS survey[13] shows a comparison of the labour forces of contractors and public-sector construction organisations.

The pay of public-sector employees is less and so probably is the number of hours worked[14] with less overtime. This would mean that the cost of the job would be less so that the value of output is less which gives a lower value of output per head.

The private sector has slightly more skilled workers than the public sector which could also partly account for the higher pay. On the other hand, the value of output per man of a skilled worker should be rather higher than that of an unskilled one.

Very important in Table 12.5 is the higher percentage of job security in the public sector coupled with a higher age. The higher age of the men in the public sector with different conditions of employment means that from a national point of view, even if they have lower productivity, their employment may be efficient. For older men who need stability of employment in a particular locality more than younger men, it might be that the alternative to working in direct labour departments would be to leave the industry, in which case their skills might not be utilised and the men's contribution to gross domestic product might be reduced. Another large difference between direct labour departments and contractors is that direct labour departments train fewer than contractors, even

	(1) Contractors excluding self-employed[a] £	(2) Contractors including self-employed[b] £	(3) Local authorities and new towns[c] £	(4) % (2) of (3)
New housing:				
Public	16 000	7 925	10 682	74
Private	27 568	13 629	..	..
Total	21 275	10 528	10 682	99
Other new work:				
Public	19 378	15 567	12 329	126
Private	19 646	15 682	..	..
Total	19 526	15 631	12 329	127
Repair and maintenance:				
Housing	18 105	13 231	7 161 (public only)	185
Other public	15 339	11 303	9 117	124
Other private	14 471	10 581	..	..
Total	16 485	12 022	8 102	148
Total all work	19 041	12 808	8 530	150

Notes and sources:

[a] DoE, *Housing and Construction Statistics 1971–1981* (HMSO, 1982) Tables 10 and 15.
[b] Sources as [a] above but self-employed allocated as shown in Table 12.5.
[c] Based on first and third quarters of year at an annual rate. DoE, *Housing and Construction Statistics 1971–1981* (HMSO, 1982) Tables 45 and 44.

TABLE 12.5   *Comparison of the labour forces of private- and public-sector construction organisations: characteristics of full-time manual employees, age 21 and over*

	Private sector	Public sector
Mean pay last week (£s)	88.9	72.5
Mean length of jobs so far (months)[a]	55	105
% of jobs which have already lasted five years or more	28	57
% classed by employer as:		
Skilled	65	62
Semi-skilled	23	20
Unskilled	12	18
	100	100
% who had completed apprenticeship	36	34
Mean age	38.3	43.3
% aged 51 or over	21	38
Base (men in sector)	815	208

Note:

[a] Excludes 109 individuals who did not give length of job. There was also a smaller amount of non-response to some of the other items in the table.

Source:

Marsh, A., Heady, P., and Matheson, J., *Labour Mobility in the Construction Industr* OPCS (HMSO, 1981) Table 10.9.

if it is assumed that self-employed train none and that the self-employed are included in the contractors (see Table 11.5). In this respect their contribution to long-term efficiency of the industry is low compared with the private sector.

Thus the data on productivity of direct labour organisations and contractors are inconclusive. The broad comparison of output per man seems to show that contractors have a higher productivity but when account is taken of the differences in mix of work, in the way the value of output is calculated and in the labour used, the difference is reduced so that it is doubtful, bearing in mind the assumptions that have to be made and the errors inherent in the figures, whether the remaining differences are significant or not. When a wider view is taken of efficiency of the two organisational types, the balance of advantage favours the direct labour organisations in some respects and contractors in others. The matters discussed above are drawn together in Table 12.6. It is over all

TABLE 12.6 *Factors affecting assessment of real productivity and efficiency of direct labour organisations and contractors and direction of adjustment*

Factors causing adjustment in contractors' favour	Factors causing adjustment in DLO's favour
	Addition to DLO's output to allow for return on capital and full overheads – say, 5 per cent
	Mix of work types (see Tables 12.4 and 12.5)
Mix of work within work types ⟶	
Possible under-counting of managers in DLOs	Men used on snow clearing, etc. by DLOs included in DLOs manpower
⟵ APTCs on non-construction work	
Larger proportion of self-employed probably used on private work than public-sector work (see Table 12.5)	
More training	Lower rate of pay and less overtime
	Higher job security
	Higher age of employees

Notes:

Centre position with arrow indicates that the factor affects both. The arrow indicates the organisational type most likely to be favoured on balance.

not possible to say whether contractors or direct labour organisations are more efficient and therefore the case for whichever side in the unfortunate dispute must be regarded as not proven. The above evidence would suggest that extreme statements on either side should be regarded with very considerable reserve. It would in any case be expected in the case of direct labour organisations, as with contractors, that the range of efficiency with the organisational types is large.

Yet the fact remains that the direct labour departments of public authorities use around 20 per cent of the labour force of the industry. It is high time the matter of their efficiency compared with that of contractors was removed from the political arena to one of calm investigation, in order to facilitate optimum resource allocation.

TRADE OF FIRM

From the DoE figures[15] and from the census of production[16] some comparison can be made of value of output per man for various trades. Unfortunately, however, these two sets of figures do not yield very consistent conclusions and the problem is compounded by lack of information on how to allocate the labour-only subcontractors. There are some data for trade of labour-only subcontractors but it is still not known whether they work for main contractors or specialist contractors. However, some observations may be made.

(a) General builders have a lower output per man than building and civil engineering contractors, combined with a lower proportion of new work and a lower net capital expenditure per head.

(b) Many of the craft trades, notably carpenters and joiners, painters and plasterers, have a low output per head, combined with a low proportion of new work and a low net capital expenditure per head.

(c) Plant hiring firms, with or without operatives, have a high output per head, the very highest of net capital expenditure per head and a high proportion of new work.

SIZE OF ORGANISATION

There are data from the DoE census for the value of work done and employment by size of firm from which output per head may be derived, and also from the census of production. In broad terms the smaller the firm, the lower the output per head. However, as in the case of trade of firm these data exclude labour-only subcontracting. Labour-only subcontracting is used across all types of work and size of firm[17] although the quantitative data are not very satisfactory. However it seems unlikely that the distribution of labour-only subcontracting would be sufficient to invalidate the broad conclusions of the increase in output per head with size of firm up to the very largest firms. One of the reasons for this conclusion is the analysis of output per head by type of work from Table 12.2 combined with the data from Table 7.2. It is clear from this that the small firms do more of the work which by its nature has a low output per head, notably repair and maintenance.

The conclusion reached in the Research Report for the Bolton Committee[18] was that small firms had low productivity because they undertook the type of work that had low productivity and that efficiency was unlikely to differ as much as productivity due to such factors as different work within work type groups, shorter hours and lower earnings in smaller than in large firms and the size of contracts.

Firms employing 1200 and over from DoE figures and 2500 and over from the census show a different situation, however. Their output per head is less than the immediately lower size groups. Presumably one of the reasons is the high proportion of APTCs employed – 36 per cent which does not go down easily if work-load falls. Some of this will be used not in construction but on design. Lastly, it is possible that the distribution of labour-only subcontracting by firms of various sizes distorts the picture. This would imply that the very large contractors employ less labour-only subcontractors than the sizes immediately below them and this is indeed possible.[19]

There are similar data for public authorities prior to 1980 from the census[20] and from the DoE for local authorities and new towns.[21] Here the pattern is more erratic than for contractors and few conclusions can be drawn.

13 Management

Management is a vital input for the construction industry at the level of the site, the firm and the total process. Because of the differences in qualifications for management and the type of management required, there are differences between building and civil engineering and these will be discussed separately where relevant. Management is interpreted as the control over operations at all levels which range from supervision of men on site to major decision-making in the firm and the total process.

SITE MANAGEMENT – BUILDING

Because of the multiplicity of inputs to a site in building, the fact that each project is a one-off operation open to the vagaries of weather and the difficulties of managing large numbers of men working together often for the first time, the number of *ad hoc* decisions that have to be taken by site managers is very great. Moreover, the diversity of conditions from one site to another and the particular characteristics of each site mean that these decisions have to be taken by the man on site often without reference to seniors at head office or to any information apart from his own personal knowledge and often in response to some particular problem necessitating quick action. This is why management on construction sites is often described as crisis management.

By comparison most factory processes are carried on by very clearly defined past practices and often are dictated by the fixed plant and machinery. There are relatively fewer management decisions and those large ones that are taken are often helped by group discussion with colleagues with a reasonable time period in which to consider.

The cost of poor management on site is measured, not in the direct costs of management, which are basically the managers' remuneration and are small as a percentage of the total costs, but by increases in total costs of other inputs to the construction process or failure to reduce costs. Poor management can increase the cost of materials, because of wastage due to bad storage, pilfering or lack of care in use. It can increase the cost of labour because of low productivity, poor workmanship resulting in the need for rectification, and wastage of time between jobs because of inadequate planning of the flow of operations. It can increase the cost of subcontractors because poor planning may mean that they cannot start on site on time and therefore can generate claims against the main contractor. It can increase the costs of plant because of low utilisation and improper maintenance. All these things taken together and combined with the need for constant vigilance on such matters as labour relations and bad weather precautions may mean that the costs to the firm of a poor management team on site are very high indeed and can turn a potentially profitable contract into one making a substantial loss.

Remarkably little global data are available about who are the managers on site, their backgrounds and the training they have received. There is even less information on types of managers who would be required if they were available and more information would assist considerably in determining appropriate training and educational programmes. Moreover, the types of managers required and their training change in relation to the types of work undertaken in the industry. In particular the repair and maintenance and rehabilitation work, which is forming an increasing proportion of the total, requires a different type of management still from new construction.

There are several paths to management on building sites, broadly classified as follows:

(a) from crafts through foremen to general foremen and hence to other levels of management
(b) entry from school as a management trainee
(c) entry with some Technician Education Council (TEC) or Scottish Technical Education Council (SCOTEC) Award or National Diploma in Building (Scotland) and thence through experience to various levels of management
(d) entry with some CIOB qualification and similar progression
(e) entry in mid-career from some other related fields.

The six categories overlap in that entrants originally from the crafts or from school may obtain TEC or CIOB qualifications and those with TEC qualifications or a degree may well take CIOB qualifications. It is unusual

TABLE 13.1 *Technician training in construction*

TEC awards	SCOTEC and National Diplomas Scotland
Certificate 3 years' day release	Certificate 3 years' day release
Higher Certificate 2 years' day release	Higher Certificate 2 years' day release
Diploma 2 years' full time	Ordinary National Diploma 2 years' full time
Higher diplomas 2 years' full time or 3 years' part time	Higher National Diploma 3 years' sandwich
Specialisations possible are	Building Technician Quantity Surveying Technician Architectural Technician

Source:

Based on Building Industry Careers Service, *Opportunities in Building Management* (Careers Leaflet) (BICS, 1981).

for construction managers to come from other industries. There are several levels of TEC training, or the Scottish equivalent, as shown in Table 13.1. These various certificates and diplomas and their predecessors in the certificate and diploma qualifications enable the student to obtain entry to the CIOB at various levels, as shown by Figure 13.1. There are various problems in the system which may be resolved by discussions going on between educationalists and the industry and the CIOB is discussing new routes to membership. In the TEC system, for example, there is no link on to further education after the higher diplomas. The system is not geared to the needs of the small firms in the industry whose staff cannot leave their work for this type of education. One difficulty in this connection is that possibilities for evening study are dying out. Moreover, even within the scheme as it operates, the original modular system in the teaching with a central core and a choice of subjects beyond that is being eroded by cuts in budgets of technical colleges and by transfer of staff on to the development of craft courses for the massive first-year YTS entry. Lastly, there are some functions within the industry, such as purchasing and foreman, for which little training is available specifically for construction. The present tendency towards increased subcontracting as well as the increased qualified entry to construction

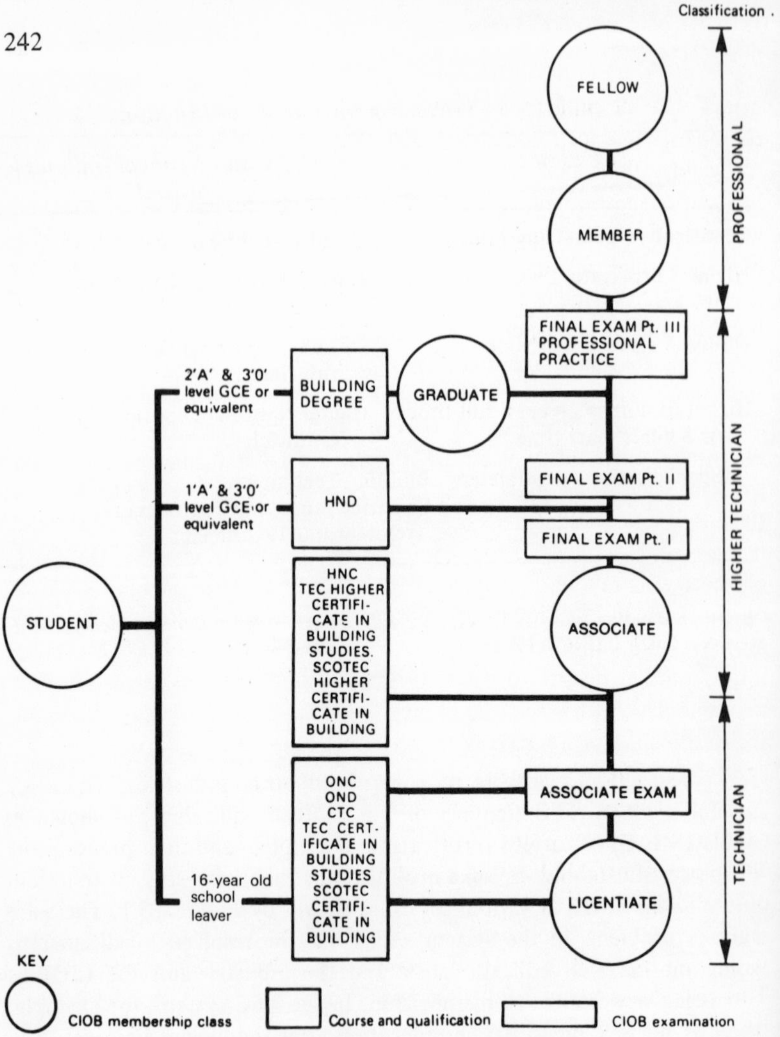

Classification .

FELLOW

MEMBER

PROFESSIONAL

FINAL EXAM Pt. III
PROFESSIONAL
PRACTICE

2'A' & 3'O'
level GCE or
equivalent

BUILDING
DEGREE

GRADUATE

1'A' & 3'O'
level GCE or
equivalent

HND

FINAL EXAM Pt. II

FINAL EXAM Pt. I

HIGHER TECHNICIAN

STUDENT

HNC
TEC HIGHER
CERTIFI-
CATE IN
BUILDING
STUDIES.
SCOTEC
HIGHER
CERTIFI-
CATE IN
BUILDING

ASSOCIATE

ONC
OND
CTC
TEC CERT-
IFICATE IN
BUILDING
STUDIES
SCOTEC
CERTIFI-
CATE IN
BUILDING

ASSOCIATE EXAM

16-year old
school
leaver

LICENTIATE

TECHNICIAN

KEY

⬤ CIOB membership class   ▭ Course and qualification   ▭ CIOB examination

Notes:

1. This diagram shows only the principal routes to Institute membership and does not include transfer routes from one course to another.

2. For admission or transfer to the classes of Member, Associate and Licentiate it is essential to comply not only with the Institute's academic requirements but also with the requirements covering practical experience in building. The regulations governing transfer from the Member class to Fellowship are obtainable on request.

Source:

Chartered Institute of Building, *Yearbook and Directory of Members 1982-83* (CIOB, 1982), p. 17.

FIGURE 13.1   *Principal routes to membership of CIOB*

means that the industry is having problems in the supply of foremen. A training scheme for foremen would assist in this respect.

Qualifications alone do not make good managers and many who have had experience of all aspects of work on site are first-class managers without any formal qualifications. Just because a man has a degree in building it does not mean that he will ever be able to manage a building site well. Nevertheless, with the increasing technological content of building and of management as such, training helps. One problem is that the sifting that now takes place in the educational system may well mean that those with general ability, including management ability, do get selected by the educational system and therefore that a craftsman is less likely now than thirty years ago to become a senior manager. If this is the case, then they must be recruited from elsewhere. Membership of the CIOB and graduates are possible sources and so are those starting as management trainees. However, a major problem with all forms of management training is that it is very difficult to develop the personality of the man in the direction of improving his ability to manage men. Moreover, for those who are learning to manage by progression from one job to another on site, the job is so demanding that it is not realistic to take one day off a week and evening courses are dying out. Yet many of the best managers are 'grown' by their employing contractors by planned site training and experience.

Some data on the jobs being done by members of the CIOB will become available from a survey currently being undertaken by the Institute. There are some 9000 full members of the CIOB and in 1975 probably only about a quarter were working on sites.[1] This would mean, if the same percentages apply, that only just over 2000 CIOB full members were working on site in 1983 and most of these were probably young. This may be compared with new orders for projects of over £500 000, many of which will last over a year, of well over 3000 in 1981. However, the CIOB is the professional institution with the most emphasis on management as a subject in its professional examinations.

Then there are the graduates who are not necessarily members of the CIOB, although most probably become so. The number of building degree students has been rising steadily year by year and in 1981–2 was over 1400 with a final year output probably about 250. In that year there were also 600 building surveying students and 2500 quantity surveying degree students, some of whom might ultimately go into construction industry management.[2]

In addition, there is a handful of postgraduate courses on construction management each with a different emphasis on the management of the project, the firm or on an understanding of the way the industry works.

The interpretation of the statistics of various types of technician training is difficult because the old system is being phased out and the TEC system is slowly replacing it. There does seem to have been a decrease in technician training in the recent past. In 1981-2 in Great Britain there were about 24 000 students on general building courses and special courses for CIOB examinations, of which 17 000 were on TEC or SCOTEC courses. Of these about half were studying for a building technician function and the other half were seeking technician training in building surveying, quantity surveying or architecture.[3] In very broad terms, about 3000 students were added each year to the stock of building technicians and another 3000 to the stock of related disciplines.

Using the data on APTCS in Chapter 12, there are probably a maximum of about 200 000 persons employed by contractors and the public authority who could benefit from some form of technician training. If each person stayed in the industry for, on average, thirty years then the requirement for technician training would be 6700 a year. The existing training would provide, say, half or rather over half that figure, the remainder being met by learning on the job, etc. But there is insufficient data on requirements in this area.

It is difficult to judge whether the current rate of increase of the stock of well-qualified persons is adequate. Certainly if comparison is made with the fifties and first half of the sixties, when there was a great movement towards improving the standards of the industry in technology and especially in management, then the present situation is very satisfactory. About four-fifths of the present degree courses in building have been established since 1965. The membership of the CIOB (then IOB) in 1965 was about half the present figure. Yet still there are signs in all sorts of ways that the industry is short of management ability and it would be difficult to find any knowledgeable person in the industry to assert that the standard of management over all is satisfactory. The real question is whether the present trends will bring sufficient improvement or whether there is need for further action. It seems that:

(a) the great majority of small new work jobs and maintenance work is, and is likely to continue to be, run by persons who have had a craft training rising to foreman and then being put in charge of a job

(b) the larger firms accept that there is a place for the building graduate in site management but not to the exclusion of all others. They are in fact recruiting increasing numbers of graduates

(c) medium-sized firms are split on the merits of employing graduates but again the trend is towards their acceptance
(d) it is generally accepted that there is a role for the intermediate type technician qualifications
(e) many large firms run their own training schemes that they regard as the best way to ensure the supply of managers.

In the light of the above a personal view on the future needs is that the present educational and professional institutions, including the CNAA, which is responsible for twelve of the twenty-one degree courses, and the CIOB, may be left to carry on their work at the rate they are now with their continued striving to improve standards. This alone may be sufficient to increase the stock of well-trained people in management to meet requirements, once the effects on the total generation of managers have worked through the system.

There may be a need to improve the supply of technicians and to provide industry training for some of the specialist head office staff. In addition, there is a shortage of foremen and general foremen which is probably a contributory factor to the increased reliance on subcontractors who are responsible for supervision, and the reliance on these subcontractors reduces the potential supply of foremen.

There remains a need to help in other areas which have little to do with formal educational qualifications. One is to upgrade the knowledge of the existing managers in the industry. The professions are currently discussing Continuing Professional Development (CPD) and the CIOB is one of the professional institutions in favour of this.[4] It is to be hoped that when their scheme is finally produced it will attract a large proportion of their members and will have a substantial management component in it. But this does nothing for the development of the non-professionals.

Various schemes have been produced to help in the improvement of management in contractors but, with the exception of the Building Advisory Service (BAS) of the NFBTE, they have mostly foundered. BAS was established after the Second World War, originally with Marshall Aid Funds, and is now part of the NFBTE. Its orientation seems to be towards training in management techniques rather than any educational role which will uplift the overall approach to management in the industry. In the early sixties a Building Advisory Service with a management bias similar to that of the then National Agricultural Advisory Service (NAAS) was proposed. The only proposal actually to emerge was for the inclusion of some management advisory role in the Construction Industry Research and Information Association (CIRIA) but this was not well supported and was soon dropped. Then the CITB was to have a major role in management training and advice, but that was reduced in one cut after another to a very small contribution. A similar fate has befallen other schemes and courses run by private consultants for the industry have been substantially reduced. The industry does not support the schemes which possibly are unsuited to the perceived requirement of the industry. But the overall need to improve management remains. In particular there is a need to improve the management of the smaller firms in the industry, who cannot afford the time during the day to obtain further qualifications, and there is no provision for them in the evening.

SITE MANAGEMENT – CIVIL ENGINEERING

The source of managers for civil engineering sites is qualified professional engineers normally members of the Institution of Civil Engineers. Until recently the ICE concerned itself very little with management either in the formal training of engineers or in its interest in research or dissemination of information to members of the Institution.

The civil engineers did not see management as a problem and this view was supported or acquiesced in by many other organisations concerned with the industry. It is interesting to speculate as to why this was so. First, civil engineering, not only in design but also in construction, has a very high technological component. The major problem of a civil engineer in charge of a site was often how it was possible technically to construct the required works at all, and if he could solve the technological problems, then he had achieved the objective. With much greater experience of complex civil engineering works, the technical problems on most works have become smaller and other needs of the client, notably construction to a cost and time budget, have increased in their relative importance. This requires more management control over resources.

Another factor is that because of the technical requirements on site and because of tradition, on a civil engineering project of even medium size are a large number of qualified civil engineers only some of whom will be required for higher management functions. It is therefore possible for a sifting process to operate so that the civil engineers with aptitude for management are sorted out from those with mainly technical ability.

Lastly, the profession of civil engineer seems to attract persons with more interest in management than the architect, for example, partly because the responsibilities of civil engineers traditionally cover the whole range of professional skills on site including measuring and cost control.

Changes are now taking place in that contractors are tending to put some other specialists, such as quantity surveyors and accountants, on civil engineering sites to perform functions previously undertaken by civil engineers, and the civil engineers are realising that they have to demonstrate expertise in these areas. Moreover, the change of emphasis of client requirements as mentioned above has introduced a need for greater control over cost and time for which better specialised training is seen as necessary. In many contracts, especially those abroad, the contractor has to be able to manage, not only the initial construction of the works, but also its operation, and here again a great variety of skills have to be brought in and co-ordinated by the managing civil engineer.

The Chilvers Report[5] recommended substantial changes in the education of civil engineers. In the professional examination part II, the engineer now is required to show the possession of a working knowledge of engineering management. However, the formal training for this, off-the-job, will not be more than at most fifteen days and this may not be sufficient for the future, although it must be realised that some engineering degress include some component of management in their curriculum. The Institution of Civil Engineers does not yet have any programme of CPD.

At a lower level of site management the TEC qualifications provide the technician entry just as in building. In addition, it is realised that there are many civil engineering graduates who will not achieve full corporate status of the Institution of Civil Engineers and they will potentially form another category of site personnel.

MANAGEMENT OF THE CONTRACTING FIRM

Most contracting firms are run at board level by persons who had a background in site management in building or in civil engineering although specialists from other branches of the industry may also play their part. The sifting process often ensures that those in charge in large firms are those who have considerable ability and knowledge of management and the firms are large enough to be able to accord the necessary specialists for detailed advice. Problems arise more at the medium- and small-size firms.

In the largest firms of contractors the civil engineer has formed a major component of management within the firm, because, until fairly recently, the builders did not have the pool of trained personnel. It would be expected that this position will slowly shift to a more balanced relationship.

The training for management in the firm consists first of the CIOB qualification which encompasses management of the firm in the final part II exam. However, those graduates who obtain exemption will not necessarily have covered this aspect of management in their degrees. Indeed most do not. Second, there are the postgraduate courses referred to under the above, some of which are helpful. Third, there are the various general management courses from the Diploma in Management Studies to postgraduate courses at universities or business schools which are more relevant to the construction firm than the construction project for which general courses have little relevance. The civil engineers do not have training specifically in the management of firms.

Once again the smaller firms have difficulty in freeing persons to attend these courses and it is they who would need help most.

MANAGEMENT WITHIN THE PROFESSIONS

Apart from the CIOB most of the professions are concerned with design and therefore need to be able to manage the design process and the design office, whether it be within a public authority, or within a professional practice or other organisation. Abilities in this respect are very mixed and the attention that the various institutions devote to this aspect of management in their training varies considerably. The RIBA has delegated most of the determination of standards and courses to the recognised schools of architecture and most of these have very little management in their curriculum. Moreover, the selection process of students for architecture tends to concentrate on those interested in design rather than on the production process and such courses on management as are on offer often have a poor take-up rate. The increasing complexity of design education, with an even greater technology component, also tends to preclude the devotion of much of the course to management. To some extent this is rectified in the professional practice final examination which includes a requirement for knowledge of running an office, design management and project control. It is, however, a very small part of the total educational process.

As in the case of building, there was in the RIBA in the sixties a great interest in improvement of management and this was evidenced in the publication of *The Architect and His Office*[6] and the *Handbook of Architectural Practice and Management* including the Plan of Work.[7] These have borne fruit in the present professional practice examination which will, as in the case of all changes in education, take a whole generation to have impact. Nevertheless, as with building, few would give high marks for architects as managers and the management component of education is not enough. This could be helped by the Professional Practice Membership scheme but as this stands at the moment it would do little to assist on the management side. It also could be helped by a scheme of CPD but the RIBA has not yet produced a practical scheme, and in the past in running seminars, etc. has been put off by poor response.

The RICS in its recent syllabuses for quantity surveyor membership has a substantial management component, and many of the degree courses that are a route to membership have a management component. An interesting development in recent years is that the RICS is the first professional institution to make CPD compulsory on new members and that some of the courses run for them are also extremely well attended by senior personnel in private practice. Few of these courses deal explicitly with management but it is planned to add this to those on offer. The merger of the IQS with the RICS may ultimately have an effect on the weighting of contractor management in the professional examinations. The CIBS has virtually no management component in its membership requirements.

The Institution of Civil Engineers has no specific reference to management within the professional firm in its professional examinations, although it may be touched on in the general management. Again the consulting engineers have appeared to be better managers than architects, partly because of the same factors as mentioned under site management and because of the high proportion of work abroad, which has perhaps forced a keen practical approach to management of the firm.

Technicians often play a substantial role in design practices. There are some difficulties in this area in most of the professions. Institutions with a Royal Charter are limited in the privileges they can give non-corporate members and at the same time the possibility of climbing the ladder has been reduced by the change in most institutions from some form of articles to degree entry with difficulties in obtaining evening study courses. The status of technicians is in a state of flux.

MANAGEMENT OF THE PROJECT

Because of the increasing fluidity in the way in which the project is run, the leader of the team can be from any original discipline (see Chapter 3). However, the qualifications to manage a building project vary considerably. If the architect is to retain his traditional role of the client's main adviser and team leader he will have to change his attitude towards management and RIBA must promote more management education and training. If this is not done, the number of important projects where he is the team leader will dwindle further. This role will be taken over by the contractor who, with the increasing number of CIOB members and building graduates, is probably better equipped on the management side to do this (although not necessarily on other counts). Moreover, his attitude is one orientated towards management. The other main contender for the role is the quantity surveyor who is striving to take a more central part in the process. His education too has, before the recent changes, lacked the breadth of view required. But the evidence from CPD is that he is anxious and willing to take up opportunities to improve the situation. He could become a strong contender for a leading role in many projects.

There seems no major threat at the moment to the civil engineer, either employed by a consultant or by a contractor as the professional leading the team in the civil engineering work, and, because of the technical nature of the work, there have been few instances of the contractor taking the lead. Another reason for this is that most civil engineering work is for a continuing public-sector client who has a substantial staff of qualified civil engineers who are able to act as the client's project manager.

However, on building projects the client's project manager may be from outside the client's organisation. It has been said earlier (Chapter 3) that the original discipline of the project manager is unimportant compared with other characteristics and this will remain true. However, the background education will help to determine these and a strong management component is important. To superimpose this at the stage of the postgraduate degree in project management is less easy if the spark is not there from previous encounters with the subject.

There is undoubtedly a need for a manager who sees the total construction project process against the background of the industry as a whole and the need for an integrated approach is argued by Andrews.[8] However, he will be of little value to the industry unless he also has a strong technical competence. In the present situation the broad management education is best provided in post-professional education by full- or part-time study for a degree or diploma and more generally by continuing exposure to new ideas in lectures and seminars. These should not be restricted to members of a particular professional background for it is in interdisciplinary discussion that most progress towards integration of the industry can be made.

14 Materials

USAGE OF MATERIALS

It is estimated in Table 10.6 that materials in 1981 accounted for about 37 per cent of the value of all construction output or about £8000 million in 1981 prices. If the DIY materials are included it is nearer £10 000 million. For new building work, however, the estimate is well over 40 per cent and this is compensated by the lower overall figure of 30 per cent for repair and maintenance and 35 per cent for new civil engineering. However, within these estimated figures for each group the range is great – from about 15 per cent for some repair and maintenance and some new civil engineering work to probably 75 per cent for some new building work involving a high proportion of expensive components.

The relative significance of various construction materials by value in the latter seventies is shown in Figure 14.1. The most important bulky materials are timber, cement (including its use in partially manufactured or manufactured products), aggregates, bricks and blocks and steel. Services use a large range of individual items that together have a high value. Estimates of the usage of some of the main materials are shown in Tables 10.4 and 10.5. Both these tables are based on extensive research by BRE (referred to in Chapter 10).

SOURCES OF MATERIALS

Materials for construction are produced mainly in Great Britain with the major exception of timber, most of which is imported. The manufacturers of construction materials, because of their great diversity, are found in a large number of industries, only some of which supply their output almost entirely to construction – for example, cement and

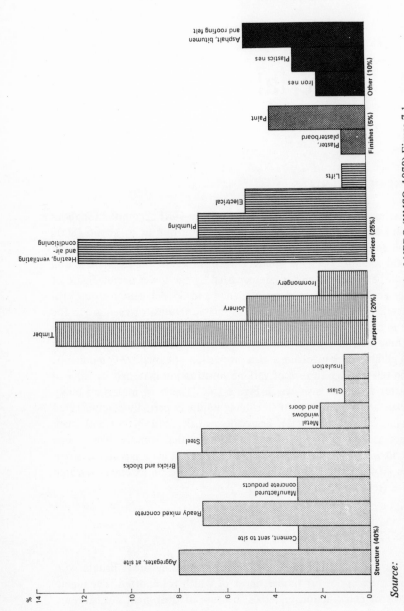

Source:

EDCs for Building and Civil Engineering, *How Flexible is Construction?* NEDO (HMSO, 1978) Figure 7.1.

FIGURE 14.1 *Estimated relative significance by value of construction materials*

concrete products, bricks and plasterboard. Many products, such as plastics and electric cable, used in building come from industries where construction is a relatively unimportant customer. The National Council of Building Material Producers represents interests of material producers on a number of construction industry organisations including the Economic Development Committees for Building and Civil Engineering and the Group of Eight.

TABLE 14.1 *Indices of imports of construction materials and components and of construction output from 1974 (1975 = 100)*

Year	Imports of materials	Output all work
1974	105	106
1975	100	100
1976	108	99
1977	97	98
1978	107	104
1979	114	101
1980	101	96
1981	100	84
1982		
1983		
1984		

Source:

DoE, *Housing and Construction Statistics 1970–1980* (HMSO, 1981) Table 61; DoE, *Housing and Construction Statistics 1971–1981* (HMSO, 1982) Table 57 and Table 1.

Imports of forty-five categories of construction materials in 1980 had a total value of £1668 million,[1] over 20 per cent of all materials used by the industry, but considerably less than 20 per cent if the DIY materials are included. Table 14.1 shows an index of the value of these imports from 1974 at 1975 prices, compared with the index of the output of construction. Thus the low level of activity in construction has not led to a decrease in material imports. To some extent this is because a large part of the fall is in civil engineering which uses few imported products. However, it would be expected that this would, at least in part, be offset by the rise in repair and maintenance work which also uses relatively little material. A more detailed investigation shows that of the forty-five materials or products listed, only thirteen have decreased in real terms while the remaining thirty-two items have increased. It is only because those that have risen less than the average include the very large items of timber – plywood, laminboard, etc. – and copper and copper manufactures, which suffer from depression of commodity prices in a world recession, that the rise in imports has been kept at reasonable levels.

The Building and Civil Engineering EDCs listed[2] five groups of imports:

(a) wood and other raw materials that are unobtainable in required quantities and qualities in the UK. These account for nearly half the value of all imports

(b) items temporarily in short supply often due to an unexpected rise in demand. Sanitary ware in the period of the hotel subsidy under the Tourism Act 1969 or plumbing and insulation materials in the housing improvement boom of the late 1970s are examples

(c) materials in which a foreign supplier has become established as a secondary source of supply, often originally in a previous shortage

(d) products regarded as superior in some way to those available domestically. Examples are architectural ironmongery, tiles, aluminium windows

(e) products that are cheaper and/or of lower quality than those available in Great Britian. Examples are wooden doors, cast-iron manhole covers, steel baths and electric cables.

Further detailed investigations of the reasons for imports was reported in a follow-up study of six product groups: wooden doors, frames, kitchen units, particleboard, ceramic tiles, cladding/decking and air-conditioning units.[3]

STANDARDS

An important element in the choice of products is the standards to which they are produced. Many products have a standard set by the British Standards Institutions (BSI). There have been considerable problems in this respect. The first is that the cost of the reports are high so that full sets will not be found in all design offices even though the membership subscription which includes an entitlement to cheaper reports is biased in favour of small organisations. Second, the BSI operates through committees of persons who are acting without pay and are busy in their own specialist fields of operation. The meetings of the committees are often held at long intervals and the whole process may be cumbersome and lengthy although in specific cases it can be speeded up. There is also the problem of at what level standards should be set and manufacturers have varying interests, dependent on the end of the market at which they operate. A high-quality manufacturer will be in favour of high standards because he can meet these, but his competitors may have problems. Others want bare minimum standards. A range is probably required with guidance on for what purpose various levels of standards are suitable. In practice, nowhere near all the products bought conform to a British Standard. It is reported that the GLC stated that at one of its establishments only 50 per cent of products delivered were actually covered by British Standards. Building regulations refer to BSI standards only in relation to health, safety, fire and energy conservation. A BRE investigation[4] showed that in most cases products tended to be at the lower end of the assessment scale. The poor degree of quality performance was often due to lack of data on performance in use. Sampling procedures were generally inadequate; and few British standards included procedures for quality control in manufacture. In addition to product standards, the BSI has responsibility for codes of practice.

Where there is no British Standard the Agrément system can be used under which a product is tested by the British Board of Agrément and if it is satisfactory a certificate is issued. The problem is that manufacturers find the time taken to undergo the process is too long, so that a market may have been lost while approval is awaited.

Government is concerned at the role of standards and the Advisory Council for Applied Research and Development set up a working group on standards. Its report, *Facing International Competition: The Impact on Product Design of Standards, Regulations, Certification and Approval*,[5] covers a broad field but included a case study on metal and plastic window frames. The DoE is concerned at ministerial level to use standards in public purchasing to make British products more competitive internationally. The Property Service Agency (PSA) is helping to implement this policy through its reviews of a large number of standards and by making some of them mandatory for PSA work. The Building Economic Development Committee is strongly supporting this work and the policy behind it.

FLUCTUATIONS IN SUPPLY AND STOCKS

The requirements for building materials clearly are dependent on the levels and types of output of the industry. A buffer in the process of

TABLE 14.2 Stock of selected materials at end of year as percentage of deliveries in year from 1970

Year	Bricks (Great Britain) %	Cement (UK) %	Clinker[a] (UK) %	Concrete roofing tiles (Great Britain) %	Plasterboard (Great Britain) %	Slate (Great Britain) %
1970	9.0	2.6	6.2	9.7	4.2	17.5
1971	4.0	2.5	5.5	9.9	5.8	18.5
1972	2.6	2.5	7.3	13.4	5.7	13.9
1973	5.2	1.7	4.2	8.7	3.3	7.6
1974	18.5	2.2	5.8	16.1	6.6	8.0
1975	9.2	2.2	6.4	11.9	5.8	9.3
1976	9.8	2.2	6.1	14.8	6.2	5.3
1977	18.3	2.3	5.5	13.4	4.2	8.4
1978	11.5	2.5	5.7	12.3	5.4	3.3
1979	11.8	2.6	7.2	11.0	5.6	7.8
1980	26.6	2.3	8.3	19.8	5.9	23.9
1981	34.2	2.8	8.9	22.5	5.1	10.9
1982	25.6	2.3	8.1	15.4	6.3	
1983						
1984						

Note:

[a] Stock as a percentage of production.

Sources:

DoE, Housing and Construction Statistics 1970–1980 (HMSO, 1981) Tables 55, 57 and 59; DoE, Housing and Construction Statistics 1971–1981 (HMSO, 1982) Tables 51, 53 and 55; DoE, Housing and Construction Statistics December Quarter 1982 No. 12 (HMSO, 1983) Table 1.11.

adjustment are stocks in the hands of manufacturers, the builders merchants, and on site. Table 14.2 shows the fluctuations in manufacturers'
stocks as a percentage of deliveries from 1970 for materials for which
these data are available. The amount held in stock varies as a proportion
of deliveries for each material and would be expected to be highest in
materials where there is diversity of product. This may for example
explain the relatively high average stocks of concrete roofing tiles
and bricks. The stocks of cement must be low because of its potential
deterioration but this is largely compensated by stocks of clinker from
which cement is made. Bricks show the largest fluctuations in stocks –
the highest level in the table being over thirteen times the lowest level.
For no other product listed does this variation exceed three times. The
increase in brick stocks at the same time as a fall in production and
consumption may be due to the increase in timber-frame housing and the
decrease in housing over all in the average size of dwellings and, of course,
wrong forecasting of these factors.

Brick production is interesting from another point of view. Table
14.3 shows the percentage of various types of brick of the total produc-

TABLE 14.3 *Percentage of production of bricks taken by various use
types from 1970*

Year	Commons %	Facings %.	Engineering %	Total th m
1970	51.6	42.1	6.3	6.1
1971	48.8	44.9	6.3	6.5
1972	46.7	47.3	6.0	6.9
1973	45.0	49.2	5.9	7.2
1974	49.1	44.0	7.0	5.6
1975	42.6	49.8	7.6	5.0
1976	39.2	53.2	7.6	5.4
1977	39.1	53.6	7.3	5.1
1978	37.5	55.5	6.9	4.8
1979	38.1	55.0	6.8	4.9
1980	34.9	57.1	8.0	4.6
1981	31.7	60.4	7.9	3.7
1982				
1983				
1984				

Sources:

DoE, *Housing and Construction Statistics 1970–1980* (HMSO, 1981) Table 55; DoE,
Housing and Construction Statistics 1971–1981 (HMSO, 1982) Table 51.

tion. There has been an increase in the share of facing bricks. This may be due partly to the increase in timber-frame construction referred to above, partly the willingness of producers in a recession to undertake production of whatever bricks are required and at the same time designers, knowing this to be so, increasing their demand for facing and special bricks. It may also be due to higher insulation requirements which may cause replacement of the inner skin of the cavity wall by other materials.

Merchants' stocks were estimated at £300 million in 1982 compared with annual sales of £2600 million.[6]

PRICES

Costs of all materials used in construction increased by a little over four times in the ten years 1971-81 – rather less than construction as a whole and than earnings in construction.[7] There was, however, a considerable difference from one material to another, as shown in Table 14.4. Quite

TABLE 14.4 *Price rises of selected materials,*
1971-81, Great Britain

Material or material group	% increase
Granite and limestone roadstone	525
Sand and gravel (delivered)	442
Cement[a]	493
All bricks	512
Pre-cast concrete products	403
Building blocks	465
Imported wood	413–465
Steel products	362–426
Aluminium plate sheet and strip	324
Copper products	252–263
Iron cast and spun pipes and fittings	483
Plumbers' brassware	395
Domestic electric heating	365
Paint	373
Bituminous and flax felts	444

Note:

[a] Calcareous other than clinker: delivered 25 miles.

Source:

Based on DoE, *Housing and Construction Statistics 1971-1981* (HMSO, 1982) Table 50.

striking is the price of bricks which has risen faster than most other materials and the small rises in copper products – tubes and sheet and strip. The price of non-fletton commons has risen faster than non-fletton facing bricks and fletton commons have also risen faster than fletton facings. This may well have added to the advantages of timber-frame construction and partly explain the increasing proportion of facings used (see Table 14.3). It is also possible that the reduction in the consumption of commons has necessitated a rise in their price.

CHANNELS OF DISTRIBUTION

The distribution of so large a variety of building materials and products, many of them bulky, is a complex process and a network of builders merchants has evolved. Builders merchants sales in 1982 were estimated at £2600 million through over 2000 outlets by the Builders Merchants Federation.[8] This would represent about a third of all contractors' supplies of materials and a quarter of all materials used. The complexity of the merchanting process is illustrated by the estimated average number of items of stock of 20 000 held by branches.[9]

It is of great value to manufacturers of materials to have a 'ready-made' distribution system. There are two ways in which manufacturers sell through merchants. In the first the supplies never actually pass through the merchant's hands but he processes the contractors' orders and arranges the payment and handles all the paper work. The goods are delivered ex-works to site. In the second case the merchant buys in for stock and sells from his own stock. One major function of the merchant is to act as a channel for credit to the industry. The merchants normally have longer credit from the supplier than the contractor or speculative housebuilder[10] and can pass on some of the advantage of this to his customer. Credit given by the builders merchant to the contractor is sometimes as long as two months or so but, in general, it is the larger mechants who can give longer credit and the small local merchants can afford only much shorter delays in payment without losing their discounts from manufacturers.[11] The average period of credit is normally under two months.

There are discounts from merchants for large quantities and in addition the large contractors are able to negotiate prices below the usual discount.

Specialist factoring organisations have emerged that act as wholesalers to merchants, especially smaller merchants, and to retailers. These are active particularly in manufactured products where a broadening of the variety of products on offer has created a need for breaking bulk. In some cases the merchant groups themselves have set up separate factoring organisations.

Large contractors will often buy from the manufacturer direct, particularly for bulky materials, and will presumably be able to obtain favourable terms.

Lastly, increasing amounts of building products are sold direct to the retailer or to the consumer. These are particularly those products for the home improvement market and the DIY trade referred to earlier.

A study carried out by GIRA (UK) Ltd[12] includes estimates of the method of distribution of the major materials and a summary of these data is shown in Table 14.5.

Those materials sold direct to contractor are mainly the heavier ones, notably ready-mixed concrete which must all be delivered straight from producer to site to avoid deterioration, but also especially bricks and blocks, sand, gravel and hoggin, roof tiles and bituminous roofing and wooden windows. Merchants handle nearly all heating and much of the plumbing products including fixtures and fittings mainly from stock. They also, surprisingly in view of its bulk, handle almost all cement, mainly ex-works, because it is the policy of the cement producers to deal through merchants. They are strong in plaster and plasterboard. Glass merchants are a specialist branch of the trade and do not normally do general business.

Notable at the retail end are bathroom and kitchen products, metal fittings, tools, decorating materials and aluminium doors and windows, going direct to the consumer with the high pressure salesmanship in replacement and supplementary windows and doors. Factors or wholesalers are especially important in electrical wiring, tools and metal fittings and locks and to a lesser extent kitchens and bathroom fittings and decorating materials.

TABLE 14.5 Estimated[a] sales and first stage of distribution for selected groups of building products and materials, 1981

Product/product group	Approx. construction market size £m	First-stage distribution – %					
		Direct to contractor	Merchant (ex works)	Merchant into stock	Factor/ Wholesale	Direct retailer/ consumer	Other
Kitchen and bathrooms	680	6	neg.	30	36	27	neg.
Heating and plumbing	430	3	6	70	11	3	7
Plumbing fixtures and fittings	300	7	6	70	6	7	4
High-volume/low-value heavyside products[b]	1 450	39	36	17	2	neg.	5
Other heavy-side products[c]	400	31	22	33	9	3	1
Joinery	220	31	5	33	8	5	19
Metal doors and windows	440	19	–	7	neg.	74	–
Flat glass	140	–	–	–	–	–	100 glass merchants
Metal fittings, locks, etc.[E]	280	7	–	14	47	32	–
Hand and power tools[E]	180	3	–	10	60	27	neg.
Electrical wiring accessories[E]	200	10	neg.	2	77	10	–
Decorating materials[E]	640	18	–	16	33	32	–

Notes:

[a] All figures are estimates – those for groups marked E are more uncertain than the others.
[b] Includes bricks, blocks and pavings, cement, sand, gravel and hoggin, ready-mixed concrete and precasts.
[c] Includes plasterboard, plaster roof tiles, bituminous roofing and loft and roof insulation materials.

Source:

Based on Denison-Pender, M. R., Barnett, G., and David Rigby Associates (Stockport), The Changing Structures of Stockholding and Distribution of Building Products and Materials in the UK (GIRA UK Ltd, London, 1982) Table 11.2.

15 Plant and Other Fixed Assets

TYPES OF ASSETS AND PLANT

Fixed assets include buildings and works, plant and machinery and vehicles. Most of the assets used by the construction industry are in plant.

The types of plant range from very large items such as tower cranes, road-building equipment, large excavators and open-cast coal equipment down to cement mixers, dumpers, pumps, etc., and even to hand tools although, since these are often owned by the operative, these are not usually included. Scaffolding and shuttering are types of plant, although not always included in this category. In civil engineering the development of plant has removed most of the hard labouring work and, because of continual development and improvement since the war, the cost of some tasks such as earth-moving have decreased in real terms and even, over long periods, in money terms. It is possible that in some of these areas the usage of plant is at its peak. This is not so, however, in other areas and there seems to be a continual development of new plant to replace or facilitate tasks previously done by hand. In recent years there have been great improvements in various forms of access plant which, for example, allow repair to be undertaken on upper storeys of buildings without the erection of scaffolding. There are improvements in existing machinery that increase the speed of operation, such as the telescopic crane, and reduce fuel consumption. Some new machines have increased capacity, others are versatile to replace a whole range of alternative equipment.[1] Over all it seems that there will be a continuing slow increase in the capital-intensity of construction.

It is estimated that over all the component cost of plant in construction output is about 5 per cent of the total (see Table 10.6). It is estimated at only about 2 per cent for new housing and repair and mainten-

ance, 4 per cent for other new building but over 20 per cent for civi
engineering. Within these groups the range is considerable.

There are three ways in which contractors obtain use of plant: pur
chase outright or with various types of hire purchase; hire; or leasing
again in a variety of forms. There is a considerable amount of data or
the purchase of plant and some information on the plant-hire industry
which is part of the construction industry. The amount of leasing, unde
which the lessee has full use of the plant but does not own it, is no
known, although it is thought that contractors do not make great use o
it. Some plant-hire firms lease plant and then hire it out. Many contrac
tors hire some plant and own or lease other types of plant.

Since no statistics are available for leasing, an apparent change in plan
usage as shown by figures of purchases or hire may in reality be a change
in the leasing component due, for example, to fiscal changes. The statistic
that are available must therefore be interpreted carefully.

Another problem in using the statistics relates to the change in the
Standard Industrial Classification. Prior to 1980 the SIC for construction
included plant-hire firms, with those with and without operatives separ
ately specified since 1976, although many firms let plant out both with
and without operatives according to the type of plant involved. From
1980 onwards the Census of Production has used the revised 1980 SIC
classification[2] which classifies plant-hire firms not hiring out operative
to Division 8 Group 842, in the services group. Since the split, with an
without operatives, was in any case rather artificial, this means that the
statistics on construction plant hire are considerably reduced in value
These firms without operatives in 1979 bought about £64 million of plan
or about 37 per cent of acquisitions of all plant-hire companies.[3] The
change of classification means that on capital expenditure there is a
break between 1979 and 1980. The CSO data in the National Income
and Expenditure Blue Book[4] is based on the 1968 Standard Industria
Classification[5] as far as possible. However, there are no data available
as yet for the construction plant hire without operatives now included
in a Service Category, so it is possible that the gross domestic fixe
capital formation figures for 1981 are affected by the change in coverage
of the Census of Production on which the CSO data are partly based.

OWNERSHIP AND INVESTMENT IN FIXED ASSETS

The ownership of fixed assets by the construction industry, including
the plant-hire industry, is low compared with other industries although

within the plant-hire part of the industry ownership of fixed assets is very high. Most of construction industry assets are plant and machinery. Table 15.1 shows the stock of fixed assets in construction (which do not include leased assets because they are not owned) compared with other industries and the total economy. The estimates are dependent on a number of assumptions and subject to considerable error. In particular, the stock of small plant is difficult to determine and its age will be very varied.

The ratios of the total stock to the annual gross domestic product are striking with construction very low at 1.0 compared with 2.3 for distribution and other service industries and 4.5 for manufacturing industry. The total economy has an even higher ratio at 5.6 because of the large stock of dwellings and other public-sector assets such as roads, railways, gas and electricity installations.

Table 15.2 shows 1981 expenditure on fixed assets. This too covers plant bought by contractors and plant-hire firms but not leased plant. It will be seen that the construction industry spent only 4.2 per cent of its GDP on investment, compared with 12.5 per cent for manufacturing industry and 30 per cent for service industries.

It will be noted comparing Table 15.1 with Table 15.2 that the net acquisitions of vehicles by construction were relatively higher than their ownership of the stock due presumably to the longer life of construction plant and equipment other than vehicles, which are probably mostly cars, trucks and lorries.

Capital expenditure in construction using the BSO figures[6] kept up well until 1979 but in 1980, even after allowing for changes in the classification, there probably was a fall in investment in real terms.

Ownership of plant or at least the sole claim on the use of plant (which is achieved by leasing too) is advantageous if the plant can be maintained at a high utilisation level, when it is normally cheaper than hiring, although in a period of recession, such as the early 1980s, plant hirers have let plant at below average cost. It also gives complete control over its deployment – especially important when there is a degree of overload on the industry.

Plant purchase is frequently regarded as a good use of capital. However, if there is a shortage of capital to invest in plant it is possible to buy on hire purchase or lease and hiring carries other advantages (see below).

There were particular reasons why plant purchase was fairly buoyant in the 1970s. First, there was a good second-hand market for plant in the Middle East and elsewhere. Second, new plant was relatively cheap

TABLE 15.1 Gross capital stock in 1981 at 1975 replacement cost, UK

Type of assets	Construction		Total manufacturing		Distributive trades and other service industries		Total economy	
	£ th m	%	£ th m	%	£ th m	%	£ th m	%
Vehicles, ships and aircraft	1.10	16.4	2.42	2.3	7.07	9.1	27.5	5.0
Plant and machinery	4.07	60.8	67.77	63.4	25.71	32.8	150.4	27.3
Buildings and works	1.52	22.7	36.64	34.3	45.66	58.2	374.0	67.8
Total	6.69	100	106.83	100	78.44	100	551.9	100
Ratio of total capital stock to GDP of sector in 1981 at 1975 prices	1.0		4.5		2.3		5.6	

Source:

CSO, National Income and Expenditure 1982 Edition (HMSO, 1982) Tables 11.9, 11.10, 2.6 and 3.1.

TABLE 15.2 *Gross domestic fixed capital formation, 1981, UK (1981 prices)*

Type of asset	Construction		Total manufacturing		Distributive trades and other service industries[a]		Total economy	
	£m	%	£m	%	£m	%	£m	%
Vehicles, ships and aircraft	183	31.4	436	7.0	1 854 (1 089)	18.3 (15.6)	4 587	11.6
Plant and machinery	341	58.6	4 797	77.0	4 980 (2 611)	49.2 (37.4)	15 581	39.6
Buildings and works	58	10.0	994	16.0	3 291 (3 276)	32.5 (47.0)	19 209	48.8
Total	582	100	6 227	100	10 125 (6 976)	100 (100)	39 377	100
% of GDP of sector	4.2		12.5		30.0 (20.7)		18.7	

Note:

[a] The figures in brackets exclude leased assets, that is, purchases of assets by financial-sector companies for leasing to other industries.

Source:

CSO, *National Income and Expenditure 1982 Edition* (HMSO, 1982) Tables 10.8 and 3.1.

in the UK because of the generally depressed conditions. Thus it paid to update the stock of plant by buying new and selling old plant second-hand at favourable prices. In addition, many companies that had a policy of not bringing profits on large projects into the accounts until the projects were complete had a substantial cash surplus to invest. At the same time the capital tax allowances were favourable.

Data are available from the BSO Census of production on net capital expenditure as a percentage of value added by trade of firm and these are shown in Table 15.3. There are problems interpreting this table, especially as to the main trades contractors and plant-hire companies. The census of production deals with undertakings and the plant subsidiaries and plant divisions of large contractors may or may not be separated from the main contractor, although it seems likely that they are. (This conclusion is supported by the apparent low net capital expenditure a head by the very large contractors, which could be explained by their hiring their plant from a separate (but owned) undertaking.)

In fact the fleets of the large contractors are very large indeed. In 1980-1 the ten largest plant-owning contractors had a gross book value of plant of about £810 million compared with about £290 million by the ten top plant-hiring companies.[7] Moreover, of the six largest contracting groups all but one were among the twenty companies having the largest plant fleets. They are George Wimpey, Tarmac, Costain, Taylor Woodrow and John Laing.[8] Thus in Table 15.3 much of the capital expenditure attributed to plant-hire companies is that of the large main trades contractors, especially the building and civil engineers often operating through subsidiaries specialising in plant hire.

The net capital expenditure is some indication of how much is owned but not how much is used. In order to know the usage of plant it is necessary to know, in addition, the distribution of plant hired between trades, but this is not available. However, it is known that the same large contractors who own large plant fleets are also among the largest customers of the rest of the plant-hire industry. The top five contractors with large plant fleets hire from elsewhere 10-15 per cent of their plant requirements.[9] The figures of expenditure are likely to give some indication of usage by specialist trades who will not have separate plant-hire divisions. There are in fact few surprises between specialist trades. The most intensive purchasers of plant are the miscellaneous group, because of opencast coal-mining, the scaffolding specialists and demolition contractors, while traditional craft trades are the lowest spenders on capital equipment.

TABLE 15.3 *Net capital expenditure as percentage of gross value added by trade of firm, average of years 1977-9, Great Britain*

Trade	%
General builders	5.3
Building and civil engineering contractors	7.7
Civil engineers	11.9
Plumbers	4.8
Carpenters and joiners	5.3
Painters	4.6
Roofers	5.7
Plasterers	4.9
Glaziers	7.9
Demolition contractors	16.1
Scaffolding specialists	16.6
Heating and ventilating engineers	8.0
Reinforced concrete specialists	4.9
Electrical contractors	3.6
Asphalt and surface dressing contractors	9.5
Plant-hiring contractors with operatives	29.1
Plant-hiring contractors without operatives	44.5
Flooring contractors	55.5
Constructional engineers	10.8
Insulating specialists	4.5
Suspended ceiling specialists	4.1
Floor and wall tiling specialists	4.6
Miscellaneous (including open-cast coal-mining)	26.2
Total industry	8.5

Sources:

Based on Business Statistics Office, *Report on the Census of Production Construction Industry* PA 500, 1977 (HMSO, 1979) Table 6; 1978 (HMSO, 1980) Table 5; 1979 (HMSO, 1981) Table 5.

PLANT HIRE

The value of the output of the construction plant-hire industry in 1981 was about £650 million[10] but it is not known how much of the plant hired by subsidiaries of contractors is included in this. The amount of plant hired as opposed to owned or leased is not known with any degree of accuracy. However, an indication is that over the six years 1974-9 inclusive, 30-35 per cent of net acquisitions of plant by the construction industry in Great Britain were by plant-hire companies with and without their own labour force (drivers and operatives).[11] Some of the plant owned by these companies, probably 10-20 per cent, will be hired to industries other than construction. However, it is likely that on average the plant hired may be used more intensively than plant owned and therefore the amount of usage of plant hire may be understated by the purchase figures. Some put the usage on site figure of plant hired as high as 50 per cent of total.

Greene & Co. put Hewden Stuart as the largest general plant-hire company and second largest in the crane hire field with about £76 million of gross book value of plant. The second largest over all is Grayston, also a general hirer.[12] The total number of plant-hire companies is between 3000 and 3500[13] but in 1980 only forty-three of them employed more than 115 persons.[14]

All large plant is hired with operators but smaller items are usually hired and operated by contractors.

The advantages of plant hire to the contractor are that he can obtain plant from a source near his site for a long or short time period. He does not need to concern himself with maintenance problems or the dislocations associated with breakdowns, and if he hires it with an operator he is relieved of the task of ensuring that he has a competent operator. Above all, as with leasing, it reduces the amount of capital locked up. Plant hire has increased the ability of small contractors to compete with large ones.

PLANT LEASING

Leasing of plant is an arrangement by which the user pays for the use of a piece of plant over its life. It is thus a way of financing some of the advantages of ownership, without ownership ever actually passing from the lessor to the lessee. The merits of leasing or hire purchase, which confer the same effective control over the plant, are largely determined at any time by the financial position of the lessee company, the various tax allowances available, the rates of interest, etc.

In particular a company that pays little corporation tax is not in a position to take full advantage of the 100 per cent capital allowances which can be set against tax in the first year. On the other hand, the leasing company is usually a bank that has little need for fixed assets in the normal course of its business and is able to set the whole of the purchase of plant against tax. This favourable tax situation enables the leasing company to charge relatively favourable rates to the lessees while at the same time still making substantial profits itself. For the small firm that needs a large capital asset the leasing option can be advantageous on account of its inability to benefit directly from capital allowances against tax if it buys. If, on other hand, the firm is paying substantial corporation tax is excess of the cost of the plant it is more likely to be beneficial to own the plant itself.

It is largely as a result of the tax situation that leasing is probably used mainly by small contractors and subcontractors and by small plant-hire firms who lease plant and then hire it out.

16 Finance for Contracting

NEED FOR FINANCE

Finance is not a resource in the same sense as manpower or materials. It is a mechanism by which requirements for capital of a person or organisation are met by drawing on savings. These savings may be internally generated or from outside the organisation. It is necessary because production and sale cannot take place instantaneously and thus there is a need to finance outgoings before receipts are obtained. Finance is needed mainly to purchase fixed assets and to use as working capital to pay for goods and services which will be incorporated in buildings and works for the period of time before payment for these is made by the client. Since the normal way of paying for construction on site is on a monthly certificate by the professional team, minus a retention, usually of 5 per cent, the time lag between expenditure and receipt of payment should be quite short and the working capital requirements consequently low.

Moreover it is part of the skill of successful contracting to keep disbursements to a minimum. This is done, first, by utilising credit available for purchase of materials from builders merchants and producers. Since the period of credit is usually six to eight weeks the contractor will probably be able to avoid financing materials with his own money. Second, the main contractor often pays subcontractors after he is paid for the work they have done. This leaves the main contractor with labour on site (as well as overheads) to finance and the main contractor increasingly subcontracts to labour-only subcontractors and probably delays payment to them as long as possible. The subcontracting firm has to find a higher amount of working capital in relation to turnover than the main contractor. Third, the contractor in pricing the bill of quantities may price the items that are relevant to work in the early stages of a contract relatively higher than that in the later stages, so that he gets the money in earlier. In addition the contractors may be able to use plant previously written off on another project. Thus the contractor may be able, once the contract is underway, to obtain receipts in excess of expenditure, in spite of the retention, thus requiring negative working capital.

This is not always how the situation works out in practice and there are often large sums outstanding from clients to the construction industry, in excess of the retention monies. The industry complains about the level of retentions as well as about other monies outstanding. The economic situation created by these two is, however, very different. If the contractor knows at the time of tendering that the client will retain 5 per cent of the value of the work done, he can plan accordingly by allowing for interest on this money in his tender and also in assessing his cash-flow position. He is providing money for the project that would otherwise be provided by the client and from the point of view of the total economy it does not matter that this is so.

If, however, the client does not, when the time comes, pay money to the contractor that is due to him, then the contractor will not have planned for this and indeed cannot have been expected to do so, unless the client has a reputation for being a late payer. Claims by contractors under their contracts outstanding at any one time are substantial, amounting for some types of work to about a third of the annual value of work done. The contractor's costs are increased by the loss of return on the money and he may in addition incur legal costs in obtaining it. In extreme cases he may not obtain the money for such a long time that he is forced into liquidation.

CAPITAL EMPLOYED

The relationship of capital employed in the business to turnover varies considerably from one type of business to another. Table 16.1 shows a comparison between construction and other industries, for large companies only, since it is only public companies that are obliged to disclose turnover. The table also shows the relationship of working capital to capital employed. The capital employed in relation to turnover is smaller in construction than in industry as a whole and of this smaller total working capital has a higher proportion. This would be expected from the analysis of fixed assets held by the industry in Table 15.1. It will be seen that, although there are differences between construction and other industries, these are small compared with differences within the construction group, between building and civil engineering companies

TABLE 16.1 *Comparison of capital employed as percentage of turnover and working capital as percentage of capital employed, large companies in various industry groups, Great Britain*

Industry group	Capital employed as % of turnover			Working capital as % capital employed		
	1978	1979	1980	1978	1979[p]	1980[p]
Construction	32[a]	36[a]	37[a]	41[a]	44[a]	39[a]
54 Public building and civil engineering companies	24[b]	25[b]	23[b]	n.a.	n.a.	n.a.
18 Private estate developers	60[b]	61[b]	61[p]	n.a.	n.a.	n.a.
All industries	42[a]	42[a,p]	41[p]	37[a]	40[a]	35[a]
Manufacturing industry	44[a]	45[a,p]	44[p]	47[a]	46[a]	43[a]
Non-manufacturing industry	39[a]	37[a,p]	38[p]	26[a]	28[a]	27[a]

Notes:

For [a], capital employed is net tangible assets plus stocks and work in progress plus debtors' prepayments and government grants receivable minus creditors and accruals. Turnover may be slightly understated thus leading to a possible overstated percentage.

For [b], the definition of capital employed adopted by Savory Milln may have slight differences to those in [a] above but insufficient to invalidate the comparison.

Sources:

Based on [a] Business Statistics Office, *Company Finance, Thirteenth Issue*, Business Monitor MA3 (HMSO, 1983) Tables 6 and 10; [b]E. B. Savory Milln & Co., *Savory Milln's Building Book 1981 Supplement: Company Operating Statistics and Ratios* (E. B. Savory Milln, 1981), pp. 10–24.

and private estate developers who have a lot of capital locked up in land and do not get paid for their construction work until it is completed. Within the building and civil engineering group there are differences as to the extent to which property and other interests are included under the umbrella of the company and this can cause substantial differences in the operating statistics.

SOURCES OF FINANCE

Finance is, in broad terms, found from shareholders, by way of equity, and from lenders, by way of borrowings. The equity or shareholders' interest is made up of the original subscription from shareholders plus ploughed-back profits, some of which may have been capitalised by scrip issues. Borrowing can in general take the form of long-term finance by way of debentures, mortgages and long-term loans or of short-term finance by way of bank loans (some bank loans, these days, are medium term), overdrafts, acceptance credits, etc.

Table 16.2 shows the source of funds for construction and industry generally by size of firm. It will be seen that all companies analysed by the BSO obtained in 1978 about 69 per cent from shareholders' interests (including minority interests and deferred taxation), about 13 per cent from debentures, mortgages and long-term loans and 19 per cent from bank loans and overdrafts and short-term loans.[1] The manufacturing companies had a rather higher proportion of shareholders' interests, with corresponding adjustments elsewhere, and the non-manufacturing companies rather less. However, the importance of short-term bank loans, overdrafts and short-term loans rises as the company size decreases, offset by a fall in debentures, mortgages and long-term loans.[2] Construction generally has a relatively larger dependence on short-term finance than other industries, especially in the medium and small companies.

All these statistics refer to a wide range of enterprises. The total number of companies in construction in the BSO statistics in 1978 was approaching 28 000 of which 105 were 'large', defined as having a capital employed of over £4.16 million. This total would include firms, according to the DoE statistics, employing less than seven persons.[3]

Although Table 16.2 shows that relatively construction relies more on short-term finance than do other industries, in relation to its turnover it is not a large customer of the banking system. This is because the mass of building and civil engineering firms employ less capital in relation to turnover than other industries. This is shown in Table 16.1 for large

TABLE 16.2 *Sources of finance for construction and all industry by company sizes, 1978 and 1979, Great Britain*

Industry group	% of finance from:					
	Shareholders'[a] interest		Debentures[b] and loans		Banks and[c] short loans	
	1978	1979[P]	1978	1979[P]	1978	1979[P]
Construction:						
Large companies	74	73	6	5	19	22
Medium and small companies	63	65	7	6	30	29
All companies	70	70	6	5	23	25
All industry:						
Large companies	68	70	14	12	18	18
Medium and small companies	73	73	5	4	23	23
All companies	69	70	13	10	19	19

Notes:

[a] Shareholders' interests, minority shareholders' interests plus deferred taxation.
[b] Debentures, mortgages and long-term loans.
[c] Bank loans, overdrafts and short-term loans.

Source:

Based on Business Statistics Office, *Company Finance, Thirteenth Issue*, Business Monitor MA3 (HMSO, 1983) Tables 1, 6, 9, 10 and 11.

companies but is probably more pronounced for the industry as a whole. The Bank of England data on advances and acceptances to UK residents by banks in the UK[4] show that in November 1982 the amount outstanding by construction was between a fifth and a sixth of that outstanding by manufacturing industry, in spite of the fact that in 1981 the contribution of construction to GDP was between a third and a quarter of that by manufacturing industry.[5] In relation to turnover, therefore, it is not so dependent on banks as manufacturing industry.

A number of sources have come to the conclusion that there is not a shortage of finance for construction companies. In the Building and Civil Engineering EDCs report *How Flexible Is Construction?* it stated that: 'The supply of capital is not generally considered to be a constraint by most contractors, although some subcontractors are concerned about the extent to which they are required to finance main contractors.'[6] It then went on to report the concern at the clients' demands for performance bonds and also to say that: 'Construction companies with relatively small bases and a high risk element cannot attract risk capital from external sources very readily. The very large companies are better able to attract funds in this way. Small companies at the outset of their operations are likely to depend to a considerable extent on personal injection of funds'.

This is in keeping with the conclusions of the Wilson Report,[7] that in general there is not a shortage of finance for industry with the exception of small and especially new firms (paras 929-30). In the special report on small firms[8] they made recommendations, some of which have now been implemented. However, the contractor has need for relatively little finance because he has low fixed assets and because of his ability to finance contracts on low working capital, but the very paucity of these fixed assets means that there is little collateral for loans and they are therefore quite rightly seen as very risky by investors.

RETURN ON CAPITAL EMPLOYED AND ON TURNOVER

The differences in return on capital employed between all construction companies in the BSO statistics and the companies in other industries are probably not significant. The returns ranged between 16-20 per cent for all size groups together in manufacturing, non-manufacturing and construction in 1978 and 1979.

However, for large companies data are available for return on capital employed and on turnover. Table 16.3 shows the available data. In

TABLE 16.3   *Return on capital employed and on turnover for large companies in various industry groups, 1978–80. Great Britain*

Industry group	Profit as % capital employed			Profit as % turnover		
	1978	1979	1980	1978	1979	1980
Construction	18[a]	14[aP]	13[aP]	6[a]	5[aP]	5[aP]
54 Public building and civil engineering companies	23[b]	17[b]	18[b]	5[b]	4[b]	4[b]
18 private estate developers	15[b]	21[b]	23[b]	9[b]	13[b]	14[b]
All industries	17[a]	19[aP]	16[aP]	7[a]	8[aP]	6[aP]
Manufacturing industry	16[a]	15[aP]	10[aP]	7[a]	7[aP]	4[aP]
Non-manufacturing industry	17[a]	25[aP]	22[aP]	7[a]	9[aP]	8[aP]

Notes:

For [a], for note on capital employed and turnover, see Table 16.1. Profit is gross trading profit minus hire of plant and machinery and minus depreciation and amounts written off.

For [b], for note on capital employed, see Table 16.1. Profit is net trading profit after deducting depreciation but before charging interest or crediting investment and other income. Whenever possible, exceptional items, such as currency and stock profits/losses, provision for contingencies, etc. have been excluded.

Sources:

[a]based on Business Statistics Office, *Company Finance, Thirteenth Issue*, Business Monitor MA3 (HMSO, 1983) Tables 6, 7, 8 and 10; [b]based on E. B. Savory Milln & Co., *Savory Milln's Building Book 1981 Supplement: Company Operating Statistics and Ratios* (E. B. Savory Milln, 1981) pp. 10–24.

general construction has a low profit on turnover although in 1980 provisional figures show manufacturing industry lower. However, apart from problems of contracting and other types of business within construction, dealt with earlier, risk is very much affected by the companies operating abroad, where the risks in spite of ECGD are substantial and the overheads of obtaining and undertaking work high, so that capital back-up is important. Indeed the risks are high in construction generally although reduced by various forms of fluctuating price contracts. In a situation where adverse circumstances can exceptionally cause cost escalation of contracts of, say, 10 per cent of turnover, that is, a contract expected to cost £10 million can cost £11 million, if the capital involved is small, the risks in relation to the capital are large.

The Savory Milln figures for the larges companies are higher for return on capital employed than for the 100 or so large companies in the BSO data. It is difficult to draw definite conclusions.

17 Research and Development

There are a number of sources of data on research and development expenditure[1] but none of them gives more than a very partial view, because in construction the research and development is undertaken often by other industries, notably building materials industries, which are not separately specified in the statistics, and by categories of organisations where no separate split of construction is possible, such as academic institutions.

It has been estimated that expenditure on research and development in construction, including project-oriented research, was of the order of £100 million in 1981[2] split about equally between public and private sectors. This represents 0.5 per cent of the total expenditure on construction in the UK compared with the national figure of expenditure on all kinds of research and development of about 2 per cent of GNP.

The public-sector research is undertaken by the research establishments, notably Building Research Establishment, including the Fire Research Station and Forest Products Research Laboratory, and the Transport and Road Research Laboratory Station. The expenditure of BRE in 1980-1 was about £13.4 million,[3] of which part was funded by private and nationalised industry for specific projects. The cost to the public exchequer was about £10.5 million. This compares with about £4.2 million in 1980-1 on highways through the Transport and Road Research Laboratory, although a small part of the expenditure on transport systems also relates to construction.[4] Public authorities including nationalised industries and the PSA undertake research and commission it. In addition, government funds are used to support research through the Science and Engineering Research Council (SERC), to place research contracts directly with the research associations, notably Construction

Industry Research and Information Association (CIRIA), the Building Services Research and Information Association (BSRIA), and the Timber Research and Development Association (TRADA). These organisations are responsible to and partly funded by their industrial members but also receive some support from the DoE. NEDO commissions some research on behalf of the EDCs.

There is also some research concerned with energy conservation in building funded by the Department of Energy through the Energy Technology Support Unit which works closely with the BRE organisation – the Building Research Energy Conservation Support Unit. The Research Directorate of the EEC is also involved with this work.

The private sector undertakes research within companies and within research organisations of industries or groups of companies such as the Brick Development Association (BDA) or the Cement & Concrete Association (C & CA), and some of these private organisations receive sub-contracts from BRE. The building material producers probably account for a substantial portion of private research in construction. The consulting engineers often have to undertake considerable research for the design of individual projects and this may be done in-house, by a university, research association or a government research organisation. The professional institutions from time to time commission research, often from their members.

ORGANISATION OF RESEARCH

A major problem with construction research is the disparate interests of the parties to the construction process and in particular the separation of design and construction. Progress in construction may depend on change in design, yet designers often have little knowledge of construction methods and contractors have very little influence over design. Furthermore, research on design might be beneficial but the professions have not the resources to finance it unless it is part of a specific project and the method of their remuneration does not facilitate reward for successful research even if they could afford it. Research in improving building materials is a more fruitful area, with finance being more readily available and rewards more easily realised.

Because of the lack of a clear commercial or professional home for construction industry research, government has traditionally in this country, and elsewhere in developed countries, played a substantial role. This is appropriate, not only because government is the only party to fill the role, but also because it is the client for 40-50 per cent of the new work of the industry and, representing society, it has an interest in a satisfactory standard for the built environment. Thus as client/owner and as a representative of society, it is the greatest beneficiary from improvements in construction technology, management and organsiation.

With cuts in government research expenditure, and continual changes in the administration of research – particularly in the government research establishments – over the last few years, it is arguable that this role of government is no longer being adequately fulfilled. Consideration should be given to the adequacy of the level of research, particularly of a fundamental nature.

In 1981 the Secretary of State for the Environment asked the EDCs to investigate *inter alia* whether research was effective in improving the performance of the industry and the organisation of research. They established a working party under the chairmanship of Sir Peter Trench which recommended[5] that the EDCs should establish a Research Strategy Committee to advise *inter alia* on 'medium and long-term priorities, funding and vehicles for research. An important role would be the encouragement of communication and application of research results.'

This Research Strategy Committee was set up in 1982. A second recommendation was for a Board of Management to advise the Secretary of State on the BRE research programme and the communication and application of the results, and on the effective management of BRE. This recommendation was accepted in the spring of 1982. One important task for the Board should be for the examination and implementation of steps required for it to exercise adequate management control and to allow BRE the necessary flexibility for commercial operations.

This would have the effect of removing BRE from the day-to-day control of the DoE which, together with cuts in expenditure, has had a stifling effect over the last few years.

AREAS FOR FUTURE RESEARCH

CIRIA has undertaken an investigation into the long-term research requirements in civil engineering,[6] and has attempted to indicate effort devoted to various subjects compared with effort required, as well as more detailed areas where research is necessary.

They are concerned that the requirements for research are far in excess of present provision and, in particular, that much of government-sponsored research is concerned with day-to-day problems and with matters of regulation of construction rather than fundamental problems. The Rothschild Report[7] which recommended that research and development should be undertaken on a customer/contractor basis so that the customer of the research says what he wants and how much he can spend and commissions the research to be done, specifically excluded from this fundamental or pure research. In construction there is a danger that this basic research is inadequate and in the long run the UK consulting engineers and others in the industry will be damaged in international competition by this lack of back-up and the built environment will be less satisfactory than it need be.

On specific areas of research, CIRIA draws particular attention to the following:[8]

(a) The long-term behavour and durability characteristics of new and traditional materials and the development of higher performance coatings with particular emphasis on actual conditions in use and exposure.

(b) The development of site investigation techniques and methods of testing and interpretation to establish relevant properties of soils and rocks.

(c) The performance of structures in-use with regard to durability, serviceability and economy.

(d) Performance data on systems of water supply irrigation, drainage, sewage treatment and coastal protection.

(e) The development of a range of improved methods of construction.

(f) The development of geotechnical and other processes for building on poor ground.

(g) The development of more appropriate forms of contract and effective systems and procedures for communication between all those concerned in a project.

(h) The development of methods of repair, maintenance, replacement and refurbishment for various types of structures and installations, but particularly buildings, bridges and sewers.

SERC is establishing priorities for the funding of this research.

Research expenditure on the economics, management and organisation of the industry has been relatively small and concentrated on a few large projects in the 1960s and 1970s. Many have been unsatisfactory and results have often not been published. Where the research project itself has been satisfactory the level of application of results has often been low.[9] With a scarcity of research funds the applied research should be orientated towards areas where action is possible. NEDO has a good record in this respect. SERC is currently funding construction management research to the sum of about £1.3 million over five years in building departments in universities and polytechnics.

In this book several areas have been identified where more information could assist in improving the operation of the industry. In some cases the data is required simply as support for a consideration of changes which need to be made. In others knowledge is required of the effects of the present situation before the nature of the changes can be formulated. In some instances there are gaps in data which can be used for a variety of purposes and it is desirable to fill those gaps. Five such areas of investigation are mentioned here:

(a) improvement of the planning of programmes in the public sector and particularly a move away from strictly annual financing
(b) the effect on subcontractors' efficiency of the present contractual arrangements, especially domestic subcontractors
(c) the possible effects of potential changes in the arrangements for self-employment in construction
(d) investigation of the type, background and training of managers and supervisory staff in construction and of the future needs
(e) a comprehensive review and interpretation of all data available on overall resource inputs for the production of various output types.

Notes and References

PREFACE

1. Fleming, M. C., *Construction and the Related Professions*, on behalf of the Royal Statistical Society and the Social Science Research Council (Pergamon, 1980).

1 THE CONSTRUCTION INDUSTRY

1. CSO, *Standard Industrial Classification*, revised 1968 (HMSO, 1968).
2. CSO, *National Income and Expenditure, 1982 Edition* (HMSO, 1982) Table 11.7.
3. DoE, *Housing and Construction Statistics, 1971-1981* (HMSO, 1982) Table 9.
4. CSO, *National Income and Expenditure, 1982 Edition* Table 1.9.
5. These figures are not quite comparable. The value of output refers to Great Britain and the GDP to the UK. Moreover the value of work undertaken abroad by the UK construction industry is excluded in the output figures for the industry but some allowance is made for it in the GDP figures. The differences do not alter the general argument.
6. CSO, *National Income and Expenditure, 1982 Edition* Table 1.9.
7. ibid, Tables 1.9 and 3.2.
8. ibid, Table 10.8.
9. Maurice, R. (ed.), for the CSO, *National Accounts Statistics: Sources and Methods* (HMSO, 1968) p. 366.
10. CSO, *National Income and Expenditure, 1982 Edition* Table 10.8.
11. DoE, *Housing and Construction Statistics, 1971-1981*, Table 15.
12. Leopold, E., 'Where Have All the Workers Gone?' *Building*, vol. 243, 22 Oct 1982, pp. 29–30.
13. Department of Employment, *Employment Gazette*, vol. 91, no. 3, Mar 1983 (HMSO, 1983) Table 1.1.
14. Business Statistics Office, *Input-Output Tables for the United Kingdom 1974*, Business Monitor PA 1004 (HMSO, 1981) Table B.
15. DoE, *Housing and Construction Statistics 1971-1981*, Tables 9 and 62.

16. CSO, *United Kingdom Balance of Payments, 1982 Edition* (HMSO, 1982) Table 3.9.
17. Business Statistics Office, *Input-Output Tables for the United Kingdom 1974*, Table C.
18. DoE, *Housing and Construction Statistics 1970-1980* (HMSO, 1981) Table 61.
19. Economist Intelligence Unit, *Capital Spending and the UK Economy*, commissioned by the FCEC (EIU, 1981).
20. Cambridge Econometrics Ltd, *Policies for Recovery: An Evaluation of Alternatives*, commissioned by FCEC, NCBMP, NFBTE, RIBA, RICS (Cambridge Econometrics Ltd, 1981).
21. Trades Union Congress, *Reconstruction of Britain* (TUC, 1981).
22. National Economic Development Office, *Construction, Public Spending and the Economy*, Press Information (NEDO, 2 Mar 1982).
23. Ministry of Housing and Local Government, *Homes for Today and Tomorrow* (The Parker Morris Report) (HMSO, 1961).

2 DETERMINANTS OF DEMAND

1. DoE, *Housing and Construction Statistics 1970-1980* (HMSO, 1981); DoE, *Housing and Construction Statistics, December Quarter 1982*, no. 12 (HMSO, 1983; CSO, *National Income and Expenditure 1981 Edition* (HMSO, 1981); CSO, *National Income and Expenditure 1982 Edition* (HMSO, 1982).
2. University of Aston, Joint Unit for Research on the Urban Environment, *Planning and Land Availability* - quoted in ref. 3, p. 76.
3. EDCs for Building and Civil Engineering, *How Flexible Is Construction?* NEDO (HMSO, 1978), p. 75.
4. ibid.
5. DoE, *The Recent Course of Land and Property Prices and the Factors Underlying It* (DoE, 1976).
6. Shaw, G., Written Answer, *Hansard* 23 Mar 1982.
7. DoE, *Housing Policy: A Consultative Document*, Cmnd 6851 (HMSO, 1977).
8. Joint Land Requirements Committee, *Sufficient Housing Land for the 1980s?* Paper 1: 'How Much Land should we Plan for?' (Housing Research Foundation, 1982). The Committee comprises members from the Volume Housebuilders' Association, the Royal Town Planning Institute, the House Builders Federation and the Housing Research Foundation.
9. EDCs for Building and Civil Engineering, *How Flexible Is Construction?*, p. 9.
10. DoE, *Housing Policy, Technical Volume, Part 1* (HMSO, 1977) Table 1.5.
11. Office of Population Census and Survey, *Census 1981 National Report Great Britain Part 1*, CEN 81 NR(1) (HMSO, 1983) Table 24; DoE, *Housing and Construction Statistics, September Quarter 1982*, no. 11 part 2 (HMSO, 1983) Table 2.20.

12. Office of Population Census and Survey, *Census 1981 National Report Great Britian Part 1*.
13. DoE, *Housing and Construction Statistics 1971-1981*, (HMSO, 1982) Table 103.
14. Specialist Research Unit, *Why New? The Motivation for House Purchase*, paper for the House-Builders Federation (HBF, 1981).
15. DoE, *Housing and Construction Statistics, 1971-1981*, Table 105.
16. Bank of England, 'Analysis of Advances and Acceptances to UK Residents by Banks in the United Kingdom', *Bank of England*, 17 Nov 1982, and subsequent issues.
17. 'Housing Attracts Investment', *The Times*, 23 Apr 1982; 'The Building Trust', *BMP Information*, 5 Mar 1982.
18. DoE, *Housing and Construction Statistics, 1971-1981*, Table 105.
19. Williams, P., *The Role of Financial Institutions and Estate Agents in the Private Housing Market* (Centre for Urban and Regional Studies, University of Birmingham, 1976). p. 6
20. Gough, T. J., *The Economics of Building Societies* (Macmillan, 1982).
21. Mayes, D. G., *The Property Boom: The Effects of Building Society Behaviour on House Prices* (Martin Robertson, 1979).
22. Gough, *The Economics of Building Societies*, p. 140.
23. University of Aston, Joint Unit for Research on the Urban Environment, *Planning and Land Availability*; Kilroy, B., 'Housing Finance – Why so Privileged?', *Lloyds Bank Review*, no. 133, July 1979, pp. 37–52.
24. DoE, *Housing and Construction Statistics 1971-1981*, Table 106.
25. Mabey, S., and Tillet, P., *Building Societies: The Need for Reform* (Bow Group, 1980).
26. Kilroy, 'Housing Finance – Why so Privileged?'.
27. EDCs for Building and Civil Engineering, *Construction for Industrial Recovery*, NEDO (HMSO, 1978).
28. Hillebrandt, P. M., *Economic Theory and the Construction Industry* (Macmillan, 1974) pp. 62–8.
29. Maurice, R. (ed.), *National Account Statistics: Sources and Methods*, CSO (HMSO, 1968) p. 364.
30. CSO, *National Income and Expenditure 1981 Edition*, Table 11.11; and CSO, *National Income and Expenditure 1982 Edition*, Table 11.7.
31. DoE, *Commercial Property Development* (The Pilcher Report) (HMSO, 1975) p. 5.
32. ibid, pp. 49–50.
33. DoE, *Commercial and Industrial Property Statistics 1979* (HMSO, 1980) Table 24.
34. Ambrose, P., and Colenutt, B., *The Property Machine* (Penguin, 1975).
35. House of Lords Select Committee on Science and Technology, *The Water Industry*, vol. 1 Report (HMSO, 1982).
36. *Government Expenditure Plans 1982/83 to 1984/85*, Cmnd 8494 (HMSO, 1982).
37. National Council of Building Material Producers, *The Need for*

Building Materials (NCBMP, 1978) Appendix 12.
38. *The Government's Expenditure Plans 1981/82 to 1983/84*, Cmnd 8175 (HMSO, 1981) p. 13.
39. Bar-Hillel, M., 'All You Ever Wanted to Know About the Underspend', *Building*, vol. 243, 19 Nov 1982, p. 10.
40. 'Why They Underspend', *Building*, vol. 243, 5 Nov 1982, p. 11.
41. Ministry of Works, *Survey of Problems before the Construction Industries: A Report prepared for the Minister of Works by Sir Harold Emmerson G.C.B., K.C.V.O.* (HMSO, 1962).
42. EDCs for Building and Civil Engineering, *The Public Client and the Construction Industries*, NEDO (HMSO, 1975).
43. Relf, C. T., *The Building Timetable: The Public Sector* (Building Economics Research Unit, University College Environmental Research Group, 1974).
44. '"Bunching" Pressure on Tender Prices', *Building*, vol. 242, 26 Feb 1982, p. 11.
45. 'Finding the Funds', *Building*, vol. 243, 3 Sept 1982, pp. 26–7.
46. ibid.
47. 'New Inner City Enterprise from DoE', *Building*, vol. 243, 18 Nov 1982, p. 11.
48. DoE, *English House Condition Survey 1981, Part 1*, Report of the Physical Condition Survey, Housing Survey, Report 12 (HMSO, 1982).
49. DoE, *Housing and Construction Statistics 1971–1981*, Tables 91 and 97.
50. ibid, Tables 91 and 92.
51. ibid, and Table 2.5 of this volume.
52. National Home Improvement Council, *Report on the Market for Home Improvement, Repair and Maintenance and DIY 1977–80* (NHIC, June 1982) Table 3a.
53. House of Lords Select Committee on Science and Technology, *The Water Industry*, Table 3a.
54. DoE, *National Road Maintenance Condition Survey 1982* (DoE, 1983).
55. House of Commons Transport Select Committee, *First Report* (HC-28-1) (HMSO, 1983).
56. EDCs for Building and Civil Engineering, *Construction for Industrial Recovery*; and *Old Buildings Eat up Your Profits* (NEDO, 1978).

3 THE PROCESS

1. Ministry of Public Building and Works, *The Placing and Management of Contracts for Building and Civil Engineering Work* (The Banwell Report) (HMSO, 1964) p. 1.
2. EDC for Building, *Faster Building for Industry*, NEDO (HMSO, 1983) para 12.23.
3. DoE, *Housing and Construction Statistics 2nd quarter 1972*, no. 2 (HMSO, 1972) Table XII.

4. DoE, *Housing and Construction Statistics 1970-1980* (HMSO, 1981) Table 94.
5. Hillebrandt, P. M., *Economic Theory and the Construction Industry* (Macmillan, 1974) p. 80.
6. Chartered Institute of Building, *Project Management in Building* (CIOB, 1982) p. 12.
7. Hillebrandt, P. M., Andrews, J., Bale, J., and Smith, T., *Project Management: Proposals for Change* (Building Economics Research Unit, University College Environmental Research Group, 1974).
8. EDC for Building, *Faster Building for Industry*, para 12.11.
9. ibid, para 12.22.
10. ibid, paras 9.10 and 9.11.
11. EDCs for Building and Civil Engineering, *The Public Client and the Construction Industries* (The Wood Report) NEDO (HMSO, 1975).
12. EDC for Building, *Faster Building for Industry*, para 1.7.
13. EDCs for Building and Civil Engineering, *Before You Build: What a Client Needs to Know about the Construction Industry* (The Wilson Report) NEDO (HMSO, 1974) pp. 14-15.
14. EDCs for Building and Civil Engineering, *The Public Client and the Construction Industries*, p. 34.
15. EDCs for Building and Civil Engineering, *Before You Build*, pp. 20-40.
16. Dept of the Environment and Welsh Office, *Review of Development Control System* (The Dobry Report) (HMSO, 1975).
17. *House of Commons Expenditure Committee Report on Planning Procedures*, vol. 1, Report Session 1976-77 (HMSO, 1977).
18. DoE, *Statistics of Planning Applications April-June 1982*, Press Notice, 15 Feb 1983.
19. Dept of the Environment, Dept of Transport and Welsh Office, *Chief Planning Inspector's Report, 1981* (DoE, 1982).
20. EDC for Building, *Faster Building for Industry*, para 11.7.
21. ibid.
22. Ministry of Works, *The Placing and Management of Building Contracts*, Report of the Central Council for Works and Buildings to the Minister of Works (The Simon Report) (HMSO, 1944).
23. EDCs for Building and Civil Engineering, *The Public Client and the Construction Industries*.
24. ibid, p. 73.
25. Hillebrandt, *Economic Theory and the Construction Industry*, p. 80.
26. EDCs for Building and Civil Engineering, *The Public Client and the Construction Industries*, pp. 100-2.
27. DoE, *Housing and Construction Statistics 1970-1980*, Table 94.
28. Newcombe, R., 'Cost of Competition', *Building*, vol. 234, 16 June 1978, pp. 95-7.
29. National Joint Consultative Council, *NJCC Code of Procedure for Selective Tendering* (NJCC, 1972).
30. 'Tender Deviations Worry NJCC', *Building*, vol. 243, 23 July 1982, p. 14; Construction Industry Research and Information Association,

Pre-Contract Delays in Civil Engineering Projects (FCEC, 1982).
31. Construction Industry Research and Information Association, *Pre-Contract Delays in Civil Engineering Projects*.
32. Hillebrandt, *Economic Theory and the Construction Industry*, p. 80.
33. Lansley, P., *Reseach and Construction: Case Studies of the Constraints to the Application of Construction Management Research* (University of Reading, 1983).
34. The constituent bodies of the Joint Contracts Tribunal are: Royal Institute of British Architects; National Federation of Building Trades Employers; Royal Institution of Chartered Surveyors; Association of County Councils; Association of Metropolitan Authorities; Association of District Councils; Greater London Council; Committee of Associations of Specialist Engineering Contractors; Federation of Associations of Specialists and Subcontractors; Association of Consulting Engineers; Scottish Building Contract Committee.
35. DoE, *Housing and Construction Statistics 1970–1980*, Table 94.
36. ibid.
37. EDCs for Building and Civil Engineering, *The Public Client and the Construction Industries*, p. 79.
38. Pover, P. E. S., *Performance Bonding of Local Authority Building Contracts in the United Kingdom*, Report for University of London M.Sc. in Science and Architecture (Building Economics and Management) (UCL, 1976) p. 27.
39. EDCs for Building and Civil Engineering, *How Flexible Is Construction?* p. 23.
40. Bentley, M. J. C., *Quality Control on Building Sites*, CP 7/81 (BRE, 1981).
41. Clark, T., *Building Clerks of Works in the NHS: Towards an Educational Policy*, CEU Working Paper (York Institute of Advanced Architectural Studies, 1982).
42. Slough Estates Ltd, *Industrial Investment: A Case Study in Factory Building* (Slough Estates Ltd, 1979).
43. EDC for Building, *Faster Building for Industry*, para 1.7.
44. Construction Industry Research and Information Association, *Pre-Contract Delays in Civil Engineering Projects*.

4   OUTPUT IN GREAT BRITAIN

1. Lea, E., Lansley, P., Spencer, P., *Efficiency and Growth in the Building Industry* (Ashridge Management Research Unit, 1974).
2. DoE, *Housing and Construction Statistics 1971–1981* (HMSO, 1982) p. 161.
3. CSO, *National Income and Expenditure 1982 Edition* (HMSO, 1982) Table 117.
4. National Home Improvement Council, *Report on the Market for Home Improvement, Repair and Maintenance and DIY 1977–80*

(NHIC, 1982) Table 1.

5. ibid, Table (3) b.
6. Wheatcroft, A., 'A New Output Enquiry for the Construction Industry', *Economic Trends*, no. 333, July 1981, pp. 99–104.
7. DoE, *Housing and Construction Statistics 1971–1981*, Table 2.
8. DoE, *Housing and Construction Statistics 1970–1980*, Table 8; DoE, *Housing and Construction Statistics 1971–1981*, Table 8.
9. Ministry of Housing and Local Government, *Housing Statistics no. 6*, July 1967 (HMSO, 1967) Table 15; DoE, *Housing and Construction Statistics, 1st quarter 1972*, no. 2 (HMSO, 1982) Table 23; DoE, *Housing and Construction Statistics, 1st quarter 1975*, no. 13 (HMSO, 1975) Table XVIII; DoE, *Housing and Construction Statistics, 1st quarter 1979*, no. 29 (HMSO, 1979) Table XX.
10. DoE, *Housing and Construction Statistics 1970–1980*, Table 96.
11. Ministry of Housing and Local Government, *Housing Statistics no. 6*, Table 9; DoE, *Housing and Construction Statistics, 1st quarter 1973*, no. 5 (HMSO, 1973) Table 22.
12. DoE, *Housing and Construction Statistics 1970–1980*, Table 88.
13. Scottish Development Department, *Scottish Housing Statistics no. 4, 4th quarter 1978* (HMSO, 1978) Table 30.
14. DoE, *Housing and Construction Statistics 1970–1980*, Table 88.
15. DoE, *Housing and Construction Statistics, 1st quarter 1979*, no. 29 (HMSO, 1979) Table XXI.
16. Cullen, A., 'Speculative Housebuilding in Britain: Some Notes on the Switch to Timber-Frame Production Method', *The Production of the Built Environment: The Proceedings of the Bartlett Summer School 1981* (University College London, 1982).
17. National House-Building Council, *Private House-Building Statistics 1982*, quarter 4 (NHBC, 1983) Table 5.
18. DoE, *Housing and Construction Statistics 1971–1981*, Table 102.
19. Rimmer, G., 'Brick Marches North', *Building*, vol 239, 28 Nov 1980, p. 47.
20. DoE, *Housing Policy, Technical Volume Part 1* (HMSO, 1977) p. 73.
21. See, for example, Bentley, M. J. C., *Quality Control on Building Sites*, BRE Current Paper 7/81 (BRE, 1981).
22. Institute of Housing and RIBA, *Homes for the Future: Standards for New Housing and Development* (RIBA, 1983).
23. DoE, *Private Contractors Construction Census 1974* (HMSO, 1976) Table 52.
24. RIBA, *Quarterly Statistical Bulletin no. 51*, June 1982 (RIBA, 1982) Table 6.2.
25. ibid, Table 6.2.
26. ibid, Table 6.3.
27. ibid.
28. DoE, *Housing and Construction Statistics 2nd quarter 1979*, no. 30 (HMSO, 1979) Table III.
29. RIBA, *Quarterly Statistical Bulletin no. 54*, March 1983 (RIBA, 1983) p. 3.
30. DoE, *Housing and Construction Statistics*, no. 30, Table IV.

5 OUTPUT ABROAD

1. 'Building Up: The Work of UK Construction Firms Overseas', *British Business*, vol. 9, no. 6, 15–21 Oct 1982, pp. 256–261; DoE, *Housing and Construction Statistics 1971–1981* (HMSO, 1982) Table 10.
2. Venus, D. H. M., 'Getting the Work: 2. The Contractors' View', paper to Construction Industry Conference Centre, Easter Conference 1979 International Construction, 5–6 April (University of Nottingham, 1979) pp. 11–13; Davis, A., 'Construction: Personal Approach Wins Arab Contracts', *The Times*, 30 Mar 1983.
3. 'Construction Overseas' *British Business*, vol. 6, no. 7, 16–22 Oct 1981 pp. 282–9; 'Building Up: The Work of UK Construction Firms Overseas'.
4. Savory Milln & Co., *Building Book 1981 Supplement Dec. 81* (Savory Milln, 1981); Savory Milln & Co., *Building Book 1982 vol. 2, Contractors, Housebuilders and Plant Hire Cos* (Savory Milln, 1982).
5. DoE, *Housing and Construction Statistics 1971–1981*, Tables 32 and 42.
6. Venus, 'Getting the Work: 2. The Contractors' View'.
7. ibid.
8. Latham, M., 'The British Abroad', *Building*, vol. 241, 23 Oct 1981, p. 23.
9. EDC for Civil Engineering, *Design and Export*, NEDO (HMSO, 1978) pp. 38–9.
10. *Export Business from Capital Projects Overseas*, Report of an Enquiry by the Rt Hon. the Earl of Cromer PC, MBE (HMSO, 1968) p. 22.
11. EDC for Civil Engineering, *Design and Export*, p. 39.
12. EDC for Civil Engineering, *Overseas Capital Projects*, a report by Sir Archie Lamb (NEDO, 1982).
13. Association of Consulting Engineers, Press Release, 22 Mar 1982; Association of Consulting Engineers, Press Release, Mar 1983.
14. Association of Consulting Engineers, *Overseas Work Entrusted to Members during 1982* (ACE, 1983).
15. Association of Consulting Engineers, *Overseas Work Entrusted to Members during 1981* (ACE, 1982).
16. Beardall, G. D., 'Getting the Work: 1. The Consultants' View', paper to Construction Industry Conference Centre, Easter Conference 1979, International Construction, 5–6 April (University of Nottingham, 1979) pp. 1–10.
17. Department of Trade: Projects and Export Policy Division, *Overseas Projects Fund Assistance: Guidance for Applicants* (DOT, 1981).

6 FORECASTING AND FORECASTS OF DEMAND AND OUTPUT

1. Sugden, J. D., and Wells, E. O., *Forecasting Construction Output from the Orders*, Building Economics Research Unit, Environmental Research Group (University College London, 1977).

2. RIBA, Statistics Section, *Quarterly Statist*
3. RICS, *Quantity Surveyors' Workload*, Qu
   Releases.
4. Wheatcroft, A., DoE, 'A New Output Enq
   Industry', *Economic Trends*, no. 333, July
5. Fleming, M. C., *Construction and the Relat*
   of the Royal Statistical Society and the
   Council (Pergamon, 1980) section 13.S.12.
6. These include the NFBTE, HBF, FCEC, HVC
7. See, for example, notes 8 and 9 below.
8. *Public Expenditure to 1977/78*, Cmnd 5519 (
9. *Public Expenditure to 1981/82*, Cmnd 7049 (HMSO, 1978).
10. Source of data to assist in public-sector housing forecasts include:

    (a) dwellings in tenders approved and approved but not started for
        local authorities and new towns in Great Britain
    (b) changes in number of dwellings started and under construction
        in Great Britain
    (c) time lag start to completion dwellings in local authorities and
        new towns and all public sector
    (a) to (c) above in DoE, *Housing and Construction Statistics*,
        annual and quarterly (HMSO).

11. Sources of data to assist in private-sector housing forecasts include:

    (a) changes in number of dwellings started and under construction
        in Great Britain
    (b) time lag start to completion private dwellings
    (c) receipts and advances of building societies and advances of
        other institutions
    (d) rate of interest on mortgages
    (e) changes in house prices – there are many indices of which one is
        published as below
    (a) to (e) above in DoE, *Housing and Construction Statistics*, annual
        and quarterly (HMSO).

12. Sources of data to assist in private-sector non-housing forecasts
    include:

    (a) CBI Quarterly Industrial Trends Survey reported in CSO,
        Economic Trends (HMSO)
    (b) Dept of Industry Investment Intentions Survey three times a
        year reported in DoI, *British Business* (HMSO)
    (c) Survey of Office Market Activity by Hillier, Parker, May and
    (d) Monthly Survey of Business Opinion by *Financial Times*
    (e) Business Indicators Poll by RICS and *Financial Times*
    (f) Survey of Office Market Activity by Hillier, Parker, May and
        Rowden.

13. Organisations undertaking forecasts of the economy include: The
    Treasury, OECD, NIESR, CBI, London Business School, Cambridge

metrics, Cambridge Economic Policy Group, The Liverpool up and the Economist Intelligence Unit.

EDCs for Building and Civil Engineering, Joint Forecasting Committee, *Construction Forecasts* (every six months) NEDO (HMSO).

15. National Council of Building Material Producers, *BMP Forecasts* (three times a year) (NCBMP).
16. DoE, *Housing and Construction Statistics 1970–1980* (HMSO, 1981) Table 142.
17. Young, G., Written Answer, *Hansard*, 23 Mar 1982.
18. DoE, *English House Condition Survey 1981*, pt 1, Report of the Physical Condition Survey, Housing Survey Report 12 (HMSO, 1982).
19. DoE, *Housing and Construction Statistics 1971–1981* (HMSO, 1982) Table 103.
20. ibid, Tables 99–103.
21. Whitehead, C. M. E., *The UK Housing Market: An Econometric Model* (Saxon House, 1974).
22. Holmans, A. E., 'A Forecast of Effective Demand for Housing in Great Britain in the 1970s', *Social Trends*, no. 1 (HMSO, 1970) pp. 33–42.
23. EDCs for Building and Civil Engineering, Joint Working Party on Demand and Output Forecasts, *Construction Industry Prospects to 1979*, (NEDO, 1971).
24. ibid.
25. EDCs for Building and Civil Engineering, *Regional Construction Forecasts to 1977*, vols 1–4 (NEDO, 1974).
26. EDCs for Building and Civil Engineering, *Construction into the Early 1980s*, NEDO (HMSO, 1976); EDCs for Building and Civil Engineering, *Scottish Construction into the Early 1980s*, NEDO (HMSO, 1976).

7 STRUCTURE OF CONTRACTING INDUSTRY

1. DoE, *Housing and Construction Statistics 1971–1981* (HMSO, 1982) Table 27.
2. Business Statistics Office, *Report on the Census of Production 1980: Construction Industry*, PA 500 (HMSO, 1982).
3. CSO, *Standard Industrial Classification Revised 1980* (HMSO, 1979) Class 50.
4. Business Statistics Office, *Report on the Census of Production 1979: Construction Industry*, PA 500 (HMSO, 1981).
5. DoE, *Housing and Construction Statistics 1971–1981*, Table 27.
6. ibid.
7. ibid, Table 31.
8. ibid, Table 41.
9. ibid, Tables 31 and 41.
10. ibid, Table 43.
11. ibid, Tables 12 and 32.
12. ibid, Table 42.

13. E. B. Savory Milln & Co., *Savory Milln's Building Book 1982, vol. 2: Contractors, Housebuilders and Plant Hire Companies* (Savory Milln, 1982); E. B. Savory Milln & Co., *Savory Milln's Building Book 1981, vol. 1: Building Materials and Builders Merchants* (Savory Milln, 1981); E. B. Savory Milln & Co., *Savory Milln's Building Book 1981, Supplement: Company Operating Statistics and Ratios* (Savory Milln, 1981).

14. E. B. Savory Milln & Co., *Savory Milln's Building Book 1969-70* (Savory Milln, 1970).

15. DoE, *Housing and Construction Statistics 1971-1981*, Tables 40 and 41.

16. ibid; and DoE, *Housing and Construction Statistics 1970-1980* (HMSO, 1981) Tables 41 and 42.

17. EDC for Building, *Faster Building for Industry*, NEDO (HMSO, 1983) paras 9 and 10.

18. DoE, *Housing and Construction Statistics 1971-1981*, Table 31.

19. ibid.

20. National House-Building Council, *Private House-Building Statistics 1982 4th Quarter* (NHBC, 1983) Table 9.

21. Hillebrandt, P. M., *Economic Theory and the Construction Industry* (Macmillan, 1974) ch. 12.

22. EDC for Civil Engineering, *Efficiency in Road Construction* (Chairman: John Lofthouse) NEDO (HMSO, 1966).

23. The Labour Party, *Building Britain's Future: Labour's Policy on Construction* (The Labour Party, 1977) p. 41.

24. The Monopolies Commission, *Report on the Supply of Buildings in the Greater London Area*, House of Commons Paper 264, Session 1953/54 (HMSO, 1954).

25. Registrar of Restrictive Trading Agreements, *Restrictive Trading Agreements*, Report of the Registrar, 1 July 1969 to 30 June 1972, Cmnd 5195 (HMSO, 1973).

26. Ball, M., and Cullen, A., *Mergers and Accumulation in the British Construction Industry*, 1960-79 Birkbeck College Discussion Paper no. 73 (Birkbeck College, 1980).

27. Jones, D. W. and Harris, F. C., 'Company Acquisitions and Business Performance in the Construction Industry', *Construction Papers*, vol. 1, no. 3, 1982.

28. This section draws on and updates the article on the subject: Hillebrandt, P. M., 'Going Bust: What are the Facts?' *Building*, vol. 232, 11 Feb 1977, pp. 52-3.

29. DoE, *Housing and Construction Statistics 1971-1981*, Table 15.

30. Leopold, E., 'Where Have All the Workers Gone?' *Building*, vol. 243, 22 Oct 1982, pp. 29-30.

31. DoE, *Housing and Construction Statistics 1971-1981*, Table 48.

32. The NFBTE includes the House Builders Federation, National Federation of Plastering Contractors, National Association of Scaffolding Contractors, National Federation of Painting and Decorating Contractors, Association of Natural Stone Industries and British Woodworking Federation.

33. National Federation of Building Trades Employers, *1878-1978: An Outline History of the National Federation of Building Trades Employers* (NFBTE, 1978).

34. The constituent associations of CASEC are: British Constructional Steelwork Association Ltd, Electrical Contractors Association, Electrical Contractors Association of Scotland, Heating and Ventilating Contractors Association, National Association of Plumbing, Heating and Mechanical Services Contractors, Metal Window Federation, National Association of Lift Makers, Scottish and Northern Ireland Plumbing Employers Federation (*CASEC Annual Report 1981* (CASEC, 1982)).

35. The constituent associations of FASS as at Jan 1983 were: Architectural Aluminium Association, Asphalt and Coated Macadam Association, British Decorators' Association, British Precast Concrete Association, British Reinforcement Manufacturers Association, Contract Flooring Association, Federation of Piling Specialists, Felt Roofing Contractors Advisory Board, Glass and Glazing Federation, Mastic Asphalt Council and Employers Federation, National Federation of Terrazzo-Mosaic Specialists, National Master Tile Fixers Association, Suspended Ceilings Association.

36. DoE, *Housing and Construction Statistics 1971-1981*, Tables 11 and 46.

37. *Local Government Planning and Land Act 1980* (HMSO, 1980).

38. Chartered Institute of Public Finance and Accountancy, *Accounting Code of Practice for Direct Labour Organisations* (CIPFA, 1981).

39. Elliot, D. A., *Direct Labour Organisations: Implications of the Local Government Planning and Land Act 1980* (CIOB, 1980).

40. ibid. p. 14.

41. Planning Exchange, *Direct Labour Organisations: The Effects of Part II of the Local Government Planning and Land Act 1980*, Forum Report no. 31 (Planning Exchange, Glasgow, 1982).

42. ibid; Elliot, *Direct Labour Organisations*.

43. DoE, *Housing and Construction Statistics 1971-1981*, Tables 11 and 46.

44. DoE, Private Communications of 16 Dec 1982.

45. Economist Intelligence Unit for CABIN, *Public Ownership in the Construction Industries* (EIU, 1978).

8 STRUCTURE OF THE PROFESSIONS

1. Kaye, B., *The Development of the Architects' Profession in Britain* (Allen & Unwin, 1960) p. 17.

2. RIBA Statistics Section, *Architects' Employment and Earnings 1982: A Report of the RIBA Survey* (RIBA, 1982).

3. *Report of the Committee of Inquiry into the Engineering Profession* (Chairman: Sir Montague Finniston FRS) Cmnd 7794 (HMSO, 1980).

4. RIBA Statistics Section, *Census of Private Architectural Practices 1980* (RIBA, 1981) p. 2.
5. ibid.
6. RICS, *A Study of Quantity Surveying Practice* (RICS, 1974).
7. Prices and Incomes Board, *Architects Costs and Fees*, Cmnd 3653 (HMSO, 1967).
8. Monopolies and Mergers Commission, *Architects Services: A Report on the Supply of Architects' Services, with Respect to Scale Fees* (House of Commons Papers) (HMSO, 1977).
9. Monopolies and Mergers Commission, *Surveyors' Services: A Report on the Supply of Surveyors' Services with Respect to Scale Fees* (House of Commons Papers) (HMSO, 1977).
10. DoE, *Housing and Construction Statistics, 1970-1980* (HMSO, 1981) Tables 50 and 51.
11. EDCs for Building and Civil Engineering, *How Flexible Is Construction?* NEDO (HMSO, 1978) p. 17.
12. DoE, *Private Contractors Census 1974* (HMSO, 1976).
13. RICS, Quantity Surveyor Committee, *The Future of the Quantity Surveyor* (RICS, 1971).
14. RICS, *Assisting Management to Build*, Leaflet (RICS).
15. Continuing Professional Development in Construction Group, *Information Sheet* (CPDC, 1982).
16. Continuing Professional Development in Construction Group, *CPDC Newsletter* no. 4 (CPDC, Dec 1981).

9 COSTS AND PRICES

1. DoE, *Housing and Construction Statistics 1971-1981* (HMSO, 1982) Table 2.
2. DoE, *Monthly Bulletin Construction Indices:* (a) Civil Engineering Works; (b) Building Contracts, Monthly (HMSO).
3. Building Cost Information Service, *Quarterly Review of Building Prices*, Issue no. 9, Feb 1983 (BCIS, 1983) p. 10.
4. Davis, Belfield and Everest, 'Cost Forecast', *Architects' Journal*, vol. 177, no. 12, 23 Mar 1983.
5. For a fuller discussion of estimating and tendering see Hillebrandt, P. M., *Economic Theory and the Construction Industry* (Macmillan, 1974).
6. DoE, *Housing and Construction Statistics 1971-1981*, Table 2.
7. Building Cost Information Service, *Quarterly Review of Building Prices*, p. 10.
8. ibid.
9. Davis, Belfield and Everest, 'Cost Forecast'.
10. Stone, P. A., *Building Economy: Design Production and Organisation - A Synoptic View* (Pergamon, 1983) pp. 20-2.

10 THE LINKS BETWEEN RESOURCES AND OUTPUT AND CAPACITY

1. EDCs for Building and Civil Engineering, *How Flexible Is Construction?* NEDO (HMSO, 1978) p. 28.
2. EDCs for Building and Civil Engineering, *Construction into the Early 1980s* NEDO (HMSO, 1976) pp. 33–4.
3. Lemessany, J., and Clapp, M. A., *Resource Inputs to New Construction – The Labour Requirements of Hospital Building* CP 85/75 (BRE, 1975); Lemessany, J., and Clapp, M. A., *Resource Inputs to Construction – The Labour Requirements of House Building* CP 76/78 (BRE, 1978).
4. EDCs for Building and Civil Engineering, *Scottish Construction into the Early 1980s* (HMSO, 1976).
5. National Economic Development Council, *The Construction Industry* (HMSO, 1964) para 74.
6. DoE, *Housing and Construction Statistics, 4th quarter 1974 no. 12*, (HMSO, 1975) Table 1.
7. ibid, Tables 45, 47, 48, 49 and 51.
8. ibid, Table 2; CSO, *Monthly Digest of Statistics no. 343*, July 1974 (HMSO, 1974) Table 169.

11 MANPOWER

1. Leopold, E., 'Where Have All the Workers Gone?' *Building*, vol. 243, 22 Oct 1982, pp. 29–30.
2. Construction Industry Training Board, *Annual Report 1981/82* (CITB, 1983) Table 1.
3. Marsh, A., Heady, P., and Matheson, J., *Labour Mobility in the Construction Industry*, OPCS (HMSO, 1981).
4. National Federation of Building Trades Employers, Manpower Study 1974 (NFBTE, 1974).
5. Construction Industry Training Board, *Annual Report 1981/82* (CITB, 1983) Table 1.
6. Marsh *et al.*, *Labour Mobility in the Construction Industry*, Table 7.1.
7. ibid.
8. ibid, Table 7.3.
9. Construction Industry Training Board, *£40,000,000 Youth Training Scheme Offers Place in Construction for 20,000 School Leavers*, press release (CITB, 10 Mar 1983) (and related leaflets).
10. Construction Industry Training Board, 'Recognition Only Given to Electrical JIB Trainees', *Construction Board News*, no. 67, Mar 1983.
11. Marsh *et al.*, *Labour Mobility in the Construction Industry*, Table 2.4.
12. Jeanes, R. E., *Building Operatives Work* (HMSO, 1966).
13. Hatchett, M., *ILEA Building Craft Student Survey 1978: A Profile of Building Craft Students in Inner London* (The Bartlett School of Architecture and Planning, University College, London, 1982).

14. Woodward-Smith, N., *A National Register of Craft Skills in the Building Industry: A Feasibility Study* (Civic Trust, 1979).
15. Fulcher, A. J., 'Achievement Measurement in the Building Sector', *Training for Tomorrow*, Report of Construction Industry Training Officers Conference (CITOC) (CITB, 1982).
16. Marsh *et al.*, *Labour Mobility in the Cosntruction Industry*, p. 8.
17. ibid, p. 11.
18. *Report of Committee of Inquiry under Professor E. H. Phelps Brown into Certain Matters Concerning Labour in Building and Civil Engineering*, Cmnd 3714 (HMSO, 1968) p. 183.
19. Marsh *et al.*, *Labour Mobility in the Construction Industry*, p. 11.
20. Hatchett, *ILEA Building Craft Student Survey 1978*, Table 8.
21. Marsh *et al.*, *Labour Mobility in the Construction Industry*, pp. 10–11.
22. ibid.
23. ibid, Table 3.4.
24. 'British Labour Fuels Dutch Black Markets', *Building*, vol. 241, 23 Oct 1981, p. 11.
25. Manpower Services Commission, 'National Training Survey', 1975 quoted in EDCs for Building and Civil Engineering, *How Flexible Is Construction?* (HMSO, 1978) pp. 40–5.
26. Marsh *et al.*, *Labour Mobility in the Construction Industry*.
27. *Report of Committee of Inquiry under Professor E. H. Phelps Brown into Certain Matters Concerning Labour in Building and Civil Engineering*, pp. 100–1.
28. Health and Safety Executive, *News Release*, 10 Nov 1982 (HSE, 1982).
29. Health and Safety Executive, *Fatal Accidents in Construction in 1978* (HMSO, 1981)
30. CSO, *Monthly Digest of Statistics*, no. 441, Sept 1982 (HMSO, 1982) Table 3.12.
31. Wood, L., *A Union to Build* (Lawrence and Wishart, 1979).
32. National Joint Council for the Building Industry, *Working Rule Agreement* (1982 edn) (NJCBI, 1982); Joint Industry Board for the Electrical Contracting Industry, *National Working Rules and Industrial Determination for the Electrical Contracting Industry* (JIBECI, 1982); The National Joint Industry Board for Plumbing Mechanical Engineering Services in England and Wales, *Constitution and Rules, National Working Rules, Grading Scheme, Training and Apprenticeship Agreement* (JIBPMES, 1982); Building and Allied Trades Joint Industrial Council, *Constitution and Working Rule Agreement* (BATJIC, 1983); Civil Engineering Construction Conciliation Board for Great Britain, *Constitution of the Board and Working Rule Agreement* (CECCB, 1982).
33. Joint Industrial Board for the Electrical Contracting Industry, *JIB 1982/1983 Industrial Determination* (JIBECI, 11 Jan 1982).
34. National Joint Council for the Building Industry, *Working Rule Agreement*, p. 178; Department of Employment, *New Earnings Survey 1981* (HMSO, 1982) Table 86.

35. DoE, *Housing and Construction Statistics 1971-1981* (HMSO, 1982) Table 23.
36. ibid, Table 27.
37. ibid, Table 25.
38. CSO, *Monthly Digest of Statistics*, no. 447, Mar 1983 (HMSO, 1983) Table 3.15.
39. Health and Safety Executive, *Fatal Accidents in Construction*, pp. 1 and 7.
40. Marsh *et al.*, *Labour Mobility in the Construction Industry*.
41. DoE, *Private Contractors' Construction Census 1976* (HMSO, 1977) Table 32.
42. DoE, *Housing and Construction Statistics 1971-1981*, note on p. 165.
43. ibid, Tables 15, 44 and 47.
44. ibid, Tables 15 and 47.

12 PRODUCTIVITY AND EFFICIENCY OF MANPOWER

1. DoE, *Housing and Construction Statistics 1971-1981* (HMSO, 1982).
2. Business Statistics Office, *Report on the Census of Production: Construction, PA 500* (a) 1974 (HMSO, 1976) (b) 1975) (HMSO, 1977) (c) 1976 (HMSO, 1978) (d) 1977 (HMSO, 1979) (e) 1978 (HMSO, 1980) (f) 1979 (HMSO, 1981) (g) 1980 (HMSO, 1982).
3. CSO, *National Income and Expenditure, 1982 Edition* (HMSO, 1982).
4. DoE, *Housing and Construction Statistics 1971-1981*, p. 162.
5. Fleming, M., 'Direct Works Departments and the Construction Industry – Trends in Employment and Comparative Productivity', *National Builder*, vol. 58, Feb 1977, pp. 13–15; Fleming, M., 'Direct Works Department and the Construction Industry: Employment and Productivity Re-examined', *National Builder*, vol. 59, Mar 1978, pp. 90–3.
6. O'Brien, D., 'Direct Works Departments: Output per Head Still Significantly Lower', *National Builder*, vol. 58, Feb 1977, p. 12.
7. Sugden, J. D., 'Direct Labour: How Statistics Have Proved Nothing', *Municipal Engineering*, vol. 155, 23 May 1978, pp. 354–7 and 371.
8. Business Statistics Office, *Company Finance 13th Issue*, Business Monitor MA3 (HMSO, 1983).
9. DoE, *Housing and Construction Statistics 1971-1981*, Table 11.
10. National Federation of Building Trades Employers, *Manpower Study 1974* (NFBTE, 1974).
11. DoE, *Housing and Construction Statistics 1970-1980* (HMSO, 1981) Table 14.
12. Lemessany, J., and Clapp, M. A., *Resource Inputs to Construction: The Labour Requirements of Housebuilding* CP 76/78 (BRE, 1978).
13. Marsh, A., Heady, P., and Matheson, J., *Labour Mobility in the Construction Industry* OPCS (HMSO, 1981).

14. National Board for Prices and Incomes, *Pay and Conditions in the Building Industry, the Civil Engineering Industry and the Construction Industry other than the Building and Civil Engineering, Report Nos. 91, 92 and 93: Statistical Supplement*, Cmnd 3982 (HMSO, 1969).
15. DoE, *Housing and Construction Statistics 1971–1981*, Tables 38 and 41.
16. Business Statistics Office, *Report of the Census of Production*, 1976–82.
17. DoE, *Housing and Construction Statistics 1970–1980*, Table 14; National Federation of Building Trades Employers, *Manpower Study 1974*.
18. Hillebrandt, P. M., *Small Firms in the Construction Industry*, Committee of Inquiry on Small Firms, Research Report no. 10 (HMSO, 1971).
19. National Federation of Building Trades Employers, *Manpower Study 1974*.
20. Business Statistics Office, *Report on the Census of Production*, 1976–82.
21. DoE, *Housing and Construction Statistics 1971–1981* (HMSO, 1982) Table 46.

13 MANAGEMENT

1. Institute of Building, *Survey of Home Members 1975* (IOB, 1976).
2. Chartered Institute of Building, *Surveys of Student Numbers 1977/78 to 1981/82* (CIOB (formerly IOB) 1978–82).
3. ibid.
4. Chartered Institute of Building, *The Challenge of Change: A Report for the Continuing Professional Development Working Party* (CIOB, 1982).
5. Institution of Civil Engineers, *Education and Training of Civil Engineers: Report of the Chilver Committee* (ICE, 1975).
6. RIBA, *The Architect and his Office* (RIBA, 1962).
7. RIBA, *Handbook of Architectural Practice and Management* (RIBA, 1964).
8. Andrews, J., *Education for the Management of Construction: The Way Ahead – From Already Behind* (Construction Industry Development Unit, University College London, 1983).

14 MATERIALS

1. DoE, *Housing and Construction Statistics 1971–1981* (HMSO, 1982) Table 57.
2. EDCs for Building and Civil Engineering, *Building Materials: Export Opportunities and Import Substitution*, NEDO (HMSO, 1980) pp. 43–4.

3. EDC for Building, *Building Products – Competing at Home and Abroad*, NEDO (HMSO, 1983).
4. Covington, S. A., *The Degree of Quality Assurance Provided with Certain Building Components and Products*, CP 8/80 (BRE, 1980).
5. Advisory Council for Applied Research and Development, *Facing International Competition: The Impact on Product Design of Standards, Regulations, Certification and Approval* (HMSO, 1982).
6. Builders Merchants Federation, *Leaflet on BMF and 'The Builders Merchant'* (BMF, 1982).
7. DoE, *Housing and Construction Statistics 1971–1981*, Table 2.
8. Builders Merchants Federation, *Leaflet on BMF and 'The Builders Merchant'*.
9. ibid.
10. Potter, G. M., 'Seller Concentration, Growth and Financial Performance of Builders' Merchants', report submitted in partial fulfilment for M.Sc. Degree in Architecture, Building Economics and Management (University College London, 1981) p. 58.
11. ibid, p. 59.
12. Denison-Pender, M. R., Barnett, G., and David Rigby Associates (Stockport), *The Changing Structures of Stockholding and Distribution of Building Products and Materials in the UK* (GIRA UK Ltd, London, 1982).

15   PLANT AND OTHER FIXED ASSETS

1. Welsh, D. O., 'The Changing Shape of Plant and Machinery', *Building*, vol. 1243, 10 Dec 1982, p. 69.
2. CSO, *Standard Industrial Classification*, revised 1980 (HMSO, 1979).
3. Business Statistics Office, *Report on the Census of Production 1979: Construction Industry PA 500* (HMSO, 1981) Table 2.A.
4. CSO, *National Income and Expenditure 1982 Edition* (HMSO, 1982).
5. CSO, *Standard Industrial Classification 1968* (HMSO, 1968).
6. *Report on the Census of Production 1974–80: Construction Industry PA 500* (HMSO, 1976–82) Table 2.
7. Greene & Co., *Investment in Plant Hire 1981* (Greene & Co., 1981) p. 8.
8. ibid, p. 9.
9. ibid, p. 10; Greene & Co., *Investment in Construction 1982* (Greene & Co., 1982) Table Q.
10. DoE, *Housing and Construction Statistics 1971–1981* (HMSO, 1982) Tables 40 and 41.
11. *Report on the Census of Production 1974–9: Construction Industry PA 500*.
12. Greene & Co., *Investment in Plant Hire 1981*, p. 12.
13. *Report on the Census of Production 1979: Construction Industry PA 500*, Table 1A; DoE, *Housing and Construction Statistics 1971–1981*, Table 31.
14. DoE, *Housing and Construction Statistics 1971–1981*, Table 31.

16 FINANCE FOR CONTRACTING

1. Business Statistics Office, *Company Finance, Thirteenth Issue*, Business Monitor MA3 (HMSO, 1983) Table 1.
2. ibid, Table 6.
3. DoE, *Housing and Construction Statistics 1971–1981* (HMSO, 1982) Table 27.
4. Bank of England, *Analysis of Advances and Acceptances to UK Residents by Banks in the United Kingdom 17 Nov 1982* (Bank of England Press Notice, 5 Jan 1983).
5. CSO, *National Income and Expenditure 1982 Edition* (HMSO, 1982) Table 3.1.
6. EDCs for Building and Civil Engineering, *How Flexible Is Construction?* NEDO (HMSO, 1978) pp. 22–3.
7. *Committee to Review the Functioning of Financial Institutions: Report* (The Wilson Report) Cmnd 7937 (HMSO, 1980).
8. *Interim Report of the Committee to Review the Functioning of Institutions: The Financing of Small Firms*, Cmnd 7503 (HMSO, 1979).

17 RESEARCH AND DEVELOPMENT

1. CSO, *Research and Development: Expenditure and Employment*, Studies in Official Statistics no. 27 (HMSO, 1976); Business Statistics Office, *Industrial Research and Development Expenditure and Employment 1978*, MO14 (HMSO, 1980); Department of the Environment and Transport, *Report on Research and Development 1981* (HMSO, 1982); Bowles, J. R. Department of Industry, 'Research and Development: Expenditure and Employment in the Seventies', *Economic Trends* no. 334, Aug 1981, pp. 94–111; Bowles, J. R., Departments of Industry and Trade, 'Central Government Expenditure on Research and Development', *Economic Trends* no. 346, Aug 1982 (HMSO, 1982) pp. 82–95.
2. Construction Industry Research and Information Association, *Long-term Research and Development Requirements in Civil Engineering*, Report of a Task Force set up by the Science and Engineering Research Council and the Departments of the Environment and Transport (CIRIA, 1981) p. 45.
3. Building Research Establishment, *Annual Report 1980/81* (HMSO, 1982) p. 2.
4. Departments of the Environment and Transport, *Report on Research and Development 1981*.
5. EDCs for Building and Civil Engineering, *Report of Research Working Party*, NEDO unpublished report 1982.
6. Construction Industry Research and Information Association, *Long-term Research and Development Requirements in Civil Engineering*.
7. *Framework for Government Research and Development 1971/72* (The Rothschild Report) (HMSO, 1972).

8. Construction Industry Research and Information Association, *Long-term Research and Development Requirements in Civil Engineering*, pp. 42–3.
9. Lansley, P., *Research and Construction: Case Studies of the Constraints to the Application of Construction Management Research* (University of Reading, 1983).

Select Bibliography

GENERAL

Bowley, M. E. A., *The British Building Industry: Four Studies in Response and Resistance to Change* (CUP, 1966).
Colclough, J. R., *The Construction Industry of Great Britain* (Butterworth, 1965).
DoE, *Housing and Construction Statistics*, annual and quarterly (HMSO).
EDCs for Building and Civil Engineering, *How Flexible Is Construction? A Study of Resources and Participants in the Construction Process*, NEDO (HMSO, 1978).
Fleming, M. C., *Construction and the Related Professions*, on behalf of the Royal Statistical Society and the Social Science Research Council (Pergamon, 1980).
Hillebrandt, P. M., *Economic Theory and the Construction Industry* (Macmillan, 1974).
Stone, P. A., *Building Economy, Design, Production and Organisation – A Synoptic View*, 3rd edn (Pergamon, 1983).

1 THE CONSTRUCTION INDUSTRY

Cambridge Econometrics Ltd, *Policies for Recovery: An Evaluation of Alternatives*, commissioned by FCEC, NCBMP, NFBTE, RIBA, RICS (Cambridge Econometrics Ltd, 1981).
EIU, *Capital Spending and the UK Economy*, commissioned by the FCEC (EIU, 1981).
Sugden, J. D., 'The Place of Construction in the Economy', in Turin, D. A. (ed.), *Aspects of the Economics of Construction* (George Godwin, 1975).
Turin, D. A., *What Do We Mean by Building?* Inaugural Lecture delivered at University College London on 14 Feb 1966 (published for the College by H. K. Lewis & Co. London, 1966).

2 DETERMINANTS OF DEMAND

Ambrose, P., and Colenutt, B., *The Property Machine* (Penguin, 1975).

Ball, M., *Housing Policy and Economic Power: The Political Economy of Owner Occupation* (Methuen, forthcoming).

DoE, *Housing Policy: A Consultative Document*, Cmnd 6851 and related technical volumes (HMSO, 1977).

DoE and National Water Council, *Sewers and Water Mains – A National Assessment*, Standing Technical Committee Report no. 4 (DoE, 1977).

EDCs for Building and Civil Engineering, Joint Working Party on Demand and Output Forecasts, *Construction Industry Prospects to 1979* (NEDO, 1971).

EDCs for Building and Civil Engineering, *Construction into the Early 1980s*, NEDO (HMSO, 1976) ch. 3.

EDCs for Building and Civil Engineering, *Scottish Construction into the Early 1980s*, NEDO (HMSO, 1976) chs 2 and 3.

EDCs for Building and Civil Engineering, *The Public Client and the Construction Industries* (The Wood Report) NEDO (HMSO, 1975).

EDCs for Building and Civil Engineering, *Regional Construction Forecasts to 1977*, vols 1–4 (NEDO, 1974).

EDCs for Building and Civil Engineering, Joint Forecasting Committee, *Construction Forecast* (every six months) NEDO (HMSO).

Marriott, O., *The Property Boom* (Pan, 1969).

National Council of Building Material Producers, *BMP Forecasts* (three times a year) (NCBMP).

National Home Improvement Council, *Report on the Market for Home Improvement, Repair and Maintenance, and DIY 1977-1980* (NHIC, 1982).

Shelter, *Housing and the Economy: A Priority for Reform* (Shelter, 1982).

Stone, P. A., *Urban Development in Britain: Standards, Costs and Resources 1964-2004*, NIESR (CUP, 1970).

House of Lords Select Committee on Science and Technology, *The Water Industry*, vol. 1 Report (HMSO, 1982).

3 THE PROCESS

The Aqua Group, *Tenders and Contracts for Building* (Granada, 1983).

Chartered Institute of Building, *Project Management in Building* (CIOB, 1982).

Construction Industry Research and Information Association, *A Client's Guide to Design and Build* (CIRIA, 1981).

EDC for Building, *Faster Building for Industry*, NEDO (HMSO, 1983).

EDC for Building, *Action on the Banwell Report* (chairman: P. G. Potts) NEDO (HMSO, 1967).

EDCs for Building and Civil Engineering, *Before You Build* (chairman: Sir Hugh Wilson) NEDO (HMSO, 1974).

EDCs for Building and Civil Engineering, *The Public Client and the*

Construction Industries (chairman: Sir Kenneth Wood) NEDO (HMSO, 1975).

EDC for Civil Engineering, *Contracting in Civil Engineering Since Banwell* (chairman: W. G. Harris) NEDO (HMSO, 1968).

EDC for Civil Engineering, *Efficiency in Road Construction:* Reports 1 and 2, NEDO (HMSO, 1966 and 1967).

McGhie, B., 'The Implications of Project Management', in *The Production of the Built Environment*, Proceedings of the Third Bartlett Summer School (University College London, 1982) pp. 2.1–9.

Marsh, P. D. V., *Contracting for Engineering and Construction Projects*, 2nd edn (in association with the Institute of Purchasing) (Gower, 1981).

Ministry of Public Buildings and Works, *The Placing and Management of Contracts for Building and Civil Engineering Work* (chairman: Sir Harold Banwell) (HMSO, 1964).

Ministry of Public Building and Works, *Organisation and Practices for Building and Civil Engineering: Report of the Working Party on Building and Civil Engineering Procedure in Scotland* (chairman: W. McEwan Younger) (HMSO, 1964).

Ministry of Works, *The Placing and Management of Building Contracts: Report of the Central Council for Works and Buildings to the Minister of Works* (chairman: Lord Simon) (HMSO, 1944).

Ministry of Works, *Survey of Problems before the Construction Industries: A Report Prepared for the Minister of Works by Sir Harold Emmerson GCB, KCVO* (HMSO, 1962).

The National Joint Consultative Committee of Architects, Quantity Surveyors and Builders, *Communications in the Building Industry: The Report of a Pilot Study*, prepared by Higgin, G., and Jessop, N. (The Tavistock Institute of Human Relations, 1963).

Tavistock Institute of Human Relations, *Interdependence and Uncertainty: A Study of the Building Industry* (Tavistock, 1966).

Turin, D. A., 'Building as a Process', *Transactions of the Bartlett Society*, vol. 6 (1967–8) (University College London, 1968).

5 OUTPUT ABROAD

Construction Industry Conference Centre, *International Construction Conference Proceedings 1979* (University of Nottingham).

Cox, V. L., *International Construction* (Construction Press, 1983).

Neo, R. B., *International Construction Contracting* (Gower, 1976).

6 FORECASTING AND FORECASTS OF DEMAND AND OUTPUT

EDCs for Building and Civil Engineering, Joint Forecasting Committee, *Construction Forecasts* (every six months) NEDO (HMSO).

EDCs for Building and Civil Engineering, Joint Working Party on Demand

and Output Forecasts, *Construction Industry Prospects to 1979* (NEDO, 1971).

EDCs for Building and Civil Engineering, *Regional Construction Forecasts to 1977*, vols 1-4 (NEDO, 1974).

National Council of Building Material Producers, *BMP Forecasts* (three times a year) NCBMP.

7 STRUCTURE OF CONTRACTING INDUSTRY

Ball, M., 'The Speculative Housebuilding Industry', in *The Production of the Built Environment*, Proceedings of the Third Bartlett Summer School (University College London, 1982) pp. 1.31-51.

Ball, M., *The Contracting System in the Construction Industry*, Birkbeck College Discussion Paper no. 86 (Birkbeck College, 1980).

Ball, M., and Cullen, A., *Mergers and Accumulation in the British Construction Industry 1960-79*, Birkbeck College Discussion Paper no. 73 (Birkbeck College, 1980).

Business Statistics Office, *Report of the Census of Production: Construction Industry*, Business Monitor PA 500, annual (HMSO).

Clarke, L., 'Subcontracting in the Building Industry', in *The Production of the Built Environment*, Proceedings of the Second Bartlett Summer School (University College London, 1980) pp. 35-53.

Fleming, M. C., 'Construction', in Johnson, P. S. (ed.), *The Structure of British Industry* (Granada, 1980) ch. 10.

Hillebrandt, P. M., *Small Firms in the Construction Industry*, Committee of Inquiry on Small Firms, Research Report no. 10 (HMSO, 1971).

Ive, G. J., from reports by Ive *et al.*, *Capacity and Response to Demand of the Housebuilding Industry: A Summary of Three Research Studies*, Building Economics Research Unit, University College Environmental Research Group (University College London, 1981).

Langford, D. A., *Direct Labour Organisations* (Gower, 1982).

Sugden, J., 'The Nature of Construction Capacity and Entrepreneurial Response to Effective Demand in the UK', in *Production of the Built Environment*, Proceedings of the First Bartlett Summer School (University College London, 1980) pp. 1-6.

University College Environmental Research Group, Building Economics Research Unit, *The Mechanism of Response to Effective Demand*, 5 vols (University College London, 1975).

8 STRUCTURE OF THE PROFESSIONS

Dolan, D. F., *The British Construction Industry: An Introduction* (Macmillan, 1979).

EDCs for Building and Civil Engineering, *The Professions and the Construction Industries*, NEDO (HMSO, 1976).

Joint Committee on Training in the Building Industry Report (chairman: Sir Noel Hall MA LLD RIBA, IOB, RICS, I. Struct E) with the knowledge of the NJCC, 1964.

Kaye, B., *The Development of the Architectural Profession in Britain* (Allen and Unwin, 1960).

Monopolies and Mergers Commission, *Architects' Services: A Report on the Supply of Architects' Services with Reference to Scale Fees* (HMSO, 1977).

Monopolies and Mergers Commission, *Surveyors' Services: A Report on the Supply of Surveyors' Services with References to Scale Fees* (HMSO, 1977).

Saint, A., 'A History of Professionalism in Architecture', in *The Production of the Built Environment*, Proceedings of the Third Bartlett Summer School (University College London, 1982) pp. 3. 10–12.

Thompson, F. M. L., *Chartered Surveyors: The Growth of a Profession* (Routledge and Kegan Paul, 1968).

10   THE LINKS BETWEEN RESOURCES AND OUTPUT AND CAPACITY

EDCs for Building and Civil Engineering, *Construction into the Early 1980s*, NEDO (HMSO, 1976).

EDCs for Building and Civil Engineering, *Scottish Construction into the Early 1980s*, NEDO (HMSO, 1976).

Hillebrandt, P. M., 'Crisis in Construction', *National Westminster Bank Review*, Nov 1977.

Lemessany, J., and Clapp, M. A. *Resource Inputs to New Construction – The Labour Requirements of Hospital Building*, CP85/75 (BRE, 1975).

Lemessany, J., and Clapp, M. A., *Resource Inputs to Construction: The Labour Requirements of House Building*, CP76/78 (BRE, 1978).

University College Environmental Research Unit, Building Economics Research Unit, *The Mechanism of Response to Effective Demand* 5 vols (University College London, 1975).

11 MANPOWER

Austerin, T., 'Unions and Wage Contracts, The Case of the "Lump" in the Construction Industry', in *The Production of the Built Environment*, Proceedings of the First Bartlett Summer School (University College London, 1980) pp. 75–80.

Bedale, C., Halford, R., and Lovejoy, B., 'Training in the Construction Industry', in *The Production of the Built Environment*, Proceedings of the Second Bartlett Summer School (University College London, 1980) pp. 64–9.

Burchall, S., 'Training: An Analysis of the Crisis', in *The Production of the Built Environment*, Proceedings of the First Bartlett Summer

School (University College London, 1980) pp. 81-6.

Carter, P., 'Problems for the Building Unions in Great Britain', in *The Production of the Built Environment*, Proceedings of the Third Bartlett Summer School (University College London, 1982) pp. 2.39-41.

Druker, J., 'The History of Construction Unions: The Process of Structural Change', in *The Production of the Built Environment*, Proceedings of the First Bartlett Summer School (University College London, 1980) pp. 69-74.

Hatchett, M., 'The Development of Building Craft Skills in Inner London with Particular Reference to Work Experience', in *The Production of the Built Environment*, Proceedings of the Third Bartlett Summer School (University College London, 1982) pp. 2.14-29.

Hilton, W. S., *Industrial Relations in Construction* (Pergamon, 1968).

Marsh, A. and Heady, P. with Matheson, J., Office of Population Censuses and Surveys, Social Survey Division, *Labour Mobility in the Construction Industry* (HMSO, 1981).

Morton, C. N., 'Collective Bargaining in Building and Civil Engineering: A Case Study of Three Major Re-development Projects in the City of London', thesis for the Degree of Doctor of Philosophy (University of London, 1979).

Report of Committee of Enquiry under Professor E. H. Phelps Brown into Certain Matters concerning Labour in Building and Civil Engineering, Cmnd 3714 (HMSO, 1968).

Wood, L., *A Union to Build* (Lawrence and Wishart, 1979).

14 MATERIALS

Bowley, M. E. A., *Innovations in Building Materials: an Economic Study* (Gerald Duckworth, 1960).

EDC for Building, *Building Products – Competing at Home and Abroad*, NEDO (HMSO, 1983).

EDCs for Building and Civil Engineering, *Building Materials: Export Opportunites and Import Substitution*, NEDO (HMSO, 1980).

15 PLANT AND OTHER FIXED ASSETS

Eden, J. F., 'Mechanisation', in Turin, D. A. (ed.), *Aspects of the Economics of Construction* (Godwin, 1975).

Greene & Co., *Investment in Plant Hire*, Annually (Greene & Co.).

Ive, G. J., 'Fixed Capital in the British Building Industry', in *The Production of the Built Environment*, Proceedings of the First Bartlett Summer School (University College London, 1980) pp. 107-19.

Mead, H. T., and Mitchell, G. L. *Plant Hire for Building and Construction* (Newnes Butterworth, 1972).

16 FINANCE FOR CONTRACTING

Business Statistics Office, *Company Finance Thirteenth Issue*, Business Monitor MA3 (HMSO, 1983).

Clarke, L., 'Subcontracting in the Building Industry', in *The Production of the Built Environment*, Proceedings of the Second Bartlett Summer School (University College London, 1980)

E. B. Savory Milln & Co.,*Building Books*, Annual (E. B. Savory Milln).

17 RESEARCH AND DEVELOPMENT

Construction Industry Research and Information Association, *Long Term Research and Development Requirements in Civil Engineering*, Report of a Task Force set up by the Science and Engineering Research Council and the Departments of the Environment and Transport (CIRIA, 1981).

Ministry of Public Building and Works, *Building Research and Information Services*, Report of a Working Party (chairman: D. E. Woodbine Parish) (HMSO, 1964).

Index

Authors, reports, etc., may be found in Notes and References and Select Bibliography.

Abbreviations: T = Table; F = Figure; n = note.

imports of, 255–6, 255T
inputs for output types, 175, 181T,
   182–3T, 184T
prices of, 260–1, 260T
producers in process, 40–1F
in repair and maintenance output, 175
and research, 283–4, 286
significance of, *see* usage of
sources of, 253, 255–6, 255T
standards, 256–7
supply and stocks – fluctuations in,
   257–60, 258T, 259T
usage of, 254F
mechanical plant operators, *see* plant
   operators
mergers, 130–1, 132T
Metal Window Federation, 300 (n34)
metal fittings, *see* ironmongery
Middle East
   British consultants in, 99
   British contractors in, 94, 96T
   second-hand plant market, 267
Ministry of Public Building and Works, 8
mobility, 205–10, 209T, 212
moratoria – on spending, 27
mortgage market, 18
Mowlem, John & Co plc, 97, 117
multi-storey housing, *see* housing –
   in flats
municipal engineers, 153

N

National Association of Lift Makers,
   300 (n34)
National Association of Plumbing
   Heating and Mechanical Services
   Contractors, 215, 300 (n34)
National Association of Scaffolding
   Contractors, 299 (n32)
National Construction Corporation, 148
National Contractors Group (of
   NFBTE), 141
National Council of Building Material
   Producers (NCBMP), 255
National Diploma in Building –
   Scotland, 240–1, 241T
National Economic Development
   Office (NEDO), 284, 286
National Federation of Building Trades
   Employers (NFBTE), 141
   constituent bodies, 144, 299 (n32)

and DLOs, 144
and JCT, 294 (n34)
organisation, 141
and subcontracts, 61
and training, 198
and wages, 214–15
National Federation of Building Trades
   Operatives (NFBTO), 213
National Federation of Painting and
   Decorating Contractors, 299 (n32)
National Federation of Plastering
   Contractors, 299 (n32)
National Federation of Roofing
   Contractors, 214
National Federation of Terrazzo-Mosaic
   Specialists, 300 (n35)
National Home Improvement Council
   (NHIC) – and warranty, 90
National House-Building Council
   (NHBC)
   members and structure, 127, 128T
   and warranty, 90
National Insurance evasion, 125–6
National Joint Consultative Council
   of Architects, Quantity Surveyors
   and Builders (NJCC), 142, 154–5
National Joint Council for the Building
   Industry (NJCBI), 141
   and training, 198
   and wages, 214–5
National Master Tile Fixers Association,
   300 (n35)
need
   definition, 9–10
   and forecasting, 106, 108–11
   for housing, 14
   for public-sector construction, 24
negotiation of contracts, 56
Newarthill plc, 117
new towns
   and APTCs, 219, 220T
   DLOs, 143–8, 144T, 145T, 146T;
      number, work done and employ-
      ment, 143, 144T, 145T; and
      operatives by trade, 197T; and
      productivity, 228–9T; and
      training, 200–1, 204T; and types
      of work, 146T
non-housing work
   and self-employment, 230
   see also public-sector – non-housing
      work, private-sector – non-
      housing work
Northern Ireland, xii